# 50 HIKES
## IN CONNECTICUT

SIXTH EDITION

Mary Anne, David, Gerry
& Sue Hardy

D1516979

THE COUNTRYMAN PRESS

A division of W. W. Norton & Company

*Independent Publishers Since 1923*

AN INVITATION TO THE READER

Over time trails can be rerouted and signs and landmarks altered. If you find that changes have occurred on the routes described in this book, please let us know so that corrections may be made in future editions. The author and publisher also welcome other comments and suggestions. Address all correspondence to:

50hikesct@gmail.com OR

50 Hikes CT Editor
W. W. Norton & Company
500 Fifth Avenue
New York, NY 10110

Copyright © 1978, 1984, 1991 by Gerry and Sue Hardy
Copyright © 1996 and 2001 by David, Gerry, and Sue Hardy
Copyright © 2019 by The Countryman Press

All rights reserved
Printed in the United States of America

For information about permission to reproduce selections from this book, write to Permissions, The Countryman Press, 500 Fifth Avenue, New York, NY 10110

For information about special discounts for bulk purchases, please contact W. W. Norton Special Sales at specialsales@wwnorton.com or 800-233-4830

Manufacturing by Versa Press
Series book design by Chris Welch
Production manager: Devon Zahn

Library of Congress Cataloging-in-Publication Data

Names: Hardy, Mary Anne, author.
Title: 50 hikes in Connecticut / Mary Anne, David, Gerry, and Sue Hardy.
Other titles: Fifty hikes in Connecticut | Fifty hikes series.
Description: Sixth Edition, Fully revised and updated edition. | New York :
The Countryman Press, a division of W.W. Norton & Company, [2019] | Series: 50 Hikes |
Previous edition: 2002. | Includes bibliographical references and index.
Identifiers: LCCN 2018056860 | ISBN 9781682682555 (Paperback : alk. paper) Subjects:
LCSH: Hiking—Connecticut—Guidebooks. | Walking—Connecticut—Guidebooks. |
Backpacking—Connecticut—Guidebooks. | Trails—Connecticut—Guidebooks. | Connecticut—Guidebooks.
Classification: LCC GV199.42.C8 H37 2019 | DDC 796.5109746—dc23
LC record available at https://lccn.loc.gov/2018056860

The Countryman Press
www.countrymanpress.com

A division of W. W. Norton & Company, Inc.
500 Fifth Avenue, New York, NY 10110
www.wwnorton.com

10 9 8 7 6 5 4 3 2 1

# 50 HIKES
## IN CONNECTICUT

## OTHER BOOKS IN THE 50 HIKES SERIES

*In memory of Gerry and David (Dave) Hardy, who so loved the woods and contributed richly to its preservation and enjoyment. Blessings to them both as they now walk the trails together.*

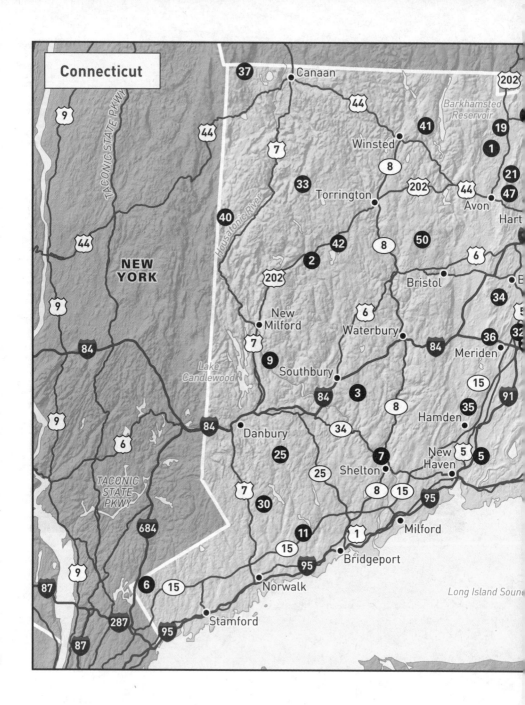

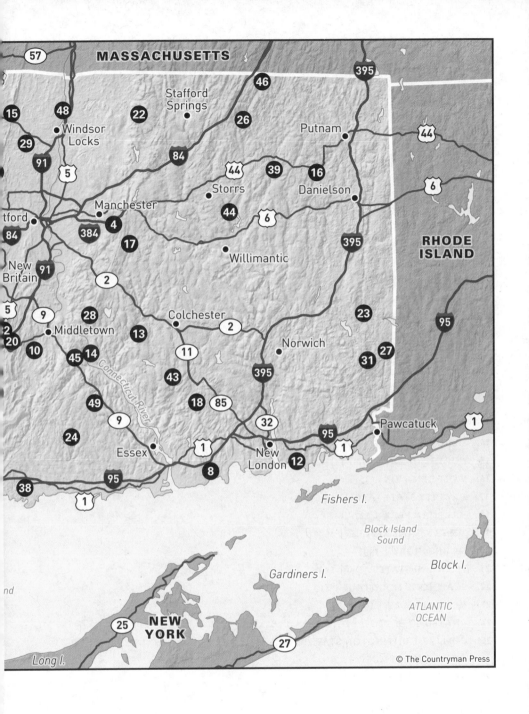

# Contents

# Hikes at a Glance

| Hike | Region | Distance (miles) | Difficulty |
|------|--------|:----------------:|:----------:|
| 1. Great Pond | Simsbury | 1.5 | D |
| 2. Mount Tom Tower | Morris | 1.5 | C |
| 3. Southford Falls State Park | Southbury & Oxford | 2 | C |
| 4. Lookout Mountain | Manchester | 2.5 | C |
| 5. Peter's Rock | North Haven | 2.5 | BC |
| 6. Audubon Center in Greenwich | Greenwich | 3 | CD |
| 7. Osbornedale State Park | Derby | 3 | C |
| 8. Rocky Neck State Park | East Lyme | 3 | D |
| 9. Sunny Valley | Bridgewater | 3 | C |
| 10. Wadsworth Falls | Middlefield | 3 | C |
| 11. Larsen Sanctuary | Fairfield | 3.5 | D |
| 12. Bluff Point | Groton | 4 | D |
| 13. Day Pond State Park | Colchester | 4 | C |
| 14. Hurd State Park | East Hampton | 4 | C |
| 15. Northern Metacomet | Granby | 4 | C |
| 16. Wolf Den | Pomfret | 4.5 | C |
| 17. Gay City State Park | Hebron | 5 | CD |
| 18. Hartman Park | Lyme | 5 | C |
| 19. McLean Game Refuge | Granby | 5 | C |
| 20. Mount Higby | Middlefield | 5 | B |
| 21. Penwood State Park | Bloomfield | 5 | C |
| 22. Soapstone Mountain | Somers | 5 | C |
| 23. Mount Misery | Voluntown | 5.25 | CD |
| 24. Chatfield Hollow State Park | Killingworth | 5.5 | C |
| 25. Collis P. Huntington State Park | Redding | 5.5 | CD |
| 26. Northern Nipmuck | Ashford | 5.5 | C |
| 27. Green Fall Pond | Voluntown | 5.7 | CD |
| 28. Great Hill | East Hampton | 6 | C |
| 29. Northwest Park | Windsor | 6 | CD |
| 30. Devil's Den Preserve | Weston | 7 | C |
| 31. Bullet and High Ledges | North Stonington | 6 | C |

| Views | Waterfalls | Good for Kids | Notes |
|---|---|---|---|
| | | ✓ | Loop around pine shoreline |
| ✓ | | ✓ | Short uphill to stone tower; summer swimming |
| ✓ | ✓ | ✓ | Waterfalls, covered bridge, and observation tower |
| ✓ | ✓ | ✓ | Hillside walk, spring vernal pond |
| ✓ | | ✓ | Woods ramble; views of New Haven Harbor |
| | | ✓ | Nature center; woods ramble |
| | | ✓ | Woods and meadow ramble; pond |
| ✓ | | ✓ | Ocean bayside walk to sandy beach |
| ✓ | | ✓ | Rocky scrambles; riverside vista |
| | ✓ | ✓ | Old woods roads leading to two waterfalls, swimming pond. |
| | | ✓ | Nature walk |
| ✓ | | ✓ | Oceanside walk; old foundations |
| ✓ | ✓ | ✓ | Summer swimming, glacial erratic boulders, woodsland waterfall |
| ✓ | | ✓ | Connecticut Riverside walk |
| ✓ | | ✓ | Traprock ridge with clifftop views |
| | | ✓ | Rock formations; fabled wolf den cave |
| | | ✓ | Woods walk through ghost town; summer swimming |
| | | ✓ | Woods walk across narrow ridges; historic fortress |
| ✓ | | ✓ | Barndoor Hill; great pine woods |
| ✓ | | | Clifftop walk along traprock ridge |
| ✓ | | ✓ | Ridgewalk to rocky outcrop; hidden lake |
| ✓ | | ✓ | Ridgewalk to summit with views |
| ✓ | | ✓ | Rhododendron swamp boardwalk; mountaintop views |
| ✓ | | ✓ | Ledges and CCC-developed park; summer swimming |
| ✓ | | ✓ | Woods roads walk along pond shores |
| ✓ | | ✓ | Rocky ridges with deep hemlock woods |
| ✓ | ✓ | ✓ | Pond walk with approach through gorge; summer swimming |
| ✓ | ✓ | ✓ | Rocky summit and ridgewalk to waterfall cascade |
| ✓ | | ✓ | Woods walk through old tobacco fields; nature center |
| ✓ | | | Woods ramble to highland vistas in nature preserve |
| ✓ | | ✓ | Eastern Connecticut Ledges |

| Hike | Region | Distance (miles) | Difficulty |
|---|---|---|---|
| 32. Chauncey Peak and Mount Lamentation | Meriden | 6 | B |
| 33. Mohawk Mountain | Cornwall | 7 | BC |
| 34. Ragged Mountain | Southington | 6 | AB |
| 35. Sleeping Giant State Park | Hamden | 6 | AB |
| 36. West Peak and Castle Craig | Meriden | 6.4 | B |
| 37. Bear Mountain | Salisbury | 6.8 | AB |
| 38. Westwoods | Guilford | 6.5 | B |
| 39. Natchaug State Forest | Eastford | 6.6 | CD |
| 40. Macedonia Brook State Park | Kent | 6.7 | AB |
| 41. Peoples State Forest | Barkhamstead | 7 | BC |
| 42. White Memorial Foundation | Litchfield | 7 | D |
| 43. Devil's Hopyard State Park | East Haddam | 7.5 | C |
| 44. Mansfield Hollow State Park | Mansfield | 8 | CD |
| 45. Seven Falls State Park | Middletown | 8 | C |
| 46. Bigelow Hollow State Park | Union | 8.5 | B |
| 47. Talcott Mountain and Heublein Tower | West Hartford | 8.5 | C |
| 48. Windsor Locks Canal | Suffield | 9 | D |
| 49. Cockaponset State Park | Chester | 10.1 | CD |
| 50. Tunxis Ramble | Burlington | 11 | BC |

## DIFFICULTY KEY

**D:** Easy terrain: little or no change in elevation, easy footing
**CD:** Intermediate between C and D
**C:** Average terrain: moderate ups and downs with some need to watch footing
**CB:** Intermediate between C and B
**B:** Strenuous terrain: steep climbs, considerable elevation gain, or some poor footing or both
**AB:** Intermediate between A and B
**A:** Very strenuous terrain: maximum elevation gain, poor footing, or hand-assisted scrambling up steep pitches or both

| Views | Water-falls | Good for Kids | Notes |
|:---:|:---:|:---:|---|
| ✓ | | ✓ | Traprock ridge walk, views of lake |
| ✓ | ✓ | ✓ | Observation tower |
| ✓ | | | Rocky trail along traprock clifftop and ridges |
| ✓ | | | Quarry views; rocky ledges; WPA Tower |
| ✓ | | | Clifftop walk on traprock ridges |
| ✓ | | ✓ | Steady acent to Connecticut's highest summit |
| ✓ | | ✓ | Scramble along rocky ledges |
| | | ✓ | Woods walk; historical stone fireplace |
| ✓ | | | Rugged hike around highland valley |
| ✓ | | ✓ | Woods ramble with rock outcrop views; nature museum |
| ✓ | | ✓ | Extensive boardwalk across shallow pond; icehouse ruins |
| ✓ | ✓ | | Hillside walk waterfall and pothole stone formations |
| ✓ | | ✓ | River walk to local ledge |
| ✓ | ✓ | | Woods walk among cascades and rocky hillsides |
| ✓ | | | Woods walk over rocky ledges and along undeveloped shoreline |
| ✓ | | ✓ | Reservoir walk to traprock ridge with famous Heublein Tower |
| ✓ | | ✓ | Easy riverside walk along old canal; open April 1 - November 15 |
| | ✓ | | Woods ramble; early fine trailwork |
| ✓ | | | Hike along the Mile of Ledges |

# Acknowledgments

This book is the outcome of over 40 years of work carried out by numerous people, all of whom were committed to the stewardship of our natural world. It all started with my parents, Gerry and Sue Hardy, when they wrote the first edition of *50 Hikes in Connecticut* in the mid-70s. Since those early days, three generations of Hardys (and Bujalskis) have continued to hike and enjoy the woods. Four subsequent editions were published through the efforts of my parents and brother, David Hardy, and now the mantle has been passed on to me. It has been a privilege to undertake this labor of love—celebrating my family and love of the outdoors.

I could not have scouted out these 50 hikes over a seven-month period without my many hiking companions, and I am very grateful for their company and assistance: the Bujalskis (Phil, Nicholas, Anna, and Julia), Steffanie Moccia-Worrell, Janet Ainsworth, Elizabeth Fiorillo, Libby Wamser, Karen Normand, Linda Valentine, Patty Hardy, George Hynes, Dan Hughes, Melissa Hall, and Ben Sanford.

For their help with hikes in the fifth edition and initial scouting for this edition, I would like to thank members of the Connecticut Chapter of the Green Mountain Club, especially Carol Langley, Sarah O'Hare, Don Hagstrom, and Dick Hart. I would also like to extend my gratitude to Sarah Williams of the Guilford Land Conservation Trust for sharing her knowledge about the important work her organization performs in order to help build a natural legacy for all to enjoy.

I would also like to thank Michael Tizzano and Róisín Cameron at the Countryman Press for their patience and perseverance in preparing this sixth edition.

Finally, the greatest thanks go to my family. None of this would have been possible without my parents. Gerry's greatest gift to me was his expansive curiosity and knowledge of the natural world, something I will always carry with me. When I examine trees, flowers, and wildlife, I will always be thinking of him. My deepest thanks as well to Sue for dragging us all out hiking over the years (I may have been reluctant as a teen, but now being in the wilderness nourishes my soul). I am also grateful to my brother, David, for trusting me to continue this family project, which he so expertly took on in the mid '90s. And for help with this edition specifically, I wish to thank my son, Nicholas, who served as my first reader and an expert initial editor. Enthusiastic conversations with him about each hike I took deepened my appreciation of the rich history and natural wonders of our beautiful state. Also endless thanks to my husband, Phil, for his patience and willingness to hike anytime. It was great to get out in the woods every week. Now that we have started this habit there is no stopping us!

# Introduction

Contrary to popular opinion, Connecticut is not all cities and suburbs. A gratifyingly high proportion of our state's woodland is preserved as state parks and state forests. In fact, the only states in New England with more miles of hiking trails are Vermont and New Hampshire.

These 50 hikes represent all areas of the state and traverse almost all its existing natural habitats. Naturally, this selection is only a sampler and, of necessity, somewhat reflects our own preferences and prejudices. We chose the hikes with an eye to hikers of all ages and abilities; most are suitable for families with young children. Keep in mind that a half-day hike for adults and teenagers may take all day with youngsters along, especially if they take time to examine their surroundings closely.

Revising a hiking guide is a never-ending task. A new edition becomes necessary whenever trails change, whether due to human activity or natural events, and outdated guides can be particularly frustrating for new hikers.

This edition reflects modifications in most of the hikes with some trails having experienced significant change (Wadsworth Falls, Day Pond, Chatfield Hollow, Northwest Park, Westwoods, Mohawk Mountain, Ragged Mountain, Tunxis Ramble, and Sleeping Giant). Several trails in this edition appear for the first time (Osbornedale State Park, Peter's Rock, and Southford Falls State Park), while the others have seen minor adjustments. The hikes in this edition represent their trail status as of 2017;

all were walked during that hiking season.

We've also reorganized the individual hike write-ups. Each opens with interesting background information—what this trail has to offer the hiker. *Getting There* provides detailed directions for driving to the trailhead from main Connecticut highways (however we also recommend that you plan your drive beforehand using a map or GPS). *The Hike* begins with a short summary of the routes you will follow and then continues in a narrative fashion, supplementing trail instructions with interesting natural and historical tidbits. *Other Hiking Options* offers suggestions for alternate trails in the area as well as ways to tailor each hike to one's fitness level and available time; these alternatives are often tagged in the general hike narrative. Since experienced hikers like the challenge of a long walk while others may prefer a shorter trip through the woods, we've tried to list a *Short & Sweet* version of every hike, pointing the easiest way to get straight to the good stuff. All the other hiking options are briefly described and often shown on the same map as the main hike.

Written comments by interested hikers like you were considered and field-checked. Such notes are important in keeping this volume up to date, and any suggestions are appreciated. You may send any questions, comments, or concerns to 50hikesct@gmail.com.

This book is intended to please both the armchair reader and the trail hiker by fleshing out directions with maps, photographs, and snippets of natural history. We have also tried to answer some of the questions that you might ask while walking. The phenomena described on these trails (some hiked many times over many years) were all experienced firsthand, and by remaining fairly observant you can witness the same things. For this reason, our descriptions are short on wildlife, which is seen only occasionally, and long on vegetation and terrain. Effective observation of animal life can require very slow movement, blinds, binoculars, and/or scopes. Although we have had quite pleasant serendipitous encounters with Connecticut fauna while just walking along the trails. In contrast, vegetation and terrain features require only an alert eye and an inquiring mind.

These hikes, which we feel represent some of the most attractive in the state, break longer trails into manageable sections. In addition to highlighting some of the best stretches of the Blue Trail System and more interesting state park trail networks, we have included a few hikes within wildlife sanctuaries and in city- and town-owned open-space areas. We have deliberately avoided including the world-famous Appalachian Trail, which is overexposed in other trail publications and overused as a result.

## CHOOSING A HIKE

Your first stop should be the Hikes at a Glance table and location map, which provide quick orientation and summaries of each hike's most important features. The hikes are presented according to their length from shortest to longest: the first, Great Pond, is a pleasant 1.5-mile walk around a wooded pond, while the final hike, Tunxis Ramble, leads you through 11 miles of varied terrain

including the scrambly Mile of Ledges. However, be aware that a trip's length in miles does not necessarily reflect the hike's difficulty, since gauging difficulty is subjective. Factors such as ruggedness of terrain, vertical rise, as well as vertical drop, should all be taken into consideration.

*Total distance* is the mileage walked if you complete the entire hike as described. *Hiking time* is computed by means of a simple formula used all over the country: 2 miles an hour plus one-half hour for every 1,000 feet of vertical rise. Thus, a 6-mile hike on flat terrain would have a three-hour hiking time, but a 6-mile hike with 2,000 feet of climbing would take four hours. If you are a beginning hiker, you may not match "book time" for a while. A fit, experienced hiker will consistently better these times. A word of caution— hiking time means just that and does not allow for lunch stops, rest breaks, sightseeing, or picture-taking.

The rating for each hike refers to the average difficulty of the terrain you traverse on the route we have described. The difficulty of a hike is relative. A tough section in Connecticut is far easier than a tough section in New Hampshire or Vermont. However, some of our rock scrambles, while shorter, can be just as difficult (such as Sleeping Giant #35 and Macedonia Brook #40). The big difference between Connecticut and northern New England is our dearth of sustained climbs. Only Bear Mountain (hike #37), the state's tallest peak, offers such an ascent.

Our rating system is the one used by the Connecticut Chapter of the Appalachian Mountain Club (AMC) and is designed for Connecticut trails. It combines such factors as elevation gain, rock scrambling, footpath condition, and steepness. Hikes rated D are the easiest, and A the most difficult. The seven categories used in our rating system are:

D: Easy terrain: little or no change in elevation, easy footing
CD: Intermediate between C and D
C: Average terrain: moderate ups and downs with some need to watch footing
CB: Intermediate between C and B
B: Strenuous terrain: steep climbs, considerable elevation gain, or some poor footing or both
AB: Intermediate between A and B
A: Very strenuous terrain: maximum elevation gain, poor footing, or hand-assisted scrambling up steep pitches or both

In an effort to limit grade inflation, an A rating is rarely given and will require the use of your hands on a steep pitch at some point in the hike. Where such a situation exists, it will be noted in the text.

When selecting a day's ramble, do not overdo it. If you have not hiked before, try the shorter, easier hikes first and build up to the longer ones. Do not bite off more than you can chew—that takes all the pleasure out of hiking. As the saying goes, "Walk till you're half-tired out, then turn around and walk back."

We have listed the United States Geological Survey (USGS) quadrangle maps and have provided a detailed map for each hike. In *Other Hiking Options* when possible we have also listed an online resource for maps (some are mobile-phone friendly).

## ABOUT CONNECTICUT SEASONS

Hiking in Connecticut is a four-season avocation. Our winters are relatively mild—we rarely have temperatures below zero Fahrenheit or snow accumulations of more than a foot. In general, the snow deepens and the temperature drops as you travel north and west. The southeastern part of the state is snow-free for much of the winter and is the first area in the state to experience spring.

Spring is usually wet and muddy, although there is also a dry period of high fire danger before the trees leaf out. Spring flowers bloom in April and peak in May. Days of extreme heat (in the nineties) can appear any time after the beginning of April—sometimes sooner!

The humid heat of summer demands short, easy, early-morning strolls and usually requires insect repellent. Our experiences have shown us that a hot, humid day can feel much cooler in the woods, especially near running water or a waterfall, and many of our hikes feature swimming options (noted in the Hikes at a Glance table) perfect for summer when the foliage is likewise lush and botanizing is at its best.

Fall, however, is the ideal hiking season, and cool, crisp days, colorful foliage, and clear air make New England's unsurpassed. A better combination of season and place may exist elsewhere, but we doubt it.

The color starts with a few shrubs and the bright reds of swamp maples. When other trees start to turn, the swamp maples are bare. Then tree follows tree—sugar maple, ash, birch, beech, and finally oak—turning, blending, fading, falling. There is no better way to enjoy a New England autumn than to explore the woods on foot.

## HOW TO HIKE

We do not mean to tell you how to walk. Most of us have been walking from an early age. Rather, we offer a few hints to help you gain as much pleasure and satisfaction as possible from a hike.

First and most importantly, wear comfortable shoes that are well broken in. Children can often hike comfortably in good sneakers; adults usually should not. We are heavier, and our feet need more support than sneakers offer. On the other hand, you do not need heavyweight mountain boots in Connecticut. A lightweight hiking boot or a good work boot is ideal. Look for footwear that has a thick rubber sole with deep indentations that improve its stability and traction (often called "lug soles"). While these soles may be hard on the woods' trails, we do recommend them, as most Connecticut hiking alternates between woods and rocky ledges, where the lug soles are very helpful. Your boots should be worn over two pairs of socks, one lightweight and one heavyweight. Wool or a wool-polypropylene blend is preferable for both pairs, as it provides warmth even when wet.

Secondly, wear comfortable, loose clothes that do not bind, bunch, or chafe. Cotton T-shirts work well but can get chilly when wet with sweat; synthetic T-shirts are more comfortable. For our day hikes, except in winter, we favor hiking shorts; they're loose and have many pockets for storing a bandana, insect repellent, a camera/phone, tissues, and a pocketknife.

Establish a comfortable pace you can maintain for long periods of time. The hiker who charges down the trail not only misses the subtleties of the surroundings, but also frequently starts gasping for breath after 15 minutes or so of hiking. That's no fun! A steady pace allows you to both see and cover more ground comfortably than the start-and-stop, huff-and-puff hiker. When you climb a slope, slow down your pace so you can continue to the top without having to stop. Having to stop is different from choosing to stop at places of interest, although the clever hiker learns to combine the two. With practice, you will develop an uphill rhythm and cover ground faster by going slowly.

## FOLLOWING THE TRAIL

There are many variations in how hiking trails are marked or blazed. Each of our hikes notes the particular trail markings for that hike. However, there are some standard symbols you will see on most hikes: in general, trails are often marked with a single blaze; trail changes are often marked with double blazes, usually offsetting the upper blaze in the direction of the turn. Here is a general key to standard trail blaze markings:

## WHAT TO CARRY

You may have read articles on the portable household the backpacker carries. While the day-hiker need not shoulder this burden, there are some things you should carry to ensure a comfortable and safe hike. Ideally, you will always carry your emergency gear and never use it.

Items 2–10 below live in our daypacks:

1. Small, comfortable, lightweight pack.
2. First-aid kit containing at minimum: adhesive bandages, moleskin (for incipient blisters), adhesive tape, gauze pads, aspirin, salt tablets, Ace bandage, and antibiotic lotion. We also always carry elastic knee and

ankle braces, which have been used more than any of our other first-aid equipment.

3. Wool or polypro shirt or sweater and a nylon windbreaker. A fast-moving cold front can turn a balmy spring day into a blustery, snow-spitting disaster, and sun-warmed, sheltered valleys may contrast sharply with windswept, elevated, open ledges.

4. Lightweight rain gear. In warm, rainy weather, hikers are of two minds about rainwear—some don it immediately and get wet from perspiration; others do not and get wet from the rain. In colder weather, wear it for warmth. In any case, if the day is threatening it is wise to have additional dry clothes in the car.

5. Water. Water found in the woods in southern New England is almost never safe to drink. Always carry at least one to three quarts (more on hot summer days) per hiker. On cool days, a thermos of hot tea, cocoa, or broth is a good thing to have with you. Also, carry some water purifier or a filter in case you need to take water from a source in the woods.

6. Food. In addition to your lunch, carry high-energy food for emergencies. Sometimes you may feel nauseated when you need a bite to eat for energy, so carry stuff you like to eat. Hiking is no time to diet aggressively or to experiment in the food department. Gorp (Good Old Raisins and Peanuts)—a hand-mixed combination of chocolate chips, nuts, and dried fruit—is a good choice.

7. Flashlight with extra batteries and bulb. You should plan to return to your car before dark, but be prepared in case you are delayed. Be aware of the shorter daylight hours of autumn and winter.

8. A well-sharpened pocketknife. This tool has a thousand uses.

9. Map and compass (optional). These items are not necessary for day hikers in Connecticut who stay on well-defined trails and use a guidebook. However, if you want to do any off-trail exploring you should learn to use a map and compass and carry them with you.

10. Other: toilet paper (always), insect repellent (in season), a hat or sunscreen lotion (always, especially on bright days), a wool hat and mittens (in winter, spring, and fall).

Winter hiking can require additional equipment and does not fall within the scope of this book. Nonetheless, it is a lovely time to hike, and we encourage you to hone your skills in mild weather, consult experienced winter hikers, and consider hiking on winter's clear, crisp, often snow-white days. For additional information on winter hiking, we recommend the AMC Guide to Winter Hiking and Camping: Everything You Need To Plan Your Next Cold-Weather Adventure by Lucas St. Clair and Yemaya Maurer.

## HIKING CONCERNS

Footing is the major difference between road walking and hiking. Roads present a minimum number of obstacles to trip you; at times hiking trails seem to present a maximum. The angular traprock cobbles on many of Connecticut's ridges tend to roll beneath your feet, endangering ankles and balance. An exposed wet root acts as a super banana peel, and lichen on wet rock as a lubricant. Stubs of improperly cut bushes are nearly invisible obstacles that can trip or puncture. All these potential hazards dictate that you walk carefully on the trail.

It is far safer to hike with a companion than to venture out alone. Should an accident occur while you are alone, you are in trouble. If you must hike alone, be sure someone knows where you are, your exact route, and when you plan to return. Do not leave this information in a note on your windshield—it is only an invitation to a thief.

Every Eden has its serpent. In warm weather, Connecticut's has its tiny biting pests. Many of us have seen horrific pictures of hikers in the Far North, their shirts blackened with bloodsucking mosquitoes. Explorers of the tropics fear not lions or tigers but biting insects most of all. In Connecticut, you can avoid this problem by hiking in winter or on chilly fall and spring days, which for other reasons are often ideal for hiking. For your summer excursions, understanding the problem and knowing its appropriate remedies will greatly enhance your enjoyment.

Most bugs can be kept at bay with insect repellent. Herbal repellents are quite effective for mosquitoes, while stronger concoctions, often containing DEET, are necessary for blackflies and for repelling deer ticks. Ticks are a concern when hiking in Connecticut as they can carry Lyme disease.

Lyme disease was named for a Connecticut town near Long Island Sound, where it was first identified in 1975. Carried by the very small deer tick (only 0.25 inch in diameter even when fully engorged with blood), Lyme disease does not affect most nonhuman animals except for dogs, which may develop joint disorders. It is now the most prevalent tick-borne illness in the United States, and the number of cases increases yearly. Originally reported only in southern New England, Lyme disease has been found (using different tick carriers in different regions of the world) in 47 states and on all continents except Antarctica. European literature almost a century ago reported a similar group of symptoms. Fortunately, only a small percentage of deer ticks are infected, so the chances of contracting the disease are not high for hikers and other outdoors adventurers; suburbanites seem much more susceptible. Usually within a month of infection, a circular rash a few inches in diameter surrounds the tick bite location. If you are uncertain about a tick bite or find the telltale bull's-eye rash, contact your doctor. Proper treatment within a few weeks of infection is very effective. While not considered a fatal disease, untreated Lyme disease produces debilitating symptoms that can persist for a lifetime. Even at this stage, the illness is treatable with antibiotics.

The best way to protect yourself against Lyme disease is to wear long sleeves and long pants tucked into your socks, use insect repellent (containing 15 to 30 percent DEET) on clothing, and check yourself for ticks. If you have been bitten, contact a physician. Yes, Lyme disease should concern hikers in Connecticut, but with proper precautions and a reasonable level of care, it should not keep you from enjoying the woods. For more information on Lyme disease, visit the federal government's Center for Disease Control website (cdc.gov).

Other hiking dangers are more common but minor. You should learn to identify poison ivy; it's a very common shrub or vine that can cause quite a bit of discomfort. If you stay on the trail, it should not be a problem. It most often appears as a vine with little rootlets clinging to the bark of a tree or a shrub along old

POISON IVY: "LEAVES OF THREE, LET THEM BE"

most efficient rodent controls continue to grace its highland home.

Bees are more of a problem. If you are allergic, you should carry a kit in case of anaphylactic shock. More than twice as many people succumb to allergic reactions to bees than die from snakebite nationwide. Some people react more than others, and many experience little more than the local swelling usually associated with mosquito bites.

## HUNTING IN CONNECTICUT

There are several hunting seasons that begin in the fall months (and select others in the spring). It is important to know that several state forests allow hunting at some point in the fall. Other areas (including Nature Conservancy and Audubon lands) may have controlled hunting to manage deer populations. It is best to inquire about any hunting in or nearby the area you are visiting to ensure a safe hike. We've noted which hikes in our book require hunting awareness.

Peak hunting activity for small game and deer occurs from the third Saturday in October through December. Early morning hours (before 9 a.m.) are the most active hunting times, especially on Saturdays and holidays. Some important safety tips to observe during hunting season include:

stonewalls or a patch of plants on the ground. Its shiny, three-leafed arrangement is fairly unmistakable. And yes, you can catch poison ivy from the bark of this shrub even in winter.

Snakes are overrated; they will not bite you unless you pick them up or step on them. Snakes by nature want nothing to do with humans and will quickly get away whenever possible. Some nonvenomous snakes can deliver a nasty bite, which will require only a good cleaning and maybe a tetanus shot. Connecticut has two native poisonous snakes and only rarely sees even one snakebite annually, and almost never among hikers. The northern copperhead and timber rattlesnake are rare creatures and very effective mousers, of which we need more to help keep the rodent population down. Rodents are not only destroyers of crops (and stealers of hikers' carelessly placed candy bars) but also hosts for deer ticks, which may be infected with Lyme disease. Although rattlesnakes are more venomous than copperheads, there have been no confirmed deaths from a New England timber rattlesnake bite. In all our years of hiking in the state, we've also never seen a rattlesnake. If you should be lucky enough to see one, enjoy the sight from a safe distance, and let one of nature's

- Wear bright clothing (400 square inches of fluorescent orange are required for hunters) to increase your visibility.
- Avoid wearing gray, brown, tan, or white when hiking in hunting areas.
- Consider using a bell on your pack, during the hunting season.

- If you see someone hunting, call out to them to identify your location.

## WATER WORRIES

Most of New England's open water sources probably contain Giardia. Warm-blooded creatures (like us) can ingest tiny Giardia cysts (about 16,500 can fit on the head of a pin) from contaminated drinking water. In the gut they will hatch, multiply, attach to the upper small intestine, and do their damage, which can include diarrhea, cramps, and visible bloating. The cysts infest many warm-blooded animals, including the now numerous beavers; some people call these symptoms Beaver Fever. However, much of the problem stems from the improper disposal of human waste and that of another commonly seen trail beast, the family dog. Both people and dogs carry Giardia, often without exhibiting any symptoms, and travel far more widely than any beaver we are aware of. Human and dog feces should be buried in a shallow hole six to eight inches deep, (a "cat hole"), at least 200 feet from water and 50 feet from the trail to reduce the spread of disease organisms.

Giardia lurks in even the clearest, coldest running water. Therefore, never drink untreated water! This means carrying your own water while day hiking and properly treating your drinking water while backpacking, with either a filter or chemical purifier like iodine. Giardiasis, once correctly diagnosed, is easily treated—but the best treatment is prevention.

## PETS

Taking the family dog on a hike seems only natural to many owners. However, dogs do reduce your chances of seeing wildlife, can spread disease by tracking animal feces into streams and ponds, can dig up fragile vegetation, and can frighten other hikers, especially children. Pet owners can ensure that hiking trails remain open to their dogs by controlling their pets, especially by burying or packing out their pets' feces and by leashing their dogs around open water and people. An important consideration for pet owners: sometimes dogs decide there is something more exciting in the woods than their human companions and take off on a trail of their own. This can lead to serious situations, including losing a treasured family pet or dealing with porcupine quills. If you decide to bring your dog, it's a good idea to carry food and water, especially on a hot day.

## POTPOURRI

- While hiking, don't litter. The AMC motto, "Carry In—Carry Out," is a good one. Carry a small plastic bag in your pack for garbage, and pick up any trash you find along the trail.
- On any hike the minerals, plants, and animals you see have been left untouched by previous trekkers. You, in turn, should leave all things for the next hiker to admire. Remember to "take only pictures, leave only footprints, kill only time."
- Connecticut has a limited-liability law to protect landowners who grant access to the general public free of charge. This saves property owners from capricious lawsuits and opens up more private lands for trails. Please respect landowners who generously allow trails to traverse their property.
- Hiking can be much more than a walk in the woods. Knowledge of natural and local history will add another

dimension to your rambles. We dip lightly into these areas to give you a sampling to whet an inquiring mind. To aid further investigation, we offer a short, descriptive Further Reading section at the end of this Introduction. Using good field guides will contribute immeasurably to a hike.

- A common sight on almost every hike in this book is the twisted limbs of the mountain laurel bush. The mountain laurel (*Kalmia latifolia*) has been the state flower of Connecticut since April 17, 1907. This beloved shrub grows thickly in the Connecticut wilds often covering hillsides with its white and pink flowers. The fragrance and richness of its blossoms during the month of June are a vivid contrast with the darker colors of the forest. A member of the heath family, the mountain laurel is an evergreen with its glossy broad deep green leaves being especially striking on stark grey winter days. The two lakes at Bigelow Hollow (hike #46) are especially beautiful when they reflect the blooms of the mountain laurel. One of the largest mountain laurels in the state can be found at Wadsworth Falls (hike #10), however there are some very large specimens on the lower loop of Devil's Hopyard (hike #43). Both Chatfield Hollow (hike #24) and Sleeping Giant (hike #35) are favorite areas for us to enjoy these blooms.
- Many of the hikes in this book are located in Connecticut state parks. The Connecticut Department of Energy and Environmental Protection website for each park has both a printer- and mobile-device-friendly map. Remember to check the date of the map before using it as there may be inaccuracies. Also as of February

2018, Connecticut has launched a new Passport to Parks program where residents have free access to state parks with the institution of a $10 fee on non-commercial car registrations. Out-of-state cars will have to pay a fee at some state parks.

- Another fascinating aspect of hiking involves observing and considering your environment. Think about why some plants are found in southern but not in northern Connecticut. Why are our woods filled with old roads and stonewalls and dotted with cellar holes? Why do some trees grow straight and tall, while others have out-flung, low branches? You will never run out of things to learn on your hikes! In these trail descriptions, we have thrown in a smattering of natural history. We have touched on only a few subjects and have tried not to repeat ourselves from hike to hike, since much of what is described in one may apply to many others.

## GOAL SETTING

Many hikers collect attractive patches to signify completion of a goal. The AMC sponsors the New Hampshire 4,000-Footer Club and the New England 4,000-Footer Club for those who have climbed the 48 mountains in New Hampshire or the 65 in northern New England that are more than 4,000 feet high. Special patches are awarded to applicants for a small fee.

Connecticut's peaks are less lofty. However, you can set some hiking goals that include "trail bagging." Completing all 50 hikes in this book will certainly earn you bragging rights but will also help you explore and learn about the diverse ecology of our state. For an even greater adventure, check out the

Blue Trails Challenge offered by the Connecticut Forests and Park Association (CFPA). With more than 825 miles of trails marked with blue rectangular blazes, the Blue Trail system offers a great way to explore Connecticut's woodlands. Many of our hikes incorporate some of these blue trails. You can set a goal of any of three challenge categories offered by the CFPA (200, 400, or 800 miles). There is no time limit—complete your goal in one season or over a lifetime of hiking. The CFPA offers a log form for keeping track and rewards your achievement with a T-shirt (200), water bottle (400), and a fleece vest (800). For more information visit the CFPA website (ctwoodlands.org).

## ABOUT TRAILS

Hiking trails do not just happen for our healthy enjoyment, and as we in Connecticut are well aware, they are impermanent at best. When the first Connecticut Walk Book was published in 1937, all the major trails in Connecticut were interconnected. The pressures of change have long since isolated most of these trails from one another. The major reason we still have good hiking trails is that hikers like rough, hard-to-reach land for their hikes, while builders prefer easily developed land. However, as time passes and populations grow, trail corridors become more and more endangered. Let's examine the history of the Appalachian Trail (AT), which mirrors the problems that beset many hiking trails.

The bane of the hiker in our uncertain world is the continual loss of hiking trails to development, land-use change, or just plain unhappy landowners. The AT had been at the mercy of changes such as these since its inception in the 1930s. By the late 1960s some 200 miles of this trail, once on private land, had been displaced onto paved roads. The volunteer Appalachian Trail Conference, located in Harpers Ferry, West Virginia, which coordinated the building and maintenance of the AT, was paying more and more attention to the loss of this wild land. Largely because of a major push by volunteers and pressure from the public, the US Congress passed the National Trails System Act, which was signed into law on October 2, 1968. While this potentially made the AT a permanent entity, no money was appropriated at that time to make the dream a reality.

In 1978, the act was amended, authorizing the National Park Service to acquire a 1,000-foot-wide Appalachian Trail corridor on the private land where about half of the original trail was located. Fortunately, Congress also appropriated $90 million to effect the needed acquisitions. A number of parcels are still to be purchased, and hopes are that it can be completed in the near future. Much has been done, but the toughest acquisitions remain. With the escalating cost of land and the uncertain attitude of recent administrations, it may take more time to complete this vital public acquisition.

What can we, the hiking public, do about this persistent problem? The hikes in this book are a direct result of the efforts of thousands of volunteers like you. Most of us do not have the time, ability, or money to make major contributions. However, we can all vote, support conservation-oriented politicians, and do some sort of volunteer trail maintenance. We must work to create an atmosphere of trust and understanding with private landowners. The hiker's cause is damaged by vandalism, rowdiness, and lack of respect for landowners' rights. But we all benefit from courteous hikers, diligent volunteer trail workers, and an understanding of landowners' concerns.

For more information about helping out, contact the following:

**Connecticut Forest and Park Association (CFPA)**
16 Meriden Road, Rock Fall, CT 06481 (860-346-TREE; ctwoodlands.org)

**Appalachian Mountain Club (AMC)**
10 City Square, Boston, MA 02129 (outdoors.org; ct-amc.org, Connecticut chapter website)

## FURTHER READING

Connecticut is a small state with pleasing outdoor diversity. The hikes in this book touch lightly on many aspects of the state's ever-fascinating landscape: flora, fauna, geology, and history. Since this is basically a hiking book, we have had neither the space nor the time to go into great detail, but we hope to pique your interest about the nature and history of Connecticut. The following texts should enhance your understanding of our state's outdoors and add to your experience hiking with this book.

Among recently released books, *The Connecticut Walk Book: The Complete Guide to Connecticut's Blue-Blazed Hiking Trails*, published by the Connecticut Forest and Park Association, covers all the Blue Trails and many others in the state. *The Appalachian Trail Guide to Massachusetts–Connecticut* covers the AT through the northwestern corner of Connecticut. Also, *AMC's Best Day Hikes in Connecticut: Four-Season Guide to 50 of the Best Trails from the Highlands to the Coast* and *Connecticut*

*Off the Beaten Path®: A Guide To Unique Places* may be of interest.

You cannot hike in Connecticut without encountering a stone wall— over 240,000 miles of stone walls once wound their way around New England. The book *Stone by Stone: The Magnificent History in New England's Stone Walls* by R. Thorson weaves together cultural and environmental history with geography and natural science and is written for a general audience, not just for academics.

Despite the fact that this corner of the nation is composed of six diverse states, people from Connecticut, Maine, Massachusetts, New Hampshire, Rhode Island, and Vermont often think of themselves as New Englanders. It follows that some background on New England as a region will certainly help increase your understanding of Connecticut itself. We recommend *Changes in the Land: Indians, Colonists, and the Ecology of New England* by William Cronon and John Demos; *Reading Rural Landscapes: A Field Guide to New England's Past* by Robert Sanford; *Forest Forensics: A Field Guide to Reading the Forested Landscape* by Tom Wessels; and *Thirty-Eight: The Hurricane That Transformed New England* by Stephen Long.

Many of the Peterson field guides are indispensable in identifying the world met along the trail. Those of special value to us include: *A Field Guide to Wildflowers* by Margaret McKenney and Roger Tory Peterson; *A Field Guide to Mammals of North America* by Fiona Reid; *A Field Guide to Ferns and Their Related Families of Eastern and Central North America* by Boughton Cobb; *A Field Guide to Reptiles and Amphibians of Eastern and Central North America* by Robert Powell, Roger Conant, and Joseph T. Collins;

and *A Field Guide to Trees and Shrubs* by George A. Petrides.

We find it difficult at times to identify trees by their leaves on our hikes, as the leafy canopy can often be high up and leaves hard to distinguish. However, you can always observe the bark of trees. For this, reason, we found Michael Wojtech's *Bark: A Field Guide to Trees of the Northeast* to be very useful. For additional reading about trees we recommend *Connecticut's Notable Trees* by Glenn D. Dreyer. This special book offers dimensions and locations for all the largest-known trees of each species found in Connecticut, as well as for several historic oaks.

Other good guides include Stokes' *A Guide to Amphibians and Reptiles* by Tom Tyning; *Newcomb's Wildflower Guide* by Lawrence Newcomb; National Geographic's *Field Guide to Birds of North America* by Jon Dunn and Jonathan Alderfer; and *Tracking and the Art of Seeing: How to Read Animal Tracks and Sign* by Paul Rezendes. Audubon Society field guides are particularly helpful because of their extensive use of photographs.

Finally, if you want to venture beyond the nuts and bolts of identification, the following books contain much of the lore so dear to the hearts of natural history buffs: *How to Know the Ferns* by Frances Theodore Parsons; *A Natural History of Western Trees* by Donald Culross Peattie and Paul H. Landacre; *Trees of the Eastern and Central United States and Canada* by William M. Halow; and *How to Know the Wildflowers* by W. S. Dana.

## MAP LEGEND

| | | | |
|---|---|---|---|
| ——— | Described trail | ═══ | Interstate highway |
| - - - - | Important trail | ══ | Secondary highway |
| ◄—— | Hike direction arrow | ——— | Minor highway, road, street |
| ——— | Perennial stream | - - - - | Unpaved road, trail |
| - - - - | Intermittent stream | +—+—+ | Railroad |
| ——— | Major contour line | —··— | International border |
| ——— | Minor contour line | --—·- | State border |
| | National/state park, wilderness | **P** | Parking area |
| | National/state forest, wildlife refuge | 🚶 | Trailhead |
| | Perennial body of water | • | City, town |
| | Intermittent body of water | | Overlook, scenic view |
| | Swamp, marsh | Å | Campground, campsite |
| | Wooded area | ⋔ | Shelter |
| | | × | Mountain peak |
| | | ▪ | Place of interest |

## 1

# Great Pond

**LOCATION**: Simsbury

**DISTANCE**: 1.5 miles

**VERTICAL RISE**: Negligible

**TIME**: 0.75 hours

**RATING**: D

**MAP**: USGS 7.5-minute Tariffville

This hike circles a delightful little body of water paradoxically called Great Pond, located in the Massacoe State Forest. The surrounding 297-acre state forest was once a multi-aged white pine plantation, established in 1932 by forestor and conservationist James L. Goodwin. In the 1950s, Goodwin's nursery was designated Connecticut Tree Farm Number One by the American Tree Farm Program. In 1964, the land was bequeathed to the state of Connecticut by Mr. Goodwin and became the nucleus of Massacoe State Forest. A network of nearly 5 miles of trails weaves through the park.

Bird watching is popular here as the pond attracts both resident and migratory populations of birds and waterfowl. Spring and fall are the best times.

You will appreciate short hikes such as this one best when you take them slowly. Adopt a silent, hesitative step to enhance your chances of surprising wildlife. Try being first out on a Sunday morning to increase your chances even more.

## GETTING THERE

From the junction of CT 167 and CT 10/US 202 in Simsbury, follow CT 167 south 0.2 mile to the next traffic light at Firetown Road and turn right. Proceed down this road for 0.7 mile and then fork left onto Great Pond Road. The dirt entrance road to Great Pond State Forest is on your right in another 1.6 miles. The road soon ends at a parking lot with a wooden trail map in a dense grove of white pines.

## THE HIKE

The hiking trails at Great Pond State Forest are unblazed but well-worn and easy to follow. We follow a clockwise loop around the park; be aware of

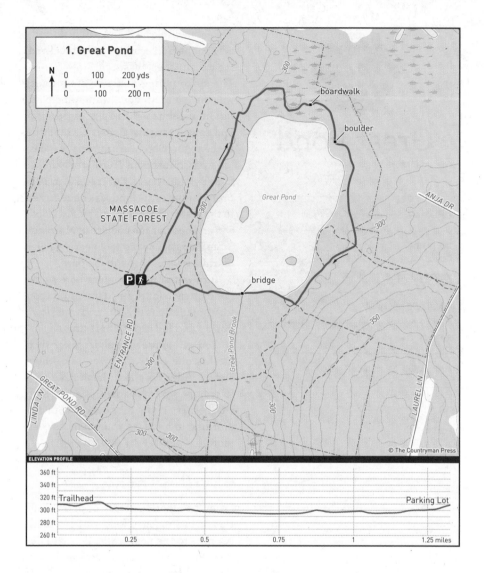

© The Countryman Press

**ELEVATION PROFILE**

numerous side trails branching off. At times, timber harvesting may be done on some of the side trails. Timber zones are well signed, and when harvest is in progress, trails leading to them are closed.

This hike starts at the far right corner of the parking lot and continues in the same direction as the entrance road. Once a tote road, the wide, horseshoe-pocked trail begins along the edge of a thick white-pine grove and then passes

through it. The pine plantation is so dense that no new pines sprout despite millions of seeds shed by opening cones. Instead, the main understory tree is the shade-tolerant hemlock. In early summer, pink lady's slippers add color to the soft carpet of pine needles.

Take the first right and head toward the pond—you'll see it through the trees. Turn left to follow the trail around the pond, keeping it to your right. Following this rule of thumb of keeping the pond on your right. You may take an occasional dead end to the water's edge without getting lost. Such inadvertent side trips will permit you to admire the pond from many viewpoints.

You will come to a fork in the trail (clearly not one of the little side trails), at which you'll bear right. You'll then cross an aging bridge over a swampy area (an arm of the pond), before a short boardwalk appears that you'll follow through marsh. You will pass a few large pines on the side of the trail, each with a diameter of two and one-half to three feet. Note a boulder off to the right of the trail: unlike most Connecticut forests, Great Pond has few large stones, making this solitary glacial erratic a point of interest. A while after the boulder, you will pass on your left a bull white pine with a diameter of four feet and enormous branches. The size of the tree's branches indicates that this pine matured in a clearing, without any competition for sunlight.

Be sure to take a side trail down to the Great Pond. There are a number at this point that lead directly to the water's edge. This shallow pond is strewn with lily pads and bordered with emergent vegetation and tree stumps gnawed by beavers. The moisture-loving royal fern stands on water-girt hummocks and grows even in the pond's shallow water. Dragonflies dance and alight with their four wings outspread. You'll also see iridescent damselflies flapping awkwardly or perching with wings clasped together above long, thin abdomens. In July and August, the rubber-band twang of the green frog serenades you.

Most of this hike features beautifully soft, pine-needle-lined trails. In fall especially, the fallen needles create interesting patterns. If the weather has been recently dry, a nice fluffy carpet of fresh needles is likely to cover these tote roads. If there have been heavy rains, the fallen needles will instead outline

GREAT POND, A SHALLOW POND STREWN WITH LILY PADS AND EMERGENT VEGETATION

A BULL WHITE PINE

the flow of runoff water. Where the water has pooled, an even layer of flattened needles tells the story.

Needles falling? But aren't pines evergreens? Yes, to both questions. A needle grows in the spring, stays on the tree the first winter—creating the evergreen effect—and is joined the next spring by a crop of fresh new needles. Eventually however, about a year and a half after emerging, needles die and fall. If you walk through a pine grove in early October, every little puff of air sends needles drifting downward.

As your path enters boggy areas, watch for the tupelo (or black gum) tree. Found from Maine to northern Florida, it has an exceptionally wide range but is found growing naturally only in swampy environs. The tupelo has glossy, leathery leaves, deeply furrowed and slightly teardrop in shape, and crosshatched bark that somewhat resembles alligator skin. As the leaves change color in fall, the tree presents a deep burgundy red. A medium-sized tree (one to two feet in diameter, with a record of five feet), the tupelo is unfit for most uses. It rots easily, and its fibers are so intertwined that it is impossible to split. This tree is fairly common along the pond's edges.

At about three-quarters of the way around the pond, you'll see on your left a side trail with what appears to be yellow blazes. A closer look will show you the blazes are actually yellow rings painted around the diameters of the trees. These trees represent a boundary line for private property which skirts the side trail until you reach Laurel Lane.

Next you'll cross a boardwalk-style bridge, after which you'll find a stand of great rhododendron,—a native relative of mountain laurel. You can tell the difference between mountain laurel and rhododendron by examining their leaves. While still evergreen and glossy, a rhododendron's are much larger. In July, this stand boasts impressive white flowers.

At first, the trail tunnels right through the stand. Then the rhododendron-lined path angles left, as you bear right to continue around the pond. Soon after, you'll pass an impressive double-trunk bull pine tree with each trunk having a diameter of more than two feet.

At the next junction, turn right to cross a causeway offering great views across the pond. You'll soon traverse a wide-plank bridge at the small cement dam on the pond's south end. Notice the beaver lodge and evidence of activity just past the dam. If you visit in October, you may discover growing on the abundant white pine branches of the forest floor small orange fungi, appropriately named Witch's Butter.

Shortly thereafter, you'll come to another woods road to your left leaving the pond. Turn left here to finish the last short stretch of your hike. You'll pass a small, rectangular stone monument with an inscription (facing hikers coming from the opposite direction) that honors James L. Goodwin for his preservation work. Continue uphill through the dense hemlock and pine grove to the parking lot.

## OTHER HIKING OPTIONS

**Additional Resources:** A state park trail map can be found at www.ct.gov /deep/massoce. The same map is displayed at a bulletin board at the start of the hike. You can lengthen the hike by exploring a number of side trails, being mindful of any timber-harvest closings.

# Mount Tom Tower

| | |
|---|---|
| **LOCATION**: Morris | |
| **DISTANCE**: 1.5 miles | |
| **VERTICAL RISE**: 360 feet | |
| **TIME**: 1 hour | |
| **RATING**: C | |
| **MAP**: USGS 7.5-minute New Preston | |

Though short, this is a rewarding half-day hike. By taking advantage of the swimming and picnicking facilities, you can profitably spend the whole day here.

One of the state's oldest parks, Mount Tom was established, along with 15 others, between 1913 and 1918 by The Connecticut State Park Comission. Charles H. Senff donated the land the park now occupies in 1911 on the condition that a permanent observation tower be maintained at the summit of Mount Tom. In 1921, a 34-foot stone tower, constructed using rough black gneiss found at the site, replaced the wooden structure that had stood there since 1881. This quick but at times rugged hike leads you to the summit of Mount Tom, 1325 feet above sea level (125 feet higher than its Massachusetts counterpart, but a much easier hike). The top of the tower offers one of the best views of the state.

## GETTING THERE

Mount Tom State Park is located just off US 202, southwest of Litchfield and 0.6 mile east of its junction with CT 341. Watch for the state park sign after you turn right on the access road (Old Town Road). You'll pass by a small, commercial summer camp on your left. Once inside the 233-acre park, follow the one-way signs to a junction with a marker directing you to the Tower Trail, just before the main picnic area. Turn right and park here.

## THE HIKE

Today's route—a gentle woods road to the summit and the option of a little more rugged trail on your descent—follows yellow-blazed trails. Be aware that there are many side paths branching off this route that are not blazed.

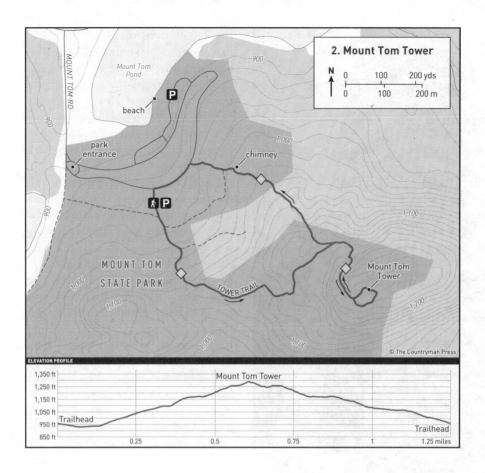

You will always, however, stay on yellow-blazed trails.

Take the yellow-blazed gravel road through a wooden gate and steadily up a gravel road (no vehicles allowed). In early spring you will see the white blossoms of the shadbush, or juneberry, so named because it flowers around the time the shad run up the rivers. This shrub, with its light gray bark, is much less noticeable at other times of the year. The juicy berries that ripen in July are edible and taste not unlike huckleberries. Native Americans used to dry and compress them into great loaves, chunks of which were broken off over the winter for use as a sweetener.

Turn right at the top of the rise and follow the ridge toward the top of the mountain as you walk along the forest road. You may notice several individual, rounded boulders scattered in the woods as you proceed. Most are glacial boulders (stones left by melting glaciers) that didn't travel very far. Occasionally, you will find a boulder or rock that is morphologically different than all other stones in the area. This is called a glacial erratic. Carried over long stretches of terrain by glacial ice, erratics can range in size from pebbles to large boulders. The more rounded they are, the further the distance they traveled.

In about 0.75 mile, the trail ends at the base of a circular stone tower over 30 feet high. Wooden stairs inside lead

MOUNT TOM TOWER

from left to right the Heublein Tower (hike # 47), the Hanging Hills in Meriden, and Castle Craig on West Peak (hike # 36). Toward the southwest, the rugged hills contain New York State's Harriman Park. On especially clear days, you can see Long Island Sound to the south and the outskirts of New York City at right.

To return by a different route, follow the same yellow-blazed woods road back down for about 0.3 mile. You'll come to a level (and frequently wet) spot where you should look for a yellow-blazed trail on your right. Follow this steep, rocky path all the way down. Once you find this trail, you should have no problem following the well-worn treadway. In late October, the evergreen mountain laurel here provides a colorful contrast with the shades of rust displayed by the oaks and beech trees of the ridge.

Near the bottom as you approach a gravel road, you'll notice a handsome stone chimney and fireplace with nearby cement foundations. This is all that remains of Camp Sepunkum's assembly hall. The camp housed the Waterbury Boy Scouts, who helped develop the park between 1916 and 1934. Continue following yellow blazes and soon you will come to the tar park road where you turn left. In about 0.1 mile you will reach your parked car.

On one occasion, as we stood by the car after this hike, a pileated woodpecker with red crest and white underwings flew overhead. This distinctive bird, as large as a crow, is the drummer that excavates great rectangular holes in unsound trees to reach infestations of carpenter ants.

Now, if you have time, head over to the pond. It's great for cooling off after

you to a cement roof—watch your head as you emerge at the top.

Below is spring-fed Mount Tom Pond, with its trucked-in sand beaches. Beyond to the northwest, you'll observe the Riga Plateau with, from left to right, Mounts Bear (hike # 37), Race, and Everett. The latter pair of mountains are in Massachusetts. To the northeast, you can see Mohawk Mountain with its radio towers (hike # 33) and beyond that, in the same direction, you can see

THE VIEW FROM MOUNT TOM TOWER

a short but hearty hike, and since it's spring fed its waters are clear, crisp, and clean. You can also relax and enjoy some lunch at the picnic tables nearby.

## OTHER HIKING OPTIONS

**Additional Resources:** A state park trail map can be found at www.ct.gov/deep/mounttom.

**Nearby:** This park is a short distance from White Memorial Foundation (hike # 42). If you want more hiking rather than a swim after your ascent of Mount Tom, check out the trail options at this wildlife sanctuary.

THE START OF THE HIKE

# Southford Falls State Park

**LOCATION**: Southbury and Oxford

**DISTANCE**: 2 miles

**VERTICAL RISE**: 400 feet

**TIME**: 1 hour

**RATING**: C

**MAP**: USGS 7.5-minute Southbury Quadrangle

Most people seem to enjoy the rush of water over and through rocks, and this hidden gem of a park offers visitors beautiful flowing waters, a covered bridge crossing the gorge, and a series of scenic waterfalls. The park also features a pleasant loop hike that will take you away from the crowds and up to an observation tower, meandering along the way through some interesting exposed geology.

Southford Falls State Park sits on the border of Southbury and Oxford, where the plunging waters from Eight-Mile Brook once powered the area's early industrial history. During the Civil War era, over a half-dozen factories, including an axe factory and grist, saw, and paper mills, were supported by the falls. Eight-Mile Brook's steady, powerful current at this site is the result of a drop in elevation from its source at Lake Quassapaug. At some point, the brook was deepened—you may note the ridge of rock between the stream and trail appears to be manmade—in order to increase the water's speed for industries taking advantage of its power. In the early 1900s, the Diamond Match Company bought up the land and built a factory for the manufacturing of cardboard matches. A series of fires ultimately culminated in the company deeding the land to the state. The state park was then created in 1932.

Southford Falls State Park offers a lovely large grassy area for picnicking, and Papermill Pond is a designated trout-fishing area managed by the state. It provides both handicapped parking and a handicapped-accessible fishing area. The path to the falls is also handicapped accessible.

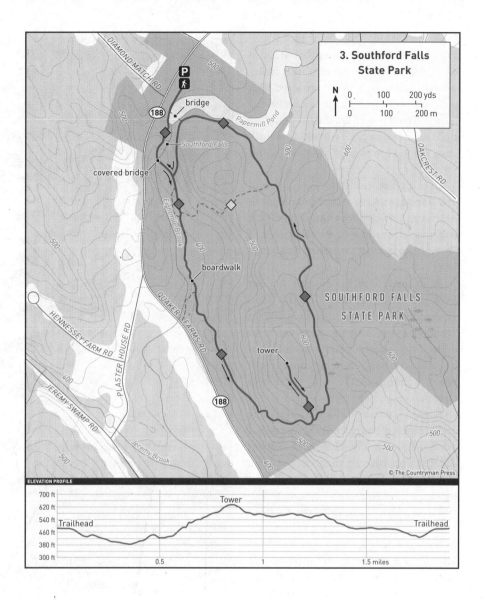

## 3. Southford Falls State Park

N

| 0 | 100 | 200 yds |
| 0 | 100 | 200 m |

bridge

188

Papermill Pond

DIAMOND MATCH RD

Southford Falls

covered bridge

Eightmile Brook

boardwalk

SOUTHFORD FALLS
STATE PARK

tower

188

QUAKER FARMS RD

PLASTER HOUSE RD

HENNESSEY FARM RD

JEREMY SWAMP RD

Jeremy Brook

OAKCREST RD

© The Countryman Press

**ELEVATION PROFILE**

| | Tower | | |
| 700 ft | | | |
| 620 ft | | | |
| 540 ft | Trailhead | | Trailhead |
| 460 ft | | | |
| 380 ft | | | |
| 300 ft | | | |
| | 0.5 | 1 | 1.5 miles |

## GETTING THERE

Southford Falls State Park is located on CT 188, 0.5 mile south of the highway's junction with CT 67, and is accessible from both I-84 and CT 8. The park entrance is clearly marked and has a sizeable parking lot that can be crowded on sunny, summer days.

## THE HIKE

The route described here is a 2-mile loop on the Red Trail with a short detour to the fire tower at the southern end of the loop.

From the southern end of the parking lot, you'll head along a crushed cinderstone path to a bridge that crosses

Papermill Pond. Take a right, following signs for the covered bridge and boardwalk. This section of trail is easily accessible and sometimes crowded with people craving fresh air and natural beauty. You'll soon pass the falls on your right as the wide path travels downhill. Take some time to enjoy the cascading waters.

Continue downhill on the path, and you'll soon see a turnoff on your right to a covered bridge above the gorge. This bridge is a reproduction of the work of Torrington bridge architect, Theodore Burr.

After the bridge, the crowds thin out as you continue downhill on the path. The walkway now shifts from cinder to crushed stone, and the path narrows a bit. You'll pass a yellow-blazed trail on your left, which can be taken if you prefer a shorter loop (see *Other Hiking Options*).

After about 0.25 mile from the start you'll reach a boardwalk that protects you from the muddy edges of the brook. After the boardwalk, the path becomes rockier, and there is an increased need to watch your footing. Continue to follow the red blazes despite any rougher blue blazes you may see on the trees. In our experience, these spray-painted blazes are not official and often signal mountain-biking routes. You should remain focused on following the rectangular red blazes. Your hike will then take you uphill where you'll pass a rocky mass on your right. This outcropping reveals a layering of dark and light minerals and is part of the geologic Collinsville Formation.

For about 0.25 mile, your path continues along the hillside on your left and parallel to CT 188 on your right, after which the trail begins to veer left as it angles around the southern end of

EIGHT-MILE BROOK ALONG THE BOARDWALK

the loop. You'll turn left (indicated by double red blazes on a tree) and then crest a hill. The trail continues to veer left and ascends again until it reaches a somewhat flat area where you'll briefly walk across a small plateau on the side of the ridge. Soon the trail ascends to the left, where you will come to the fire tower. Although red-blazed, this left-hand turn is a 0.1-mile detour off the main trail. The view from the fire tower is of the wooded forest around you. To your south is a U-shaped valley that was steepened and widened by the grinding of rocks in ice, the result of glacier flow over 15,000 years ago.

Retrace your steps down the hill back to the main trail. Turn left, but pay attention. The path is well worn, but the red blazes are somewhat faint at first. You'll travel downhill through a forest studded with mountain laurel. The dark, evergreen leaves are striking in the fall and winter amidst the bare hardwoods around you. The trail flattens out around the base of the hill leading you through a few small stands of young hemlock. The path here is heavily scattered with medium-sized rocks, so watch your step. You'll descend until you reach a wide, wooden-plank bridge as the trail travels through a wet, rocky area. On your left, you'll pass the yellow trail, mentioned earlier, where you'll rejoin the red trail if you take the shorter loop (see *Other Hiking Options*).

Your path will soon run parallel to a stone wall and then pass another large outcropping on your left. Papermill Pond will be visible on your right. On a recent, late-November afternoon, the pond was laced with a sheer pattern of ice, a harbinger of the winter cold to come.

Soon you come to an open, grassy area with a large picnic pavilion on your left. Walk across the grassy area to the bridge you crossed at the beginning of

SOUTHFORD FALLS

PAPERMILL POND

the hike. Turn right to cross the bridge and return to your car (although another quick visit to the falls might be a nice ending!).

## OTHER HIKING OPTIONS

**Additional Resources:** A state park trail map can be found at www.ct.gov /deep/southfordfalls.

**Short & Sweet:** You can see the falls and the covered bridge while enjoying a much shorter, 0.5-mile loop. Soon after passing the covered bridge, you'll notice on your left a side trail blazed in yellow. Follow this trail for 0.2 mile east across the park until you rejoin the red blazes. Turn left on the red trail, passing Papermill Pond and returning to the bridge and your car.

# Lookout Mountain

**LOCATION**: Manchester

**DISTANCE**: 2.5 miles

**VERTICAL RISE**: 350 feet

**TIME**: 1.5 hours

**RATING**: C

**MAP**: USGS 7.5-minute Rockville

Lookout Mountain is located in the Case Mountain Recreation Area in Manchester. This popular park encompasses over 600 acres of open space and watershed lands maintained by the Manchester Conservation Commission, Connecticut Forest and Parks, and a variety of concerned volunteers. There are three mountains in the park: Lookout Mountain, Case Mountain, and Birch Mountain. The latter two have wooded summits, while Lookout Mountain's is cleared, flat, and spacious, offering an excellent place to have a snack while admiring the view.

A visit to Case Mountain Recreation Area is an enjoyable outing. Its well-maintained network of trails is easy to hike, run, or bike. Lookout Mountain is great for family hiking with the kids. For those looking for a more extended hike, trails connect this recreation area with Gay City State Park in Hebron (hike #17). Adjacent to the trailhead parking lot on Spring Street and also worth a visit is a waterfall with an arched stone bridge and stone walls.

Formerly known as Highland Springs or Highland Park, the recreation area was once home to various mills and mining operations that took advantage of the power of Wyllys Falls. The Case family bought the property in 1889. Calling it the Tonica Springs Company, they intended to develop Highland Park as a spa with hotels and cottages for guests. Their plans did not materialize; however, they did bottle clear spring and mineral waters, which were sold throughout the country. In the early 1900s, the Case family constructed a "wilderness park," which included a carriage path, stone walls and bridges, and a public spring area. Much of the stone construction remains to this day, but the spring has been sealed up.

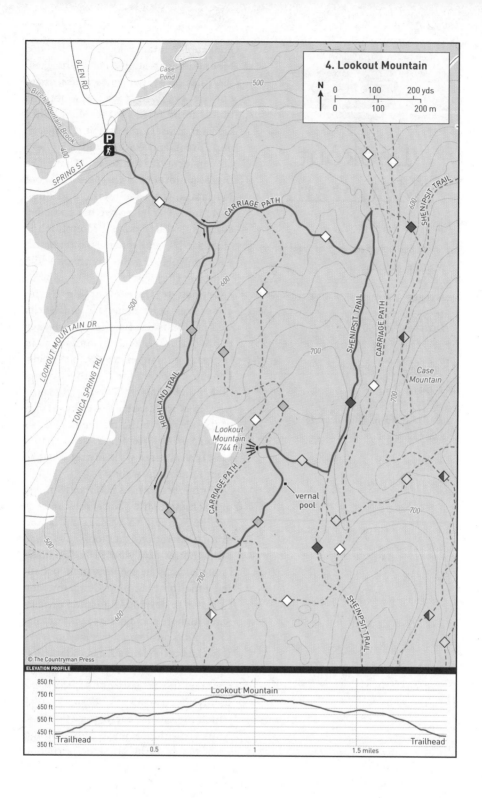

### 4. Lookout Mountain

GLEN RD

Case Pond

Birch Mountain Brook

SPRING ST

CARRIAGE PATH

SHENIPSIT TRAIL

SHENIPSIT TRAIL

CARRIAGE PATH

LOOKOUT MOUNTAIN DR

TONICA SPRING TRL

HIGHLAND TRAIL

Lookout Mountain (744 ft.)

CARRIAGE PATH

vernal pool

Case Mountain

SHENIPSIT TRAIL

© The Countryman Press

**ELEVATION PROFILE**

Lookout Mountain

Trailhead

Trailhead

850 ft
750 ft
650 ft
550 ft
450 ft
350 ft

0.5    1    1.5 miles

CASE POND

## GETTING THERE

This loop hike begins at the Spring Street parking lot. From eastbound I-384 in Manchester, take exit 4 (Highland Street). From the end of the exit ramp, turn right onto Spring Street. Proceed for 0.2 mile until you reach the small parking lot at the bottom of the hill on your left. From westbound I-384, take exit 4. At the end of the ramp there is a stop sign, turn right. Then continue to the traffic light where you turn right onto Spring Street. Crosss over the highway and proceed as above.

## THE HIKE

This loop hike begins on the white-blazed Carriage Path. From there, it will take the pink-blazed Highland Trail, then the yellow trail to the blue-blazed Shenipsit Trail, and finally travel back to the white-blazed Carriage Path.

From the parking lot, head over to the white-blazed Carriage Path near the covered bulletin board. Keeping the chain-link fence on your right, you'll walk uphill on this paved road which soon becomes a wide, gravel path. This part of the hike was once notable for a majestic hemlock grove to the left of the path, which was salvage-logged after succumbing to the woolly adelgid. The forest has a few spectral hemlocks still standing but is now primarily wooded with birch, maple, and beech and carpeted with lush fern undergrowth.

After 0.2 mile, you'll reach a bench and the intersection with the pink-blazed Highland Trail. Turn right on this loop trail. Continue along, turning

ARCHED STONE BRIDGE AND WATERFALL FROM CASE POND

right at the fork and following the pink blazes. The trail continues uphill but not as steeply. You'll cross a wooden footbridge before walking through a stand of the ever-ubiquitous mountain laurel (Connecticut's state flower). The trail then levels out and curves slowly around to the left toward the summit of Lookout Mountain. On your right, just before you reach it, there is a mysterious clearing where only sedges and mosses grow. Surrounding the opening are numerous highbush blueberry plants,

when in season are heavily laden. Unfortunately, these berries, though beautiful, are extremely sour, perhaps due to the very acidic soil. No woody plants grow within the opening. In the spring, the annual, snowmelt floods creates a large vernal pool in this spot, provideing a breeding habitat for a host of amphibians and insects. Black-masked, tan-colored wood frogs are the earliest spring breeders of Connecticut's native amphibians. Although probably more numerous than the familiar spring

east of the Connecticut River. In the foreground is the town of Manchester but because of its wooded streets, this city of 58,000 people is hard to see. You should be able to view the broad, flat-roofed box of the high school and the white spire of Center Congregational Church. To your right, if facing north, you can see Buckland Hills Mall and a tall, narrow, light-blue water tower beside it. On the clearest of days, you can see the white finger of Heublein Tower rising from Talcott Mountain (hike #47) northwest of Hartford.

East from the summit, take the yellow trail for 0.1 mile until you reach the blue-blazed Shenipsit Trail. Follow the yellow blazes carefully; there are many unmarked side trails in the woods. Turn left to continue on the Shenipsit Trail north along a ledge below the summit. To your right, the land drops off quickly in stepped ledges toward the flat forest floor. The thin, poor soil along the exposed ledges of the ridge dries out quickly and is largely treed with chestnut oaks, which are more tolerant of these conditions than the moisture-dependent hemlocks. With their deeply furrowed, dark gray bark, these oaks are distinctive at any season.

The trail now slopes downward. After bearing right downhill, you will follow the trail to your left, near the end of the ridge. After 0.5 mile further on the blue-blazed trail, you will come to an intersection with the white trail (a bench also sits at this intersection). Take a hard left here, following the small sign that says SPRING STREET PARKING. As you walk along, you'll see a sign for the CARRIAGE PATH, although its surface is not yet the gravel road we hiked upon earlier. The trail will lead you through more mountain laurel and then down to a footbridge, where

peepers, they lack the high-pitched carrying cry of the latter and are therefore not as well known. You often hear the low quack-like croaks of the wood frog in this area as early as mid-March. The tadpoles in this poind, though safe from most predators, must go through their metamorphosis and become small frogs quickly, since the cleared area is dry by early summer.

After exploring this clearing, walk a short distance to the summit of Lookout Mountain (744 feet). You'll have one of the best views of the Hartford skyline

VERNAL POOL NEAR THE SUMMIT OF LOOKOUT MOUNTAIN

you'll see another vernal pond on your left. After 0.3 mile, the path reaches the gravel road. Turn right to continue on the white-blazed Carriage Path. Once again, you'll come to the intersection with the pink-blazed Highland Trail you took earlier. From this point, you'll retrace your steps on the white-blazed Carriage Path back to your car.

## OTHER HIKING OPTIONS

**Short & Sweet:** Instead of taking the yellow trail on the summit over to the Shenipsit Trail, you can continue on the pink-blazed Highland Trail back down to the intersection with the white-blazed Carriage Path, turning left to retrace your steps back to the car. This will shorten your hike to about 2 miles.

**Interesting Side Trips:** If you wish, you can include a side trip to the eastern end of Case Pond by turning right on the white-blazed trail from the blue-blazed Shenipsit Trail. Continuing on this path will bring you to the Case Pond parking lot on West Center Street in Manchester. Once you reach the pond, take the unmarked woods roads left alongside the pond until you reach the waterfall at the western edge of Case Pond, not far from your car.

If you have time after your hike, explore the arched stone bridge, waterfall, and Case Pond. Wide, unmarked paths lined with stone walls traverse along its southern edge.

# Peter's Rock

**LOCATION**: North Haven

**DISTANCE**: 2.5 miles

**VERTICAL RISE**: 500 feet

**RATING**: B/C

**MAP**: USGS 7.5-minute Branford Quadrangle

At 373 feet above sea level, the craggy summit of Peter's Rock is the highest point in North Haven and part of a 20-mile chain of trap-rock ridges stretching from New Haven to Massachusetts. Peter's Rock has gone by many names over the centuries. During colonial times, it was called Indian Rock, as it was reported to be a Native American look-out post. It has also been called Great Rock as well as Rabbit Rock or Rabbit Rock Hill, in reference to the large number of rabbits populating the area.

According to local legend, Peter's Rock is named for Peter Brockett, an American Revolutionary veteran, who reportedly became a hermit after a war injury and built a shelter at the summit where he lived out his days. In the early 1900s, four businessmen erected an elegant sportsman's club here, known as the Hermitage, which was used for several years before it was destroyed by fire. The only remains of the clubhouse are its wine-cellar ruins, which you can see on the steeper trail leading to the summit.

Today, Peter's Rock offers extensive, heavily wooded hiking trails just 4 miles from downtown New Haven and remains the largest tract of open space left in North Haven. The property is maintained by the Peter's Rock Association, which sponsors hikes, clean-up weekends, and park festivals throughout the year.

## GETTING THERE

Peter's Rock Park is located in North Haven on CT 17/Middletown Avenue in the Montowese part of town. From 91N, take exit 8 (Middletown Ave/North Branford). Off the exit ramp, bear left to

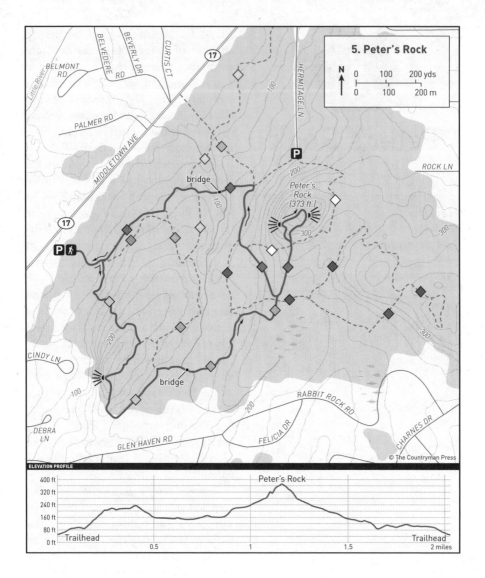

5. Peter's Rock

ELEVATION PROFILE

Peter's Rock

400 ft
320 ft
240 ft
160 ft
80 ft
0 ft

Trailhead

Trailhead

0.5 1 1.5 2 miles

© The Countryman Press

17N/103 (not a hard left). You are now on Middletown Avenue. Follow this road for 1.6 miles, passing an intersection with CT 103, and turn right into the First Fuel gas station. Bear right onto a short gravel connector at the rear end of the First Fuel lot into Peter's Rock park.

From 91S take exit 8 (Middletown Ave/North Branford). At the end of the ramp, turn left, following signs to 17N/80E. At the next light, after you pass beneath the highway, turn left onto 17N (Middletown Avenue). Follow for 1.6 miles as noted above to the park entrance.

## THE HIKE

Our hike is a 2.5-mile loop that follows the light-blue, orange, and red trails. Most of the blazes in this park are the traditional rectangles painted onto tree trunks.

Head to the gazebo from the parking

VIEW OF SLEEPING GIANT FROM THE SUMMIT OF PETER'S ROCK

lot, and turn left to the trail entrance at the edge of the woods. This entrance leads you directly onto the red trail, which you'll follow up a modest incline. Soon you will turn right onto the light-blue trail; watch for a blue arrow on a tree alerting you to the turn. The light-blue trail starts off fairly level as it parallels Middletown Avenue for a short distance. The trail then veers left (indicated with an arrow on a post) before traveling steadily uphill through a second-growth, mixed-hardwood forest of maple, beech, and oak. The shaded forest provides a pleasant hiking path lined with fallen leaves.

At the top of the hill, the trail again turns left. Continue to follow the light-blue blazes. You will intersect various unmarked paths throughout this hike. The park is adjacent to private homes, and over time informal paths have been created between these residences and the trails of Peter's Rock.

You'll continue upward through a grassy area before the trail takes a sharp left at 0.4 mile. Take a short detour here—walk straight ahead for 20 feet to enjoy a serendipitous view. To the south (left) is the New Haven Skyline and East Rock with its needle-like monument. To the north (right) is the silhouette of Sleeping Giant in Hamden (hike #35). After enjoying the view, retrace your steps and bear right to return onto the light-blue trail. You'll head downhill and come to a brushy T-junction at 0.5 mile, where you'll turn left. You'll soon come to another junction. Again, turn left. This trail is unmarked at the turn, but soon you'll see a light-blue blaze. The trail then levels out and you'll continue along a pleasant path, comfortably padded with leaves. Hike quietly through

LITTLE RIVER AT PETER'S ROCK

this area, and you're likely to see some local wildlife. Deer frequently cross these trails.

Next you'll reach a junction with the orange trail, which you'll take by turning right. Soon you'll reach Little River (a lovely stream), and bearing slightly left you'll cross a sturdily constructed boardwalk and bridge—an Eagle Scout project by John Carafeno and Todd Richards.

About 1 mile from your start, you'll come to an open area where the orange trail bears right on a less trodden path. You may see dark green blazes on your left, but turn right to stay on the orange trail. The trail travels steadily uphill. Be sure to bear left as you travel up this incline—a wide, heavily eroded path on the right also climbs the hill. You'll find that a number of trails at Peter's Rock are wide and somewhat deteriorated, and in a few spots re-routing has been done to avoid these eroded trails. The erosion is a result of illegal ATV use in the park, which has been curbed since the Peter's Rock Association reclaimed the land in the early 2000s.

After a short distance, you'll come to the end of the orange trail, as indicated by a pair of horizontal orange blazes on a tree. Just ahead is the intersection with the dark-green and red trails. Bear right, and then take a sharp left on the red trail heading toward the summit. At first, you'll walk along a gradual incline, but after the white trail veers off to your right, the red trail will begin to climb steadily.

Eventually, you'll come to a fork in the trail. Bear left. The fork to the right also goes to the summit but is unmarked and much steeper (see *Other Hiking Options*). From here, you'll have a short but somewhat difficult climb up to the summit. Be cautious of the leaves on

the trail; they can be slippery and hide loose rocks underneath. After the steepest portion, the trail curves around to the right, climbing more gradually to the summit. Red blazes can be found on the rocks, though some have been painted over. You'll reach a false summit, at which point you can head left a few dozen feet to a viewpoint. To the northwest, you can again witness the distinctive shape of Sleeping Giant State Park. To the north, you'll see the hills of Meriden and to the south, New Haven Harbor and Long Island Sound.

As you leave the viewpoint outcropping, turn left and continue a bit further to reach the actual summit with an elevation of 373 feet. After you enjoy the vista, retrace your steps back down the red trail. You will be following the red trail now for the remainder of the hike as you head back to your car. You'll again pass the white trail, this time veering off to your left. You'll then come to the intersection with the dark-green trail; bear right and then bear more sharply to the right when you see the orange trail on your left. Keep to the red trail. As you continue downhill, the path travels along a deeply eroded woods road. Perhaps this was the main route to the summit and the Hermitage? You'll see the white trail merge from the right and the dark-green trail from the left as you continue along your route back.

At 2 miles from the trailhead, you'll come to an open area in the woods. Straight ahead is a trail blazed in red with white dots that heads out to Hermitage Lane, and next to that on the left is the pink trail. You will take a hard left to stay on the red trail. In 0.1 mile, you'll bear right over Little River again, this time over a more simply constructed wooden bridge. You'll hike up a small incline and at the top bear right on the red trail, passing the intersection with the yellow trail. Again the trail will be quite wide with a nicely padded, leafy path shadowed by large maple, beech, and oak trees. You'll pass an intersection with orange blazes, but continue on the red trail.

After another 0.1 mile, you'll pass the light-blue trail coming into view on your left. This is where you turned at the start of your hike. Continue on the red trail, bearing right as you head downhill to the trail entrance and parking lot.

## OTHER HIKING OPTIONS

**Additional Resources:** In addition to information about clean-up days and festivals, Peter's Rock Association offers a nice color trail map on their website (petersrockassociation.org).

**Short & Sweet:** You can take the red trail directly up to the summit and retrace your steps back to the car. Be mindful of various twists and turns in this route, and take care to follow the red blazes throughout. The total distance up and back is 1.8 miles.

**For a Challenge:** You may choose a steeper ascent of the summit, take a detour off the red trail soon after the white trail intersects. When you begin your ascent, bear right at the fork. This unmarked trail is short but steeper and requires some scrambling. You'll come upon a foundation on your left, which is all that remains of the wine cellar from the old Hermitage sportsman's club. Continue on the path past the ruins, passing through a small grassy area before reaching the clear rocky summit.

**Extending the Hike:** There is a network of more than 6 miles of trails at Peter's Rock. You can extend the loop by incorporating the dark-blue, dark-green, lime-green, violet, and khaki trails into your hike.

# Audubon Center in Greenwich

**LOCATION**: Greenwich

**DISTANCE**: 3 miles

**VERTICAL RISE**: 300 feet

**TIME**: 1.75 hours

**RATING**: C/D

**MAP**: USGS 7.5-minute Glenville

Mention Greenwich, and you may invoke visions of high-walled estates surrounded by dense, urban areas and ribbons of concrete. New York City has spilled over into the southwestern corner of Connecticut, and this intrusion of the urban has shaped this county's ties to nature. Thus, a visit to the 285-acre Audubon sanctuary, established in 1943, is a pleasant surprise. Its woodland beauty compares favorably with that of many wilder, less accessible areas of the state. Rolling hills, large hardwoods on rich bottomland soil, swamps, a small river, and a pond attract many kinds of birds as well as hikers. This main sanctuary is one of seven in Greenwich managed by the National Audubon Society. Soon after opening, the park established itself as the National Audubon Society's first environmental education center. Even on a cold, wintery day, you can see ample evidence of Audubon's activities in managing birds and other wildlife. Open 365 days a year, the center maintains a 7-mile network of hiking trails.

Note that during the late fall and early winter on weekdays and before 9:30 a.m. on weekends there may be trail closings due to a management program in effect to reduce the local deer population and its impact on native flora and fauna. Call the center directly at 203-869-5272 to confirm before planning a hike in the winter months.

## GETTING THERE

To reach the sanctuary, take exit 28 off the Merritt Parkway (CT 15) and turn north (right) onto Round Hill Road. After 1.5 miles, turn left onto John Street. Drive for 1.4 miles to Riversville Road; the Audubon Center entrance is a sharp right at this intersection. After

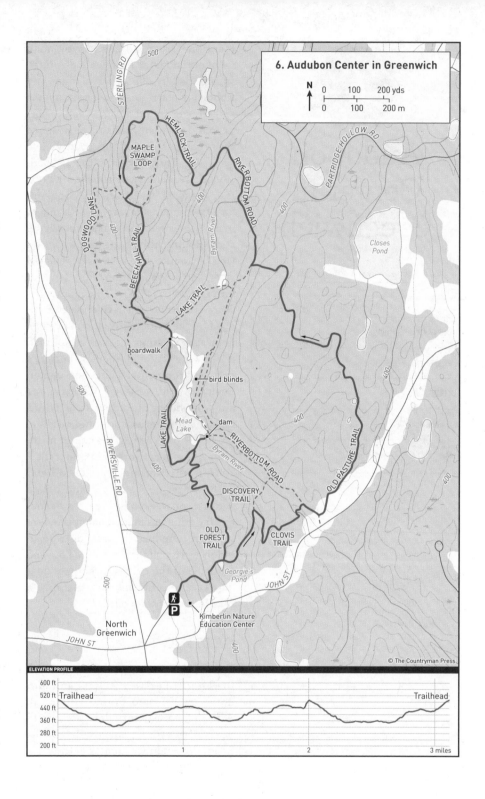

**6. Audubon Center in Greenwich**

N

| 0 | 100 | 200 yds |
| 0 | 100 | 200 m |

STERLING RD

HEMLOCK TRAIL

MAPLE SWAMP LOOP

RIVERBOTTOM ROAD

PARTRIDGE HOLLOW RD

DOGWOOD LANE

BEECH HILL TRAIL

Byram River

Closes Pond

LAKE TRAIL

boardwalk

bird blinds

LAKE TRAIL

Mead Lake

dam

RIVERBOTTOM ROAD

Byram River

OLD PASTURE TRAIL

RIVERSVILLE RD

DISCOVERY TRAIL

OLD FOREST TRAIL

CLOVIS TRAIL

Georgie's Pond

JOHN ST

North Greenwich

JOHN ST

Kimberlin Nature Education Center

© The Countryman Press

**ELEVATION PROFILE**

| 600 ft | | | |
| 520 ft | Trailhead | | Trailhead |
| 440 ft | | | |
| 360 ft | | | |
| 280 ft | | | |
| 200 ft | | | |
| | 1 | 2 | 3 miles |

a short distance on the entrance road, you will see the large Kimberlin Nature Education Center and parking area.

## THE HIKE

There are 7 miles of trails at the center. Our loop takes you along nine trails through the sanctuary: Discovery Trail, Clovis Trail, Old Pasture Trail, River-bottom Road, Hemlock Trail, Maple Swamp Loop, Beech Hill Trail, Lake Trail, and Old Forest Trail. The route is a lovely overview that can be extended or shortened as desired (see *Other Hiking Options*).

Before you begin walking, pick up a map of the trail system at the center. Painted blazes on the trails are inconsistent, but there are signs at all the trail junctions.

Start by following the paved trail to your left downhill past the large education center and through an orchard dotted with birdhouses. As the road curves right, you'll see Georgie's Pond on your left. You'll leave the road and go around the pond (either to the right or left—there are paths on both sides). On the far side of the small pond, you'll see a sign for THE OLD FOREST TRAIL AND THE DISCOVERY TRAIL. Follow the Discovery Trail (you'll come back on the Old Forest Trail). The Discovery Trail soon turns right. On a recent hike, we found the path here marked with irregular, long, teal-colored blazes on trees along the side of the trail.

In a short distance the trail becomes surrounded by thick undergrowth, especially blackberry canes with their formidable thorns. The trail tends downhill. Level log steps partially embedded in and perpendicular to the trail retard the erosion that running water causes as it courses downward. Without the steps, this well-traveled path would rapidly erode. The wood chips you find

CROSSING THE BYRAM RIVER, UPSTREAM OF MEAD LAKE

FROZEN MEAD LAKE

elsewhere on the trail are likewise there to protect it.

Two giant tulip trees serve as your introduction to the great trees of the preserve. The bark of the tulip tree is distinctive with its prominent lattice-like texture. Most of this sanctuary, with its large, mature forest, is made up of rich bottomland hardwoods—beech, ash, tulip tree, oak, and maple. The woods are left to their own natural growth and eventual decay. Dying trees and fallen branches are left to rot where they fall, recycling their nutrients into the surrounding soil and contributing to the diversity of life in the sanctuary.

Turn right onto the Clovis Trail. Follow this trail to the small stream draining Georgie's Pond. Turn sharply left just before leaving the woods, and eventually you'll cross the stream before walking downhill to the Byram River. Cross the river as well. You'll soon reach an old woods road, Riverbottom Road, and turn right. Bear left onto the Old Pasture Trail and follow this old woods road past ponds and rock outcroppings. If you find yourself hiking along this trail in winter, keep an eye out for a large holly tree on the right side of the trail; its dark evergreen leaves stand out conspicuously against the leafless hardwood forest. You'll pass through old pastures where evergreen, eastern red cedars, and various briars thrive in the sunlight.

Descend the hillside to Riverbottom Road. Its overgrown condition, a surprising development in recent years, is another example of nature absorbing our impact on the landscape. One of the more conspicuous plants found here is the greenbrier. The stem of this thorny vine remains green year round, but its tangled masses are particularly distinctive during the leafless months. Turn right onto Riverbottom Road (turning left is a shorter alternative—see *Other Hiking Options*), and follow it to cross the Byram River on a long boardwalk-like bridge, upstream of Mead Lake.

The muddy floodplain on the far side of the river is liberally dotted with skunk cabbage, a rather unattractive and malodorous plant that blossoms very early in spring. Its shape and smell are specially adapted to attract the only insects available for pollination this early—carrion flies that search out the carcasses of animals that died the previous winter. Allured by the plant's fetid odor and the dark-reddish color of its hood-like spathe, the flies mistake the skunk cabbage flower for a dead animal. In the process of investigating, the flies pollinate the tiny flowers inside the spathe.

After crossing the river, follow the trail up the slope through a large grove of beech trees. Riverbottom Road terminates at the top of this rise. Proceed to your left on the Hemlock Trail. To your right, the Hemlock Trail skirts part of Maple Swamp before rising sharply to its junction with the Maple Swamp Loop. Turn right to circle more of the swamp to your left. At this point, you are at the northern-most section of our loop. You'll see private homes and a town road through the trees beyond the edge of the sanctuary property.

The Maple Swamp Loop climbs steadily to the Beech Hill Trail. Bear left here. This trail ascends to the ridge and then drops gradually to merge with Dogwood Lane, which you will follow to your left toward Mead Lake. You pass

more large beeches here. Unfortunately, defacing initials carved on the smooth, tender bark can still be deciphered after the passage of many years.

At a fork, turn left. You are now on the Lake Trail. Follow signs for the Lake Trail, toward the boardwalk. The numbers and variety of plant species growing in this swampy area are truly amazing. Pass poison sumacs to your right along the boardwalk. The plant's compound leaves are some of the first to turn color in early autumn.

Soon you'll reach the west side of

THE BOARDWALK NEAR MEAD LAKE

Mead Lake. Elaborate bird blinds hug the far shore. The trail follows another boardwalk, after which you will take a sharp right onto the Lake Trail. But consider taking a little detour here: turn left beyond the boardwalk and continue for a short distance to visit the dam, rebuilt in 1998. Enjoy early fall views across the pond of the spectacular foliage surrounding you. Return to the Lake Trail and follow its zigzags until you reach the Old Forest Trail. This trail will lead you directly to Georgie's Pond. You'll walk around the pond to return to the paved road that will lead you back to the parking lot.

## OTHER HIKING OPTIONS

**Additional Resources:** A full-size trail map can be picked up in the Kimberlin Nature Education Center, the main building adjacent to the parking lot. Inside is a bookstore and gift shop where maps are included free with the park small entrance fee.

There is also a smaller trail map and other interesting information about the sanctuary on the Audubon Center's website (greenwich.audubon.org).

**Short & Sweet:** At a little over 1.5 miles, this short loop follows our described hike until you reach your second intersection with Riverbottom Road. Instead of turning right, turn left on this old woods road. You'll follow the trail until you reach the start of the shrubby wetlands of Lake Mead. At a fork in the trail, bear right onto the Lake Trail. This will take you along the eastern side of Lake Mead (passing some cool bird blinds on your right). Continue along the Lake Trail and over the dam to rejoin our original route. You'll zigzag down the Lake Trail, bear left onto the Old Forest Trail, and end up on the far side of Georgie's Pond. Circle this small pond around to the paved road, and follow the road back to the center and the parking area.

# Osbornedale State Park

| | |
|---|---|
| **LOCATION**: Derby | |
| **DISTANCE**: 3 miles | |
| **VERTICAL RISE**: 400 feet | |
| **TIME**: 1.5 hours | |
| **RATING**: C | |
| **MAP**: USGS 7.5-minute Ansonia Quadrangle | |

Osbornedale State Park encompasses over 400 acres of land in the Naugatuck Valley Hills on the eastern bank of the Housatonic River in Derby and Ansonia. The land was once the lushly forested hunting grounds of the Paugussett Indians. Settlers cleared the land for farming and set up a trading port, taking advantage of their location on the Housatonic and Naugatuck Rivers. After the Revolutionary war, the lands within the park near Silver Hill Road were mined for silver, but the enterprise was never commercially successful and was thus short lived. A spring water business was also once located on this land.

The park is the former estate of Frances Osborne Kellogg, granddaughter of John W. Osborne, one of Naugatuck Valley's early industrial entrepreneurs. Controversially, Frances (then the unmarried Miss Osborne) took over the family business when her father died in 1907. Despite prejudices against women in business at that time, Frances was very successful. She gradually purchased surrounding properties, piecing them together to form the over 400-acre estate. Later, Frances and her husband Waldo Kellogg ran two very successful farms, one for breeding prize-winning Holstein cows and the other an excellent milk-producing farm of Jersey cows. When she died in 1956, Frances Osborne Kellogg deeded the land for Osbornedale State Park to the people of Connecticut.

Activities at the park include hiking, picnicking, fishing, and cross-country skiing in the winter. Ice-skating is also popular on Pickett's Pond, with its night lighting and a warm-up hut. Osbornedale State Park is likewise a great place for any geology enthusiast. The park harbors several different rock types, as well as geologic folds,

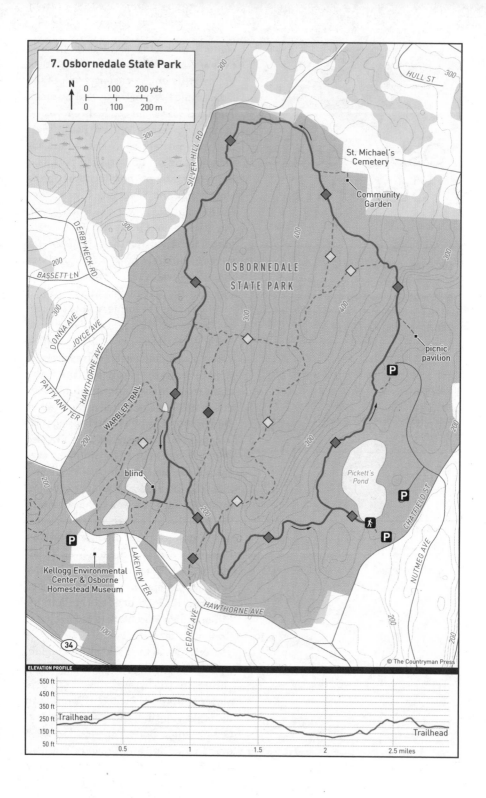

**7. Osbornedale State Park**

N
0   100   200 yds
0   100   200 m

HULL ST

St. Michael's
Cemetery

Community
Garden

OSBORNEDALE
STATE PARK

SILVER HILL RD.

DERBY NECK RD.

BASSETT LN

DONNA AVE

JOYCE AVE

HAWTHORNE AVE

PATTY ANN TER

WARBLER TRAIL

blind

picnic
pavilion

P

Pickett's
Pond

P

P

CHATFIELD ST

P

LAKEVIEW TER

Kellogg Environmental
Center & Osborne
Homestead Museum

NUTMEG AVE

CEDRIC AVE

HAWTHORNE AVE

34

© The Countryman Press

**ELEVATION PROFILE**

550 ft
450 ft
350 ft
250 ft
150 ft
50 ft

Trailhead

Trailhead

0.5      1      1.5      2      2.5 miles

MAINTAINED MEADOW TRAILS AT OSBORNEDALE

quarries, and abandoned mines. More information can be found at the Kellogg Environmental Center and on the Connecticut Department of Energy and Environmental Protection's website for the park.

## GETTING THERE

Osbornedale State Park is a short distance from CT 8. If southbound, take exit 17 and then a left at the end of the exit ramp. Take another left at the light onto Division Street. In 0.75 mile the park will appear on your right, across from Derby High School. If driving northbound on CT 8, take exit 18 and then a left at the end of the exit ramp. Drive approximately a 0.5 mile to the park.

## THE HIKE

Today's route is a 3-mile loop on a red-blazed trail around this little gem of a park. You'll pass numerous side trails, some unmarked and others blazed in yellow or blue. The hike meanders through meadows, open forest with glacial boulders, denser forest thick with undergrowth, and marshland adjacent to ponds.

From the parking lot, walk down to the Pickett's Pond and follow the path west along the stonewall. The path then veers left—away from the pond and across a grassy field—toward the woods. You come to a break in the woods where you'll see a trail signpost. Turn right. You'll proceed though the woods, then an overgrown field, and then again through the woods (returning on the trail that went left at the signpost). You are on the red trail. Although you may see some spray-painted red marks on a few trees, at this point, the path is not well blazed.

The trail soon comes to a junction; turn right to go over a boardwalk-style bridge. Notice the hill on your left has a large outcropping of rock. This is schist, a metamorphic rock that has undergone intense heat pressure and the actions of hot fluids. This outcropping has interlayered gray, rusty, weathering schist with parallel fractures and folds.

You'll see more schist throughout the hike today.

The trail then circles around the north edge of Pickett's Pond. You'll be walking through a densely wooded area lush with undergrowth. You'll see many large oaks and maples. Also look for the unusual lattice bark of a large tulip tree on your left.

In 0.25 mile, you'll come to a fork. Bear left to follow the red trail (right will take you to a parking lot). The trail soon leaves the woods through a meadow along a well-maintained path. Enter a small stand of trees, and you'll see a picnic pavilion further up on your right. As the trail departs from the trees, it enters another grassy field. When you are directly opposite the picnic pavilion, you'll notice a trail post and a path leading uphill to the left. Take this left to reenter the woods. You'll experience a short steady climb uphill, and a stone wall will soon parallel the trail to your right. This is still the red trail, but you'll find the blazes occur sporadically. Soon you'll come to a junction with the yellow trail. Continue straight ahead on the red trail. The path here is level at first but then slowly descends. Eventually you'll see the edge of the Community Garden through the woods on your right. Over the next 0.5 mile or so, the trail continues to enter small stands of trees and then moves through open meadows. If you look closely at the trees, you'll see stone walls in those stands. Annual mowing helps maintain the fragmented meadows and additional, more frequent, mowing create the well-defined paths. These connected meadows are clear evidence of Frances Osborne Kellogg's work in acquiring land piecemeal to build up her estate.

You'll reach another junction (again with the yellow-blazed trail). Turn right at the signpost following a mowed trail through the meadow. Soon you'll see St. Michael's Cemetery on your right through another thin stand of trees. The mowed trail then joins a well-worn woods road. Veer left to stay on this woods road. You'll see occasional red blazes on posts, but they are difficult to see in late summer when overgrown with vegetation. Soon after joining this woods road, you'll see a grassy road on your right. Keep left to stay on the more trodden path. As you hike along the road and head downhill, you'll notice the road's surface changes to old, fragmented macadam. Houses are visible through the trees on your right, and the ruins of an old stone house are on your left. After the ruins, as you reach the bottom of the hill, the road veers to the right. You'll see a trail entrance on your left with a signpost. Turn left here. If you miss the turn, you will come to Silver Hill Road and a wooden gate spanning across the worn dirt road.

Continue to follow the red trail as it skirts the northern border of the park. The path now proceeds again through open woodland with stone walls and numerous glacial rocks and boulders scattered about. The stone walls may be evidence of previous mining activity in the area, possibly constructed from loose boulders that were excavated.

You'll now enter a large stand of mountain laurel. The trail then veers a bit to the left around a large boulder and descends. Ferns border the trail to your left. As you hike through this rocky-floored, open-woods land, you'll pass a few unmarked spur trails on your right; these all lead to Silver Hill Road. You should continue to follow the red-blazed trail.

Soon on your left you'll see a stream (dried-up in late summer) as the trail

THE DISTINCTIVE LATTICE BARK OF THE TULIP TREE

PICKETT'S POND

descends. There is another trail junction punctuated with a bridge on your left. Continue on the red trail by keeping right. The wide, worn path continues through open woods land and a rocky hillside on your left. Shortly thereafter, a trex bridge opens a new trail on your right. This currently unmarked trail may be one that is under construction. It appears to lead toward Hawthorne Avenue and the Kellogg Environmental Center, skirting the western side of two unnamed ponds. Do not follow this trail; instead continue along the red-blazed trail.

Next you'll reach a Y junction. Taking a left will keep you on the red-blazed trail. But first take a detour to a wildlife-viewing blind by turning right along a mowed path that runs through a well-maintained meadow. You'll pass numerous birdhouses and perhaps see a bluebird on your trek. You'll then come to a four-way junction of mowed paths; turn right. The path then veers right, downhill, and around a bend to the viewing blind that overlooks the two unnamed ponds and the surrounding marshland.

Retrace your steps back through the meadow, turning left at the meadow-path junction and turning right after entering the woods to continue on the red trail. You will gently ascend before coming to a junction with the blue trail; again keep on the red trail as you turn

descending on the red trail. This is a short but steep descent, returning you to the heavily overgrown woods of earlier in the hike. Prickly briars border the cleared path. You'll then approach a trail post at the edge of a meadow. Veer left uphill as the trail hugs the edge of the woods. Soon you'll arrive at the junction where we began our trek into the woods. Turn right here heading back to Pickett's Pond and your car.

## OTHER HIKING OPTIONS

**Additional Resources:** A state park trail map can be found at wwwct.gov /deep/osbornedale. The printer-friendly map dated 2016 shows side trails in yellow and green, but we found both were blazed in yellow. The blue trail on the map was blazed true to color in the park.

**After the Hike:** Visit both the Kellogg Environmental Center and the Osborne Homestead Museum. From the park entrance, continue south on Chatfield Street and turn right onto Hawthorne Avenue. In about 0.5 mile, the entrance for both will be on your left. The Kellogg Environmental Center offers workshops, exhibits, nature activities, and lectures for the general public. It is open Tuesday through Saturday. Call to confirm hours at 203-734-2514. The Osborne Homestead Museum celebrates the life of Frances Osborne Kellogg with a restored interior (containing a significant collection of antiques and fine arts) and beautifully landscaped grounds. The house has limited hours and free admission. Call 203-734-2513 for more information.

right and walk downhill for a stretch. Ultimately the path levels off as you walk along a wooded hillside. Next you'll arrive at a T junction. Turn left to walk uphill on the red-blazed trail. (Note: the right turn is also blazed in red, but will take you to Hawthorne Avenue.) Soon you'll come to another trail post where you'll turn right and ascend, curving back around to the left. You'll then be walking along the top of a hill with numerous stone walls lacing through the woods.

You'll reach a junction with the yellow trail on your left. Turn right,

# Rocky Neck State Park

| | |
|---|---|
| **LOCATION**: East Lyme | |
| **DISTANCE**: 3 miles | |
| **VERTICAL RISE**: 150 feet | |
| **TIME 1.5 HOURS** | |
| **RATING**: D | |
| **MAPS**: USGS 7.5-minute Old Lyme, Niantic | |

Located on Long Island Sound in the town of East Lyme, Rocky Neck State Park is bound on the west by a tidal river and on the east by a broad salt marsh. As a result, the area is abundant with fish and wildlife, and was an especially desirable location for early colonists and Native people. In the 1920s, the state began the process of purchasing the land but was slow to do so. There was great concern that the opportunity to preserve the land would pass. The East Lyme Historical Society website states, "Ten men, including members of the State Park and Forest Commission, were so determined that the property be set aside for the enjoyment of the public that they risked their own money to hold the property until the Assembly voted to approve the purchase in 1931." Soon after it was established as a state park.

Today the 710-acre park is a popular recreation area. Clear waters and a stone-free beach make the park an ideal choice for summer sunning and swimming. There are many beautiful picnic locations scattered throughout the park, and diverse trails within provide interesting walks to salt marshes, wooded areas, grassy fields, and a scenic ridge. There are opportunities to fish for mackerel, striped bass, blackfish, and flounder, and bird-watching is popular. During migration periods, it is common to spot osprey, cranes, herons, and mute swans. Rocky Neck also offers family camping within walking distance of the beach: 160 wooded and open campsites can be reserved in advance. Although the park is a popular beach destination, it is nevertheless delightful year-round, and each season provides different natural wonders for the hiker.

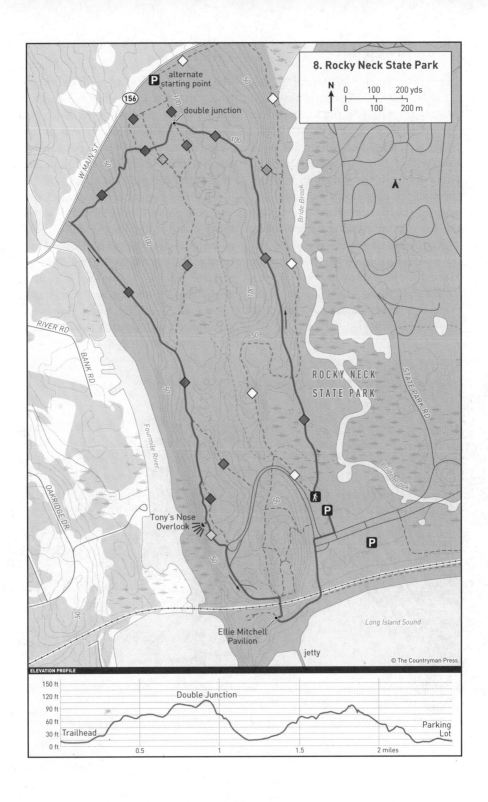

## 8. Rocky Neck State Park

N

| 0 | 100 | 200 yds |
| 0 | 100 | 200 m |

alternate
starting point

double junction

156

W MAIN ST

Bride Brook

ROCKY NECK
STATE PARK

STATE PARK RD

Bride Brook

RIVER RD

BANK RD

Fourmile River

OAKRIDGE DR

Tony's Nose
Overlook

P

P

P

Ellie Mitchell
Pavilion

Long Island Sound

jetty

© The Countryman Press

**ELEVATION PROFILE**

Double Junction

Trailhead

Parking
Lot

150 ft
120 ft
90 ft
60 ft
30 ft
0 ft

0.5          1          1.5          2 miles

## GETTING THERE

The park entrance is located off CT 156, 2.7 miles west of CT 161 in Niantic. If you are traveling on the Connecticut Turnpike (I-95), take exit 72 (Rocky Neck) to CT 156 and follow the signs east (left) off the exit ramp to the park. After entering the park and passing through the entrance kiosk, bear left toward the beach area. Drive into the first grassy parking area on your right, 1.2 miles from the entrance, just beyond the bridge over Bride Brook. Head for the far northwest corner, back and to the left as you enter, near the picnic tables and a small outhouse obscured by trees.

## THE HIKE

The network of hiking trails at Rocky Neck State Park is color-coded. Our hike is a loop combining the red, blue, and yellow trails. This loop ends at the western shoreline of the park near the historic Ellie Mitchell Pavilion, a public works project completed in 1937.

The hike begins to the right of the outhouse; a trail post displays a red arrow going straight and a white arrow going left. Follow the red trail. Blazes are infrequent, but will appear as colored, wooden squares hammered into the trees. These markings are often quite weathered. Trail junctions, however, are marked with posts. The well-worn

WINTER VIEW OF THE CAUSEWAY AND BRIDGE THROUGH THE MARSH AT THE START OF THE HIKE

SUMMER VIEW OF THE CAUSEWAY AT THE START OF THE HIKE

paths are easy to follow, but avoid taking unmarked side trails unless following a map.

The trail passes quickly through a fringe of beeches, maples, and oaks to a short causeway leading across a marsh. You then enter a shady wood that will provide relief from the summer sun. Throughout this hike, you'll find abundant mountain laurel—some of the largest groves we've seen in Connecticut—as well as blueberry, huckleberry, and sassafras in the underbrush of the forest.

About 0.25 mile along, you'll cross a white-blazed trail. Stay on the red-blazed trail. After another 0.4 mile, you'll traverse a small footbridge before reaching a junction with the purple trail. Again, stay on the red-blazed trail. Soon after the junction with the purple trail, you'll see an unmarked side trail on your right. Feel free to take a short detour: this short trail takes you to a large balancing rock perched on a larger flat boulder.

Back on the red trail, enjoy a gentle climb along the ridge above the brook.

Here, about 1 mile into the hike, you'll reach another two-part junction with the blue trail. The first junction post indicates a left turn on red will bring you to the pavilion. Bear right instead, and immediately you'll see another junction post. Turn left here following the blue trail toward Four Mile River. (If you begin your hike at the alternative starting point on CT 156, you'll enter onto the blue trail from the right—see *Other Hiking Options*.)

You'll now pass through a grassy field called the Shipyard (labeled on a post in the field). Be cautious of poison ivy as you walk along this section of the trail. Your path will cross the orange trail, but continue on the blue. The trail will reenter the woods and begin to descend in gentle switchbacks, exiting the ridge you were walking along. After skirting CT 156, the path turns left and widens into an old woods road with stone walls bordering on the left. A boatyard will be visible through the trees on your right.

Follow the woods road gently uphill passing a junction with the red-blazed

VIEW OF LONG ISLAND SOUND FROM TONY'S NOSE

trail on your left (about 0.5 mile from where you started on the blue trail). For almost 0.2 mile, the blue and red trail run together, and are marked by double blazes. The red trail then veers left. Continue on the blue trail by keeping right. On a snowy December day, we were treated to many sightings of woodpeckers along this stretch: hairy, downy, and even the elusive pileated woodpecker—the largest woodpecker species found in Connecticut, recognizable by its distinct, pterodactyl-like crest.

After the trail levels out, you come to a junction with the yellow-blazed trail. Take a right to follow the yellow trail and ascend a rocky ridge toward the ocean. Views of Four Mile River and the open bay await you from a vista called Tony's Nose. The vista is, yes, partially obscured by oak foliage, but not in winter—another reason to try and experience Connecticut hiking in all seasons!

Continue along the path. At the end of the open ridge, the trail leads directly toward fenced-in train tracks but then veers to the left to meet a tar road.

The internal woodwork includes pillars made of great tree trunks: at least one trunk was taken from each then-existing state park in Connecticut.

Return to the arched bridge and descend the paved path toward the pavilion's rear garage. Pass through the stone archway under the pavilion, and then bear left toward the picnic area and the beach. A rocky fishing jetty thrusts out into the water before you, and beyond it spreads a graceful curve of beach. The rocky arms at either side of the bay provide shelter from all but the roughest storms. From the beach, follow the walkway under the railroad bridge on your left. Swamp roses adorn the embankment here. Continue on the road straight past the pavilion and back to your car.

## OTHER HIKING OPTIONS

**Additional Resources:** Hiking maps can be found at the entrance kiosk, at the park office inside the pavilion near the parking lot, or at www.ct.gov/deep /rockyneck.

**Alternative Starting Point (CT 156):** If you are going only to hike, you may choose to avoid the day-use fee by parking on CT 156 about 0.5 mile west of the main park entrance and beginning your hike at the log gate there. This entrance is just past the Camp Niantic KOA on the opposite side of the street. You'll enter on the blue trail and soon pass the green trail junction on your right as you head straight to the red/blue junction. From there you will turn right on blue toward Four Mile River and follow the hike narrative above.

Proceed on the tar road to your right through a parking lot to the paved uphill walkway. Walk over the train tracks via an arched footbridge to an imposing building. This is the Ellie Mitchell Pavilion, a public works project of President Franklin Roosevelt's Works Progress Administration (WPA). The walls of this massive building are made of fieldstone, and large fireplaces cheer the inside.

# 9

# Sunny Valley

**LOCATION**: Bridgewater

**DISTANCE**: 3 miles

**VERTICAL RISE**: 700 feet

**TIME**: 2 hours

**RATING**: C

**MAP**: USGS 7.5-minute New Milford

A hike can be far more than just a bit of exercise in the woods or a chance to chin with a variety of like-minded folks. The woods are a wonderland where limitless understanding can feel in reach. The trees, the low-slung plants, the animals of chance encounter, the geologic clues, and our impact on the landscape are all there for us to witness. The nicest thing about reading from nature is that, for the ever-curious amateur naturalist, there are no tests, and no one to satisfy—only oneself! Some things you see are seasonal and some have been around for decades. Some features you'll encounter date to colonial times, and still others go back to the Ice Age and earlier. An encyclopedia would be needed to detail each hike you take, especially if you take the time to look closely and return each season. In this hike description, we will touch briefly on three of these categories of wonder—the Ice Age, trees, and traces left by the original colonists.

The Sunny Valley Preserve encompasses 1,850 acres of farmland, forests, wetlands, and meadows on 19 parcels of land. The preserve's trails are one facet of a multiple-use land management plan overseen by the Nature Conservancy and several private landowners. This hike takes you through the Silica Mine Hill parcel down to Lake Lillinonah. Named after the daughter of Chief Waramaug, a leader of the Pootatuck Indians, Lake Lillinonah is a 14-mile-long, man-made body of water spanning across six different towns. The second largest lake in Connecticut, Lillinonah was constructed by the Connecticut Light and Power Company, as part of a solution to channel hydroelectric power from the Housatonic River.

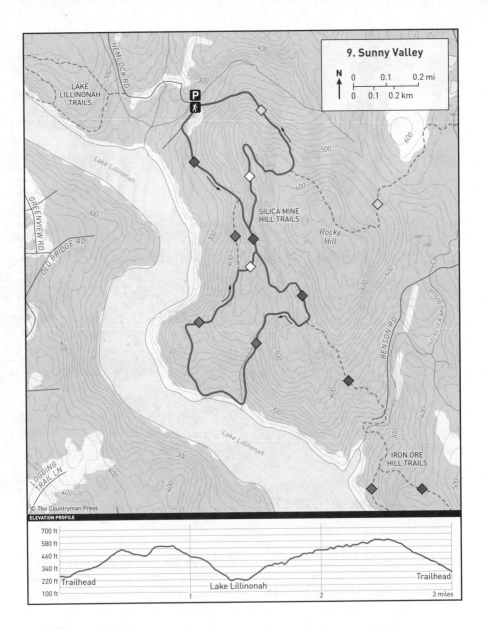

**9. Sunny Valley**

## GETTING THERE

From the junction of CT 67 and CT 133 in Bridgewater, head south on CT 133 about 0.7 mile, and then turn right at a stop sign to follow Hat Shop Hill Road. After 0.6 mile, turn left onto Christian Street, then right onto Hemlock Road, which you'll follow for 1.5 miles. Soon after the road narrows and bears sharp left, you'll find parking at the Anthony and Vanda Ficalora Nature Preserve on your left. If you reach a gated, private road, you have gone too far.

LAKE LILLINONAH

## THE HIKE

This hike follows the blue-blazed Silica Mine Hill trail for about 1 mile, and then the red trail down to Lake Lillinonah. You'll continue along the water on the red trail and then return to the blue trail—following a white-blazed connector between the two. After proceeding on the blue trail for a short distance, you'll take another white connector to the top of Silica Mine Hill and the yellow-blazed Silica Mine Hill Trail. You'll then follow the yellow blazes back to your car. All the trails are well marked with blazes, laminated maps, and signage posted on trees. You may also see laminated numbers posted along the trails. These correspond to numbers on the Nature Conservancy map, downloadable from their website (see *Other Hiking Options* for a link). Note that this hike traverses Sunny Valley's Silica Mine Hill section, and all trails within the section take its name, no matter the color of the blazes.

From the parking area, you'll see the yellow-blazed Silica Mine Hill Trail in the woods in front of you. This is the trail

to the lookout, which will be part of your return route. Continue along the blue-blazed trail, passing numerous chips of quartz from the nearby silica mines along the path. You'll soon pass an old stone foundation to your left (which may look like a sink hole until you notice the carefully placed stones supporting the sides of the pit). During your descent you'll pass another white trail on your right, and continue to follow the blue trail as it levels out.

The trail again gently descends and then bears left through a swampy section. You'll cross the small swamp over puncheon bridging made of local logs, at the end of which you'll come to a large blue-blazed tree with the distinct holes created by pileated woodpeckers. Your path will then curve up to the left to climb a small ridge. After descending the ridge, you'll note a deep, swamp-filled ravine on your left.

The glaciers that covered Connecticut more than 10,000 years ago left many traces. There are thousands of these geologic reminders throughout the state—glacial erratics, old kettle holes, and dying ponds. The swamp you encounter here—once a long, narrow pond on the side of the mountain—is such a remnant. The ice sheet gouged this depression in the ledge, the bottom of which is relatively impervious to water. The natural demise of all ponds comes sooner or later, depending on their original depth. Aquatic vegetative growth and wind- and water-borne debris have all contributed to the filling of this pond. Its surface scum and the trail's wending through the pond's former outlet are signs of an imminent return to dry land.

As you begin to descend toward Lake Lillinonah, the blue trail veers right and then takes a quick left, well marked with

you will come down on your return. To start, hike up the road, following blue blazes. When you reach a gated road, the blue-blazed Silica Mine Trail turns left into the woods. The trail proceeds southward uphill. Climb the gently graded woods road, continuing to follow the blue blazes. Shortly thereafter, your path levels and proceeds along an old tote road before climbing again. Gradually, the grade steepens before reaching a red-blazed trail on your right. Continue straight and uphill on the blue trail.

As the trail levels off, you will come to a white trail on your left. This is the trail

DISTINCTIVE HOLES CREATED BY PILEATED WOODPECKERS

Lillinonah. Turn right at the water, and cross a small brook. We spotted a mink at its edge on a recent hike here! Follow the trail, climbing away from the water's edge, crossing through an opening in a stone wall and paralleling the shoreline northward. You'll turn right and ascend a series of ridges, traveling away from the lake through thick, hemlock woods.

Hemlock forests tell an interesting story. Take a moment to look beneath this dense stand. The thick, acidic bed of the hemlocks' fallen needles and twigs, together with the trees' tightly interwoven, light-intercepting foliage, have banished all other plants from the forest floor, so that now only young hemlocks can grow here. A climax forest is then maintained until fire, ax, or by introducing another cycle.

Just as the ascent eases, you'll come to a white-blazed connector trail. Turn right here to follow the white trail for 0.1 mile, climbing again to the crest of a ridge. From there you'll descend briefly to a woods road, which is the blue-blazed trail from the beginning of the hike. Across from you are the old silica (quartz) mines that colonists carved in the hillside. These abandoned mines are indicative of the lack of mineral resources in New England. When Connecticut was first settled, dreams of mineral wealth led to much part-time prospecting in the state. Limited amounts of cobalt, iron ore, garnets, silica, and gold lured these early prospectors. Most of the holes they dug, however, have since filled in. In a few places, some small successes inspired larger diggings, where activity nevertheless faded after the discovery of richer lodes elsewhere. This silica mine is a case in point. Like other local mines, it's just a relic from the past to stimulate our curiosity.

blazes and laminated signs. You'll then soon reach a junction. Take the red-blazed trail to your right, or continue on the blue trail if you wish to pursue a longer loop (see *Other Hiking Options*). Follow this trail down a short, steep route into a ravine. The trail will continue steadily downhill, winding left and right along the sides of the ravine and paralleling a stream until it reaches Lake

Following the blue blazes, the route now turns left. Soon you will arrive at the junction with the other white-blazed connector trail. Turn right to follow it toward the lookout on Silica Mine Hill (or for a shorter option, continue on the blue back to your car—see *Other Hiking Options*). The blue-blazed trail climbs along the hillside with a steep drop-off on your left. The path then levels out, and you will see a side trail to your left that leads to the lookout. The view here is mostly overgrown, but it is still a nice spot for a break.

As you leave the lookout, turn left to follow the trail and then turn right as you continue to follow the white blazes. Your path proceeds along a ridge and then curves leftward downhill. Continue to follow white blazes as the trail bends left and right. You'll soon arrive at the junction with the yellow-blazed Silica Mine Hill Trail. Turn left here, and follow an old woods road steadily and somewhat steeply downhill to your car.

## OTHER HIKING OPTIONS

**Additional Resources:** You can learn more about the Sunny Valley Nature Conservancy and download a trail map from by visiting their site (nature.org/sunnyvalley). The map that covers the area of this hike is the Lake Lillinonah, Silica Mine Hill, Rocky Hill, and Iron Ore Hill map.

**Short & Sweet:** You can cut out the second loop of our hike for a 2.5-mile trek. Follow the blue blazes as noted to the red trail, and down to the lake. Leave the lake by continuing on the red trail, eventually joining the blue trail via the white connector. Instead of taking the second white connector to the lookout, just head back to your car on the blue-blazed Silica Mine Hill trail.

**Add Another Loop:** You can add in the Iron Ore Hill loop to lengthen this hike to 5.5 miles by remaining on the blue-blazed Silica Mine Hill trail instead of turning right downhill to Lake Lillinonah (you'll visit the lake on the way back). You'll come to a parking area and continue following the blue blazes (now the Iron Ore Hill trail), which you lead you past another parking area. You'll then reach a junction with a red-blazed trail (about 1 mile from the first parking area you passed). Turn right on the red trail. After 1 mile, you'll meet the blue trail again. Turn left at this junction, passing again the first parking area. After about 0.75 mile, you'll come to the red-blazed trail that turns left to head toward Lake Lillinonah. From here, continue to follow the original hike narrative to the lake and lookout on Silica Mine Hill.

# Wadsworth Falls

| | |
|---|---|
| **LOCATION**: Middlefield | |
| **DISTANCE**: 3.5 miles | |
| **VERTICAL RISE**: 200 feet | |
| **TIME**: 2 hours | |
| **RATING**: C/D | |
| **MAP**: USGS 7.5 minute Middletown | |

Moving water holds a special fascination for humankind, perhaps rivaled only by that of the flickering of fire. The ebb and flow of ocean waves mesmerizes us, boiling rapids and cascades captivate our attention, and waterfalls enchant us wherever they occur. This hike features two notable waterfalls, best visited during spring's heavy runoff, but also worthy of a trip in any season. Both occur along the Coginchaug River, which flows north along the western border of the park. Historically, this river provided industrial waterpower, but now only the sluiceway of a textile mill remains.

The Rockfall Corporation gave Wadsworth Falls State Park to Connecticut in 1942. The will of Colonel Clarence Wadsworth, a noted linguist and scholar, established this nonprofit group to administer his plans for the land. His former residence, the Wadsworth Mansion on Long Hill Estates, sits adjacent to the park and is accessible by the purple trail (Bridge trail). The grounds there feature additional walking trails.

Wadsworth Falls State Park's 285 acres offers pond and stream fishing, swimming, and picnicking facilities along with numerous trails for hiking and mountain biking. A great park to visit on a hot, summer day, the woods here provide natural air-conditioning for your trek, after which you can go for a swim.

## GETTING THERE

From the junction of CT 66 and CT 157 in Middletown, take CT 157 Southwest, following signs to Wadsworth State Park. You will reach the park entrance on your left in 1.6 miles.

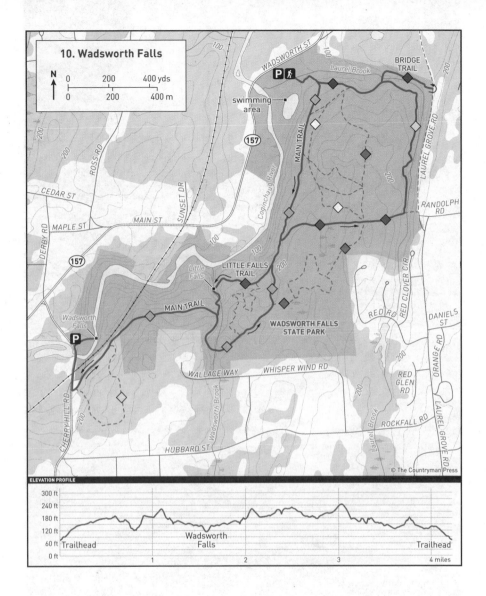

10. Wadsworth Falls

ELEVATION PROFILE

## THE HIKE

This hike takes you from the main entrance along the orange trail (Main Trail) to the blue trail (Little Falls Trail), then back to the orange trail. You'll then proceed to Cherry Hill Road to visit the main falls, before returning to the orange trail. Next, you'll follow another part of the blue trail to the yellow trail (Laurel Brook Grove Trail). At the end of the hike, you'll take the purple trail (Bridge Trail) to return to your car.

Just beyond the entrance, you'll find a nice map of the park's trails. From this spot, walk uphill through the picnic grove to the main trail, which begins by a culverted stream; this trail is blazed with orange. Do not cross the covered bridge near the parking lot—that path

THE LITTLE FALLS FLOWING OVER PORTLAND ARKOSE

goes to the swimming area and will not lead you to any trails. This is where, if you wish, you can head for a swim after your hike.

After you cross an earthen bridge, you will walk uphill to a well-marked trail intersection. Turn right to continue on the Main Trail, blazed in orange. Cedar, maple, birch, and poplar make up the wooded backdrop, while sweet fern, yarrow, blackberry, and poison ivy line the path. On your left, the trail passes one of the largest mountain laurels in the state (noted with the sign GIANT LAUREL).

A little further on, you'll come to a second small stream. The stone bridge here is supported by sidewalls of masonry cloaked in lush mosses and lichens. It is said that Colonel Wadsworth himself used the bridge, and two dates are edged into the rock: 1910 and 1945. Here the woods are composed of tall, straight hickory, oak, black birch, and skeletal hemlocks that have been ravaged by the woolly adelgid. Red squirrels chatter loudly from their perches far above the trail, while woodpeckers hammer away at the old dead trees scattered sporadically throughout the woods. Every so often, unmarked side trails leave the well-worn main path, inviting exploration.

About 0.4 mile from the start, you'll see the blue trail enter on your left. Continue on the orange trail. In less than 0.1 mile, you'll turn right onto the blue-blazed Little Falls trail. Follow the blue blazes downhill as you wind through beautifully treed ravines. Eventually, your path will run parallel to the small stream as it glides over mossy ledges. About 0.75 mile from the start, you'll reach Little Falls. These falls flow over Portland Arkose, the famous brownstone quarried for years in Portland,

Connecticut, used for many buildings built across the state. Arkose is a type of sandstone, made up mostly of quartz, but also of feldspar, whose red color is a result of the iron present within it.

Cross Wadsworth Brook below the falls and climb the steep hill on your right. Be careful, since this compacted soil can be slippery when wet. On the hilltop, there is an overlook to your left. When you have finished admiring the

BEAUTIFUL STONE WALLS ALONG THE PURPLE (BRIDGE) TRAIL

WADSWORTH FALLS

falls, return to the side trail, which continues to rejoin the nearby Main Trail. Turn right. Less than a 0.25 mile from the falls and about 1 mile from the start, railroad tracks and power lines appear below on your right. In another 0.5 mile, you'll reach the paved Cherry Hill Road. Turn right here to cross the railroad tracks. A short walk along the tracks in summer will reveal the bluebells of the creeping bellflower, and in season black raspberries tickle the pallet. Great banks of multiflora roses and a few striking Deptford pinks will also attract your attention.

Continuing on Cherry Hill Road, cross a new bridge over the Coginchaug River. If you walk down below the bridge, after crossing it, you'll see an old stone sluiceway. The river used to provide hydropower to drive a textile mill by the falls. Nearby industries once included pistol and gunpowder factories, which operated for nearly 100 years before exploding in 1892.

On the far side of the bridge, you'll cross a field beyond the parking lot to your right, and then descend on a path to your left. This will take you to the river at the base of Wadsworth Falls. On hot summer days, the falls cool the air considerably. The fenced-in overlook provides yet another view.

For the return leg of your hike, retrace your steps on Cherry Hill Road and make your way back to the orange-blazed trail. After a 0.5 mile, you'll pass on your left the blue-blazed trail to

Little Falls you took earlier. Note that the intersection is not well marked—it appears as a side trail going down the hill. Continue to follow the orange trail. After another 0.35 mile, you'll reach another intersection with the blue trail, which very briefly merges with the orange trail before veering off to your right. Take this right onto the blue trail, and follow it to the trail's end (0.37 mile) where you will turn left onto the yellow trail. The yellow trail parallels Laurel Grove Brook to the north and then runs west for 0.45 mile until it reaches the purple trail (Bridge Trail). Turning left onto the purple trail will bring you back to your car—but before concluding your hike, take a short detour by following the purple trail to the right so as to enjoy its full length. You'll find pleasure in the sight of the beautiful old stone bridges that Colonel Wadsworth rode upon while surveying his estate. Once you reach the end of the purple trail (meeting up with the hard-packed dirt Laurel Grove Road), turn around and continue along the purple-blazed trail, back over the stone bridge to the main trail and parking lot.

## OTHER HIKING OPTIONS

**Additional Resources:** A state park trail map can be found at www.ct.gov /deep/wadsworthfalls.

**Short & Sweet:** Park at the Cherry Hill Road entrance and walk down to the main falls. You can then visit the little falls by walking south on Cherry Hill Road over a highway bridge. Cross the railroad tracks, and you'll reach the trail entrance on your left. Follow the orange trail (Main Trail) for 0.5 mile and then turn left on the blue trail (Little Falls Trail). Note that this turn is not well marked with blazes. A steep, downhill walk will lead you to the little falls. After visiting them, retrace your steps back to the car.

**Extending Your Hike:** On your way back from the main falls, take a detour from the orange trail soon after entering the woods on the yellow trail. This adds 0.3 mile to the hike and takes you through land still owned by the Rockfall Corporation.

**Check Out Nearby Trails:** Do you have the time and energy to explore further? When you reach the end of the purple trail (Bridge Trail) on Laurel Grove Road, cross the hard-packed dirt road to reach the back entrance of Long Hill Estates. There is a 1.5-mile perimeter trail and 0.5-mile inner trail on this park land. Hiking here is a treat if you enjoy interesting trees: in 1900, Colonel Wadsworth planted thousands, many of them unique specimen plantings. A trail map and notable trees brochure can be found online (wadsworth mansion.com).

# Larsen Sanctuary

**LOCATION**: Fairfield

**DISTANCE**: 3.5 miles

**VERTICAL RISE**: 100 feet

**TIME**: 2 hours

**RATING**: D

**MAP**: USGS 7.5-minute Westport

Here is a hike that is perfect for all ages and abilities. The natural beauty of the Connecticut Audubon Society's Roy and Margot Larsen Sanctuary can be explored over 7 miles of trails and boardwalks. The property features streams, ponds, forest, and fields that are managed for their diverse plant and animal communities. Because of the predominance of low, marshy lands so attractive to birds, the sanctuary makes a particularly fine bird-watching area.

The trails include the mile-long Edna Strube Chiboucas Special Use Trail. Opened in 1999 and designed for wheelchair use, the trail was the first project undertaken by the Wheels in the Woods Foundation. The trail is five-to-seven-feet wide and paved with finely crushed rock. It circles through the sanctuary's 155 acres, following an easy grade through the woods, along the edge of a meadow, and over several streams and swamps. The trail is ideal for wheelchairs or strollers, but is also designed for people who use canes or walkers, or for anyone who wants to walk through the woods without worrying about tripping on roots or rocks. Interpretive signs stand at intervals along the way, and there are numerous benches for sitting.

Adjacent to the sanctuary is the Connecticut Audubon Society Center in Fairfield. The center is a hub for environmental education activities and events throughout the year. The grounds there feature a butterfly garden and live Birds of Prey Compound. The center also harbors exhibit areas, and a nature store offering a wide variety of birding and nature-themed merchandise. Trails are open seven days a week, year-round, from dawn to dusk. The center is open Monday through

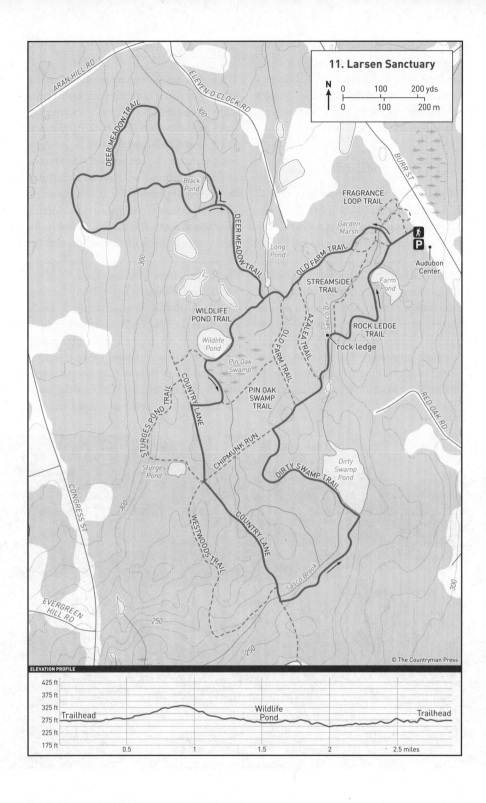

## 11. Larsen Sanctuary

N

| 0 | 100 | 200 yds |
| 0 | 100 | 200 m |

ARAN HILL RD

ELEVEN O'CLOCK RD

BURR ST

DEER MEADOW TRAIL

Black
Pond

300

300

Long
Pond

DEER MEADOW TRAIL

FRAGRANCE
LOOP TRAIL

Garden
Marsh

OLD FARM TRAIL

Audubon
Center

STREAMSIDE
TRAIL

Farm
Pond

WILDLIFE
POND TRAIL

Wildlife
Pond

Pin Oak
Swamp

AZALEA TRAIL

Sasco Br.

ROCK LEDGE
TRAIL

rock ledge

OLD FARM TRAIL

STURGES POND TRAIL

COUNTRY LANE

PIN OAK
SWAMP
TRAIL

CHIPMUNK RUN

Sturges
Pond

DIRTY SWAMP TRAIL

Dirty
Swamp
Pond

300

RED OAK RD

CONGRESS ST

WESTWOODS TRAIL

COUNTRY LANE

Sasco Brook

300

EVERGREEN
HILL RD

250

250

© The Countryman Press

**ELEVATION PROFILE**

| 425 ft |
| 375 ft |
| 325 ft |
| 275 ft |
| 225 ft |
| 175 ft |

Trailhead                Wildlife
                          Pond                    Trailhead

0.5        1        1.5        2        2.5 miles

Saturday from 10 a.m.–3 p.m. Brochures and trail maps are also available at the center. There is a nominal admission fee for nonmembers of the Audubon Society or nonresidents of Fairfield. Pets are not allowed in the sanctuary.

## GETTING THERE

To reach the sanctuary, take exit 44 in Fairfield off the Merritt Parkway (CT 15). If traveling east toward New Haven, turn right (west) immediately at the end of the ramp. If traveling west toward New York, turn left at the end of the ramp, take another left to pass under the parkway, and then immediately turn right. Either way, you are now on Congress Street, which you follow for 1.2 miles to Burr Street, where you'll turn right and proceed for 1.1 miles. The sanctuary entrance will be on your left.

## THE HIKE

The sanctuary is crisscrossed with a wide variety of trails labeled with metal trail signs. The trails have intriguing names such as Cottontail Cutoff, Dirty Swamp Trail, and Old Farm Trail. Blazes vary from unformed, painted blobs to arrows (on circular metallic disks or rectangular pieces of plastic). For the most part, the trails have been well traveled and are thus easy to follow. This hike leads you through each of the habitats present at the sanctuary. You'll take the Old Farm Trail, Deer Meadow Trail, Wildlife Pond Trail, Country Lane, Dirty Swamp Trail, Chipmunk Run, Chipmunk Trail, the Rock Ledge Trail, and then return along the Old Farm Trail. Portions of this hike will also travel along the Special Use Edna Strube Chiboucas Trail, which overlaps other trails in the park including some of those named above.

CATTAILS AT DIRTY SWAMP

DIRTY SWAMP TRAIL

Enter the sanctuary through a small, sheltered gateway to the right of the nature center. Pick up a trail map on your way through. The map highlights in blue the route to follow for the Special Use Chiboucas Trail; although the map shows other trail names along the special use route, the trail is labeled with metal signs saying CHIBOUCAS TRAIL. Follow the trail to your left, and pass the Fragrance Loop Trail on your right. Cross a bridge and turn right onto the Old Farm Trail (labeled as the Chiboucas Trail), passing Garden Marsh Pond on your left. As you pass the pond, almost hidden by shrubs, trees, and undergrowth, note the nesting boxes on trees and poles around you. The larger boxes are for wood ducks. You will also pass some fenced-in hackberry trees, planted for birds and butterflies. The fence keeps the growing deer population from eating the trees' twigs and buds until they grow out of reach.

Continue on the Old Farm (Chiboucas) trail past the Azalea Trail (on your left), and turn right onto the Wildlife Pond Trail (also labeled Chiboucas). Just after crossing the Sasco Creek by means of a large bridge, leave the Chiboucas Trail to turn right onto the DEER MEADOW TRAIL. The trail sign appears about 10 yards in along the Wildlife Pond trail, just before a small stand of spruce trees. If you come to a bridge and then a DEER MEADOW LOOP sign, you've gone too far—go back across the bridge and look for the first Deer Meadow Trail turn. Follow this woodland path past Black Pond (an overgrown, swampy area not readily identifiable as a pond) and follow the bog bridges. The trail then brings you to an open meadow, which is maintained by annual mowing. The pathway of the trail is mowed more regularly to make it easier to follow.

Make your way to the observation deck, the highest point on the sanctuary. This is a wonderful spot to view migrating raptors in the early fall months. The meadow lived up to its name early one October morning when we saw eight white-tailed deer at once!

Follow the mowed path through the meadow and reenter the woods. More bog bridges lead you once again past Black Pond to complete your loop. You'll return to the Wildlife Pond Trail (Chiboucas), where you will turn right proceeding to the Wildlife Pond. This pond, like many within the sanctuary, is not designed for human enjoyment. Instead it is overgrown with shrubs, which offer concealment for young waterfowl, great blue herons, and muskrats. Take time to enjoy any wildlife you may spy and to read about the pond's purpose on interpretive signs placed along the trail.

After you pass the Wildlife Pond, you'll see the Sturges Pond Trail on your right and soon after the Trillium Trail on your left. Take the left turn onto the short Trillium Trail, following a boardwalk along the western edge of Pin Oak Swamp. This boardwalk not only keeps your feet dry, but also protects the trail. Were it not so elevated, the thousands of tramping feet would soon turn the path into a quagmire. Future hikers would then edge to either side to avoid the swampy mess, further widening the path. This interesting little trail is the work of an Eagle Scout project.

The Trillium Trail then rejoins the Chiboucas Trail. From here, you'll need to cut across to Country Lane. The Trillium Trail is supposed to connect to Country Lane, but on a recent visit we could not find the continued trail. Instead, we turned right onto the Chiboucas Trail and soon saw a mowed path to our left. Turn left onto the mowed path and very soon you'll reach Country Lane. (Note that there will be another mowed path on your left soon after the first that you can take as well.)

When you reach Country Lane, an old woods road, turn left. You'll next come to a multi-branched intersection. You'll need to veer left at about 30° to remain on Country Road. A hard left will take you down Chipmunk Run. The St. Timothy's loop (Westwoods Trail) is on your right at the intersection, and you'll see a cleared gas pipeline (marked with yellow posts) running straight through everything. Notice that Country Lane is flanked on both sides by stone walls. In earlier days, the stone fences on either side separated farmer's fields from the roadway, limiting the wandering of their farm animals. A route flanked on both sides by stone walls is almost surely a town road. Originally, the farmers

erected wooden fences. Wood, however, eventually became scarce, and was more useful for buildings, and for heating and cooking. So the farmers piled the ever-plentiful stones from their fields along the fences. Eventually, the wooden fences rotted away, leaving the stone fences in their place.

After about 0.25 mile, you'll pass on your right the southern loop of the Westwoods trail, but continue on Country Lane. You'll crossing over a brook and then immediately turn left onto Dirty Swamp Trail. This trail provides distinctive, circular, red metallic blazes with arrows, but can sometimes be difficult to follow. You will parallel the brook upstream to Dirty Swamp Pond. When you reach the pond, you'll turn left over a wooden bridge and then continue over an earthen dam, passing some cattails on your right. Pause for a moment to enjoy the sounds of the green frogs that

ROCK LEDGES AND CAVES NEAR WOOD POND

populate this pond. We find they sound like twanging rubber bands.

The trail then weaves in and out of the woods, through meadows and swampy areas. You'll travel over a number of bog bridges. Then you'll cross the pipeline again and turn right onto Chipmunk Run, another significant woods road. As you continue on Chipmunk Run, you'll pass Old Farm Trail on your left (continue to your right), go over a bog bridge, and then up a short rise to a trail junction (Azalea Trail) where you'll turn right onto the Chipmunk Trail.

Just before using a large, wooden bridge to cross the brook below Wood Pond, take a brief detour to your left and explore the cave-like rock ledge above. When you're done exploring, cross the bridge and immediately proceed to your right uphill onto the Rock Ledge Trail (the Steamside Trail goes left). At the top of the rise, bear left and follow the twists and turns of the Rock Ledge Trail. Shortly thereafter, the two paths (Rock Ledge and Steamside) rejoin, and you'll cross a fancy stone and concrete bridge right by Farm Pond. Farm Pond was created to be a protective habitat for ducks and geese that have suffered injuries and thus have limited flying abilities. This pond also serves as a stopover for migrating waterfowl, who require open water to keep a safe distance from predators. During the winter months, the Audubon center runs a bubbler to insure ducks and geese continue to have open water year-round. In addition to being a safe haven for waterfowl, Farm Pond is also a perfect habitat for frogs. In the summer months, you can enjoy a raucous symphony of green and bullfrogs.

At the junction after the pond, turn right and continue past the Garden Marsh Trail (on your left) to the entrance and your car. If you have time, visit the Nature Center and the Birds of Prey Compound.

## OTHER HIKING OPTIONS

**Additional Resources:** You can find two useful resources—a trail map and a birding checklist specific to the sanctuary—on the center's website (ctaudubon.org /center-at-fairfield). Although it was early March when we first explored this sanctuary, it was alive with birds. A trio of ducks flew overhead, and several other species sang from the trees and underbrush. We heard the distinctive flutter and owl-like coo of the mourning dove and the cheerful (though far from melodious) chatter of that fateful harbinger of spring, the red-winged blackbird.

**Accessible Trail Option:** The Edna Strube Chiboucas Special Use Trail is a mile-long loop that will introduce you to many of the diverse features of the Larsen Sanctuary. It is paved with finely crushed stone so is ideal for wheelchairs, strollers, or anyone who prefers to walk on an even path without small obstacles that need to be avoided. The Chiboucas Trail is marked with trail signs but does overlap alternately named trails. Recently we found that the maps available in the entrance gateway had the Chiboucas trail highlighted. If you are following the trail map provided by the center, the Chiboucas Trail runs along the Old Farm Trail, bears right onto the Wildlife Pond Trail, proceeds onto the Pin Oak Swamp Trail, and then turns left back onto the Old Farm Trail. From there, you head back to the entrance and your car.

# 12

# Bluff Point

| | |
|---|---|
| **LOCATION**: Groton | |
| **DISTANCE**: 4 miles | |
| **VERTICAL RISE**: 100 feet | |
| **RATING**: D | |
| **MAP**: USGS 7.5-minute New London | |

A combination of historical circumstances and heavy demand for shoreline property has kept most of Connecticut's short coastline inaccessible to the public. One of the very few state parks on the shore, Bluff Point State Park offers over 800 undeveloped acres to roam. The only such sizable acreage on the Connecticut coast, Bluff Point is a special place for the hiker—free of concessions, cottages, and campsites.

There are an amazing variety of natural habitats to be found here. This diverse park includes coastal woodlands, beach and dune grasslands, coastal plain ponds, a coastal bluff, tidal wetlands, intertidal mud flats, and offshore eelgrass beds. A variety of plants and animals live here, some of which are rare or endangered. It is thus important to stay on the trails and not disturb the plants, animals, or rocks.

In the 1700s, this land was farmed by descendants of Governor John Winthrop; the main trails of today's park follow the original farm's old horse and cart paths. The lower roads accessed the salt marshes and beach areas while the upper roads led to the farmhouse and fields. The land continued to be farmed until the 1950s. Evidence of the park's former life is found in its many stone walls and rough roads. In 1975, the state of Connecticut purchased the land to preserve it for public use and enjoyment. Today the park and coastal reserve are protected from any further development.

## GETTING THERE

There are signs to direct you to Bluff Point. From the intersection of CT 117 and US 1 in Groton (access by US 95), drive west 0.3 mile on US 1 to Depot Road. Turn left, following the street past Industrial Road and under the railroad

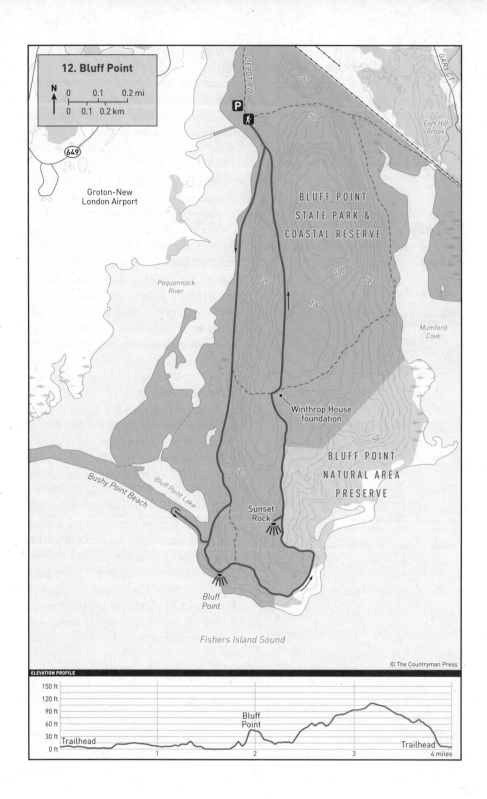

## 12. Bluff Point

N

| 0 | 0.1 | 0.2 mi |
| 0 | 0.1 | 0.2 km |

649

Groton-New
London Airport

DEPOT RD.

GARY CT.

50

Fort Hill
Brook

BLUFF POINT
STATE PARK &
COASTAL RESERVE

50

100

100

50

50

Mumford
Cove

Poquonnock
River

Winthrop House
foundation

BLUFF POINT
NATURAL AREA
PRESERVE

50

50

Bushy Point Beach

Bluff Point Lake

Sunset
Rock

Bluff
Point

Fishers Island Sound

© The Countryman Press

**ELEVATION PROFILE**

150 ft
120 ft
90 ft
60 ft
30 ft
0 ft

Trailhead

Bluff
Point

Trailhead

1          2          3          4 miles

VIEW OF FISHERS ISLAND SOUND FROM BLUFF POINT

tracks where the paved surface will end. Continue until you reach a large parking lot about 0.7 mile from US 1. You will know you've arrived when you spy a sign listing park regulations. There is an ample picnic area to the right of the gate.

## THE HIKE

The following route is fairly level. It proceeds along a dirt road, passing Bushy Point Beach after about 1 mile, and soon thereafter reaches the low bluffs. The trail then loops around and follows north up the center of the peninsula, advancing past both Sunset Rock and the Winthrop House Foundation on the way back to your car.

Proceed on foot down the gated dirt road. Given the park's proximity to civilization, you'll share the roads and park with joggers and bicyclists, as well as with horses and fishermen. Fishing boats ply the bay to your right, and windrows of dead eelgrass, one of the few flowering plants that grow in saltwater, line the rocky shore. The brandt, a smaller relative of the Canada goose, feeds almost exclusively on this plant. When a mysterious blight in the 1930s all but exterminated the eelgrass, the brandt nearly went too. The emaciated flocks subsisted on a diet of sea lettuce until the grass came back. If you walk this way in the colder months, you may see a few of the hundreds of brandt wintering along the shore of Long Island Sound.

You'll also see several side trails cut off from the main road during your hike. Due to the pervasive influence of the sea, the woods of Bluff Point are more varied than most inland forests. The understory is a tangle of vines and brambles—grape, red-fruited barberry, rose, blackberry, black raspberry,

BUSHY POINT BEACH

honeysuckle, Oriental bittersweet, and greenbrier. Look closely at the leaves lining the forest floor, you may see the spectral Indian Pipe or Ghost Plant. Often thought to be a fungus, this member of the blueberry family does not depend on photosynthesis and thus can live on the darkest forest floors. Various oaks, cherries, long-thorned hawthorns, tight-barked hickories, Shagbark hickories, sumacs, and blueberries represent the deciduous trees, and an occasional cedar represents the evergreens.

During an April visit you may hear the mating chorus of male peepers and toads. Upon breaking hibernation, these dry-land dwellers congregate in various temporary waters to breed. The peeper has a high-pitched, two-note call, hence its name. The American toad produces a long trill.

The most common tree in this narrow strip of woodland is probably the sassafras, usually recognized by its mitten-shaped leaves and greenish-barked twigs. Sassafras leaves usually come in three shapes—like a mitten with no thumb, one thumb, or two thumbs—often all on the same branch. As a rule, the leaves nearest the end of the twig have the fewest "thumbs." Native Americans made infusions from the root bark of the sassafras to treat fevers, diarrhea, and rheumatism. However, sassafras also contains the volatile oil safrole, which recent studies have shown to be carcinogenic.

About 0.5 mile from the start, the trees clear for a short stretch of the road. Enjoy the view of the Poquonock River on your right. This river is a 2-mile estuary of mixed salt and fresh waters. On your left, notice the lush tidal wetland.

Shortly thereafter, the road will meander back into the woods.

After another mile, you'll come upon a path to the beach on your right. Take a short detour now to explore Bushy Point Beach. Wandering by the water, you'll see cast-off treasures from the sea: blue mussel shells; great, whorled whelk shells; marble-sized, periwinkle shells; scallop shells; the rectangular shells of razor clams; flat, wide strands of kelp; bladder-floated algae (seaweed); crab husks and legs; and the everlasting, ever-present debris of plastics—the bane of all the world's oceans. Further down the beach are roped-off areas protecting Connecticut's threatened shorebirds, the piping plover and the least tern. Great care must be taken on this part of the beach, especially during the nesting months of April through August. When you have satisfied your yen for beachcombing or have reached the end of this beach, retrace your steps, following the sprawling masses of delicate beach peas and non-native rosa rugosa—the ubiquitous beach roses—back to the bluff. Before your walk back to the main trail, pause for a moment among the wild primrose and beach plums. You are standing on a terminal moraine. This pudding-mix of rocks and sand was dumped here some 10,000 years ago upon the retreat of a glacier that once completely covered present-day New England.

Once you return to the road, continue a short distance to the low bluffs. At the beginning of the side paths to them, you'll see an informational sign about Bluff Point State Park and Coastal Reserve. Take any side path down to the bluffs to enjoy the beautiful view of Fishers Island Sound. You'll see Groton Heights to your right and Groton Long Point to your left. Fishers Island, part of New York State, lays right-of-center, while Watch Hill in Rhode Island is left of center. However, be cautious while walking down to the water, as dense vegetation crowds the path and poison ivy can also be found here.

Follow the road around to the east. Soon after leaving the shore, take the better-worn path inland to your left before bearing right at the fork 50 yards further on. The trail to the left soon connects with the outward-bound leg of your hike. Rounding the point, you'll overlook a cattail swamp. These swamps are being taken over throughout the state by the giant reed phragmites (pronounced frag-MI-tez). Here the waving fronds of the Phragmites stand sentinel by the sound. Across the bay, a seemingly solid wall of cottages stands in stark contrast to this wild oasis.

The trail now moves inland to follow the center ridge of the peninsula. Stone walls stand in mute evidence of colonial cultivation. On your left you will see a well-signed side trail to Sunset Rock. Before the 1938 hurricane, vacationers renting summer cottages along the shore came to this boulder for Sunday religious services. At that time, this area had all been open farmland, and this large glacial erratic afforded service-goers a clear, open view of the setting sun across the sound.

The trail forks after approximately another 0.5 mile. Near this junction, keep an eye out for the foundation of the old Winthrop house. Built around 1700 by Governor Fitz-John Winthrop, grandson of the famous Massachusetts Bay Governor, the house had a 300-foot tunnel to the barn and a room-sized, brick chimney in the basement for protection from Native American raids.

INDIAN PIPE OR GHOST PLANT (*MONOTROPA UNIFLORA*)

Note that you are now about 100 feet above sea level, and at one of the highest points in the park.

Leaving this area, take the left fork (the path to the right heads over to Mumford Cove, a nice side trip if you have time). The path proceeds again through the woods for about 0.9 mile before delivering you back to the parking lot.

## OTHER HIKING OPTIONS

**Additional Resources:** A state park trail map can be found at www.ct.gov /deep/bluffpoint.

**Short & Sweet:** You can trim your hike to 3 miles by heading directly to the beach and the bluff, and then retracing your steps back along the main trail.

**Extending Your Hike:** If you want to incorporate a visit to Mumford Cove in your hike, you will go right at the fork at the Winthrop house foundation. The trail will cut across the peninsula, reaching the cove in about 0.5 mile. The trail then turns left until it reaches the Groton Cross-Town Trail. There you'll turn left, reaching your car after 0.4 mile.

**Explore Groton Further:** Check out the 6-mile cross-town trail. It begins at Bluff Point State Park and ends at the Mortimer Wright Preserve. It follows bright-blue blazes and meanders through coastal forest for most of the 6 miles. The cross-town trail connects two state parks, three land-trust properties, and a town park and preserve. You can do the trail by "spotting cars" (that is leave one car at the end and drive another to the start—just don't forget the keys to the ending point car!). Or you can hike this out and back using one car for a beautiful 12-mile hike.

# Day Pond State Park

| | |
|---|---|
| **LOCATION**: Colchester | |
| **DISTANCE**: 4 miles | |
| **VERTICAL RISE**: 500 feet | |
| **TIME**: 2.5 hours | |
| **RATING**: C | |
| **MAP**: USGS 7.5-minute Moodus | |

New England's forests, rock formations, and hills make a very nice setting for our hikes. We even have one feature that is world famous—our glorious fall colors! Westerners may rave about their yellow aspen, but here we have not only yellows (including aspen), but a riot of other colors, beautiful in themselves and magnificent together. What a grand and pleasant surprise it must have been for the Pilgrims to be greeted their first New England fall in 1621 by our magnificent colors!

Around Labor Day, the sumac and the red maple turn scarlet. Then the yellow of popple (Yankee for aspen) and birch appears, followed by seemingly translucent ash (perhaps our favorite), with deep purple on top of the leaf and yellow beneath; the wind ripples this two-toned effect beautifully. Our crown jewels, the sugar maples, with their fantastic range of hues from yellow through to orange to deep-red, burst into brilliance, and finally the various oaks, with their deep, long-lasting rusts, complete the tapestry.

The only area in the world with colors to rival ours is eastern China, but our far greater number of trees makes New England's autumn show unsurpassed. You may wonder why only these two areas, half a world apart, are so blessed. One reasonable theory is that many millions of years ago, at a time when our present trees were developing between ice ages, Greenland was a warm, forested island that served as a bridge over the pole between northern Asia and North America. The return of the ice pushed the forest south into both areas. The color genes have thus been derived from a single source spreading into both eastern China and eastern North America.

A hike at Day Pond State Park is an

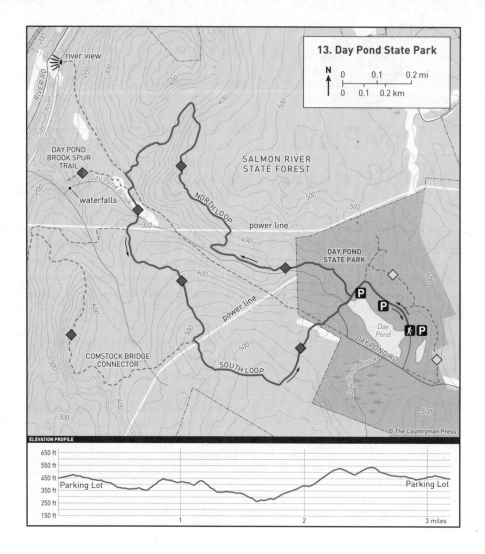

Elevation Profile

| | Parking Lot | | | | Parking Lot |

enjoyable few hours no matter the time of year, but it can be especially beautiful in the fall. In addition to the park's dense, hardwood forests, visitors will find stone walls and foundations, remnants of the colonial era when water from the pond powered a local sawmill. The pond was originally constructed by a pioneer family named Day. It is now stocked with trout and is a favorite spot for fishermen. The pond also makes for a lovely summer day trip, with a cordoned-off swimming beach, picnic facilities, and approximately 5 miles of trails for hiking and mountain biking.

## GETTING THERE

To get to Day Pond, take exit 16 off CT 2 in North Westchester and head south on CT 149. In 3 miles, take a sharp right onto Peck Lane at the sign for Day Pond State Park. After proceeding 0.4 mile, take the first left onto Day Pond Road, then turn right at the gate for Day Pond State Park. The park is 1.1 miles north

WATERFALLS FOUND OFF THE DAY POND BROOK SPUR TRAIL—WORTH THE DETOUR!

of CT 149. There is ample parking along the road around the pond. Park your car before you reach the dam, as there is limited parking at the end of the gravel road.

## THE HIKE

Today's hike is a lovely loop through the park following the Salmon River Trail, first along the North Loop and then returning on the South Loop. There is a side trail extra (detailed in *Other Hiking Options*) that is worth the extra mileage for the views they afford.

Begin by walking along the gravel entrance road around the pond, where you'll pass a large picnic shelter on your left. You'll also pass a restroom building, also to the left. After curving around the beach, the gravel road ends

about 20 yards before the dam. Continue towards the dam, and just before it on your right you'll see a sign for the Salmon River Trail/North Loop where you'll turn into the woods. This blue-blazed trail leads downhill on an old tote road. If you choose the latter part of October for this hike, you will find that the shorter hours of daylight (rather than frost, as is commonly believed) have painted the foliage lavishly in a spectrum of reds and orange.

In about 0.1 mile, the trail turns sharply left off the tote road; you are still following the blue blazes. Keep slightly to your left to cross a linear clearing carrying a buried transcontinental cable; then continue downhill toward the stream.

The outlet stream from Day Pond lends a cheery background to the first part of this hike. The stream moves quickly downhill, matching the trail and forming a series of gentle rapids on its way to Salmon River. The trail passes through mountain laurel with blooms in May and June, and sweet pepper bush with fragrant blooms in July and August. About 0.5 mile from the pond, turn sharply right onto the blue-blazed trail, walking uphill and away from the stream. Do not take the unblazed trail to the left that crosses the brook and continues to the road bisecting the Day Pond Loop.

It is interesting to note the young beech at this point in the hike. Depending upon how late in the autumn you are walking, many of the trees may have lost their foliage. The red maple leaves often fall before the other colors have fully developed. The various oaks will usually hold their leaves until well into winter. However, young beeches will often hold their leaves into early spring. By then, the leaves are bleached almost white, but still they cling to their branches.

Cross under the power lines, and then follow the trail uphill for a short stretch. It then levels out, goes downhill a bit, and then continues climbing. The rock-strewn area (glacial erractics) you are hiking through culminates in a small rocky knoll. The path starts down the other side, where a few cedars still reach the sun.

After several minor ups and downs, the trail changes its northerly direction and heads west (left) downhill, crossing a stone wall. As you descend into the woodland valley, the trail continues to bear left and you will cross a small stream over a simple two-log bridge. As the valley cuts deeper into the local water table, another stream becomes visible, growing as you proceed downhill. As you continue, note the number of stone walls and foundations along this stretch. Once you reach the stream, the trail turns right and crosses over a bridge. Soon after traversing the stream, you will come to a woods road. Turn left, walking uphill for about 100

LILY PAD–STREWN DAY POND NEAR THE DAM

VIEW OF DAY POND FROM THE DAM

feet. The path then turns right into the woods, passes through a stone wall, and comes to a trail junction. At the crossroads there is spur trail on your right that leads to Day Pond Falls. See *Other Hiking Options* for a detour to a lovely cascade of falls on Day Pond Brook.

If you take the detour when you return to the junction, continue straight to follow the blue blazes onto the south loop of the trail. Otherwise, at the junction turn left to begin the south loop as the trail gently descends.

At the bottom of the hill, the rough tote road you have been following runs into a well-defined old road, where you'll turn left and walk uphill. After again crossing the smaller stream that you followed down the valley, turn right onto another woods road to continue along the blue-blazed trail.

Follow the blue-blazed trail into the woods and across the larger stream from Day Pond; this crossing has been tamed by a small bridge utilizing old stone abutments. You are now more than halfway around the circuit. Go right uphill away from the brook. Cross under the power line and wind slowly uphill. You are now hiking through what at first glance appears to be an almost featureless woodland. However, our woodlands are never featureless! Look around you and you will see a large expanse of white pine interspersed with dying hemlock and a young deciduous forest filling in any open space. At your feet you'll find the upright leaves of wild lily of the valley as well as scattered mounds of mosses, raising their spore stalks like banners.

After almost 1 mile of gentle upgrade hiking, you'll crest the hilltop and come to a junction. Turn left to immediately cross another linear clearing and continue downhill. After crossing a bridge over a small stream at the bottom of the valley, the blue-blazed trail resumes its gentle upward slope.

Pass on your right a 400-ton glacial erratic. This impressive rock is decorated with a patina of lichen and also supports young black birch seedlings on its top, and a clump of polypody ferns clinging to a foothold on its side. Have you ever come across a large boulder in the woodlands and wondered about its weight? You can estimate the weight of a boulder like this by considering a small section first—a cubic foot would weigh about 200 pounds (water weighs about 64 pounds per cubic foot) and then consider its over-all size as 20 feet square by 10 feet high. These measures help us to calculate the volume at about 4,000 cubic feet which translates into a weight of 800,000 pounds or 400 tons.

After you ponder this great boulder, continue on the trail as it heads gently downhill and eases into a fairly level grade. As you reach the end of the loop, the path meets, parallels, and then crosses a stone wall. You soon cross an old tote road whose dirt surface is below much of the surrounding land—erosion from past heavy use. Shortly, you'll reach the park road just south of the dam.

Cross the pond's outlet stream as you walk over a large two-part dam with a bridge separating the two parts. Take a few minutes to consider the ingenuity of the dam's designer. The two-part dam provides two outlets for the pond's overflow. The first outlet you cross is lower so that it will always carry some of the pond's overflow with its cheery burble. The second outlet is higher, but much wider than the first. In case of heavy floods, this outlet can drain off a large amount of water, while the smaller outlet is more limited. The two outlets prevent an excessive buildup of water against the dam, which could result in overflow and erosion if the smaller outlet were unable to drain off the accumulating water. This pond, then, has the best of two worlds—it has the advantage of a small, compact outlet, with a safety valve that comes into play in case of heavy floods.

After crossing the dam, follow the park road to where you parked your car.

## OTHER HIKING OPTIONS

**Additional Resources:** A state park trail map can be found at www.ct.gov /deep/daypond.

**Day Pond Falls Spur Trail:** Take a right-hand turn just after you join up with the south loop of the Salmon River Trail. This spur trail is well marked with blue and red blazes and is the work of an Eagle Scout candidate. Follow it for a pleasant 0.2-mile walk through soft footing in a pine forest to the brook. You'll note the end of the spur trail when you come upon two horizontal blazes on a tree. The series of cascades are found just down the hill from that spot and are well worth exploring. When you're ready to return to the hike, retrace your steps the 0.2 mile back to the start of the spur trail. At this junction continue straight to rejoin the south loop of the Salmon River Trail.

# Hurd State Park

| | |
|---|---|
| **LOCATION**: East Hampton | |
| **DISTANCE**: 4 miles | |
| **VERTICAL RISE**: 600 feet | |
| **TIME**: 2.5 hours | |
| **RATING**: C | |
| **MAP**: USGS 7.5-minute Middle Haddam | |

A trip to Hurd State park offers the day hiker a delightful variety: a peaceful walk on the Connecticut River as well as dramatic ledge views, the tranquil cascades of Hurd Brook alongside marvelous remains of stone walls and old quarries. Hurd State Park lies in the busy cluster of state parks that congregate around the Connecticut River Valley, and is one of the oldest in Connecticut, established in 1914 only one year after the State Park Commission was established. The park began with 150 acres along the Connecticut River designated for public use but has grown to almost a thousand acres of land that includes primitive river camping reserved for canoers and kayakers.

More than any other hike in this book, a walk through Hurd State Park is an encounter with the Connecticut River. New England's main waterway, the Connecticut flows down from Quebec Province to Long Island Sound. One could argue that this long, placid waterway is the defining natural feature of the state: the very name Connecticut is a corruption of a Mohegan term meaning "place by the long tidal river." The Connecticut River has also played a major role in the state's history. The waterway served numerous early native communities, facilitated exploration and trade during the colonial period, and drove agriculture and industry well into the twentieth century. Today's hike showcases the Connecticut River as a site of both natural splendor and human labor.

The park is named after the Hurd family, early settlers from Scotland who moved to Middle Haddam from Massachusetts in 1710. The land here is geologically distinguished by its ridges of granite veined with feldspar. Before it became a park, small quarrying operations mined these minerals along with

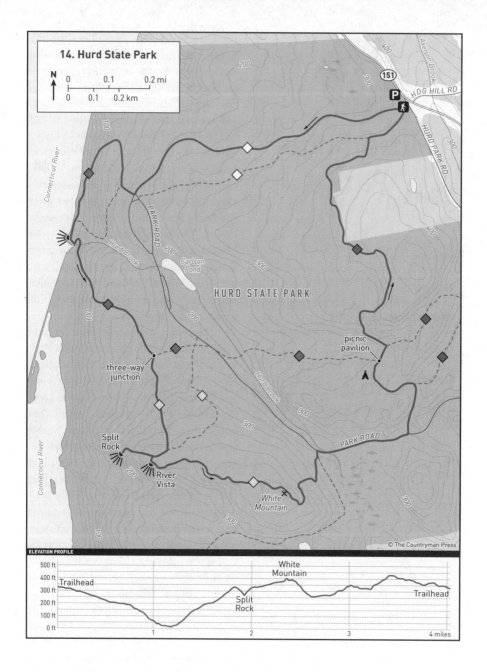

**14. Hurd State Park**

HURD STATE PARK

ELEVATION PROFILE

flint and mica. This conflicted identity between public, natural landscape, and private mining concerns reached its head in the 1930s, when a legal battle erupted over persisting claims to the land's mineral resources. The resulting court decision fortunately ruled in favor of the state, preserving the park for the enjoyment of future generations. Since then, efforts by the Civilian Conservation Corps, with ongoing support from the state, have helped turn the park into

VIEW OF THE CONNECTICUT RIVER FROM THE SPLIT ROCK RIDGE

a destination for recreation, building access roads and planting pine trees.

## GETTING THERE

From the junction of CT 151 and CT 66 in Cobalt, drive South on CT 151 for 2.4 miles to a traffic light at a four-way junction. At this junction, take a hard right into a parking lot. This is the cross-country skier parking lot (open year round) for Hurd State Park. The road to your right leads to the main park entrance. Note that main entrance closes after the first snow falls and opens after the snow melts in the spring.

## THE HIKE

The park has an extensive trail system. The map posted at the main park entrance (which matches the map found online) does not fully capture the current trail system. It appears that mountain bikers have "improved" the trail network, going so far as to blaze their own trails. To add to the confusion, the white trail from the DEEP map now seems to be blazed green. Our hike will describe the route to take following the actual blazes and landmarks seen in the park. Unfortunately, because of this history of outside intervention in the Hurd Park trail system, be warned that the blazes may be further changed without warning.

Our route starts with the white-blazed trail (not the one noted previously) down to the River Trail blazed in red, then to the yellow trail (Split Rock Trail). From there, you'll walk along the park road to the Picnic Pavilion and join up with the green trail (previously blazed in white) back to your car.

In the parking lot, you'll notice a yellow metal gate. Don't follow the woods road behind the gate, and instead follow the road to the right of the gate through the woods. Your path will be marked with white blazes. Notice the macadam surface you are walking on is slowly breaking up after years of disuse. Also you will see the glitter of mica and quartz along the road, evidence of early mining activity.

You'll soon pass a trail to your left; keep straight and gently descend, continuing to follow white blazes. The hemlocks along this road look very unhealthy, and many have died, victims of the hemlock looper and the woolly adelgid. These pests feed on hemlock needles and twigs, respectively. Southern Connecticut hemlock stands, particularly along the Connecticut River, are noticeably affected. Salvage logging began in 2000 to remove some of the trees; and you can see small seedlings of maple, beech, and birch vying for sunlight in their place.

About 1 mile from the parking lot trail, you will come upon the paved park road—take a right here onto the red-blazed River Trail (see *Other Hiking Options* for a side trip to Carlson's Pond along the paved road). Follow the River trail down the steep hillside treed with black birches, beeches, tulip trees, and more unhealthy hemlocks. In the winter and early spring before the trees leaf up, you'll have an inviting view of the Connecticut River during most of your descent.

Emerge at the bottom into a clearing along the Connecticut River. Take your time and enjoy the view, scooting down short side paths to the river. Follow the river downstream to your left. Soon you'll come to a grassy clearing used mostly by boaters plying the river. Across the river to the right is the United Technologies jet engine facility.

In addition to private craft, tugs pushing rusty barges occasionally chug by. You may also hear the clanging of a logging operation across the river. Spend a while exploring the riverside, enjoying the scenery and looking for wildlife. Wandering off to the right on a recent hike, we saw two young, black ducks in a quiet spot. The trees here are different from those in the surrounding hillsides: sycamores, dying elms, tall sassafras, cottonwoods, silver maples, and willows form this canopy. Podded milkweeds fringe the open areas; look for the Monarch butterflies that favor this plant. Across the river to your left is Bear Hill (hike #45). Only power lines mar this view of the hills along the river. Opposite the river in the woods beside you, beautiful Hurd Brook cascades through the forest.

Before continuing on the Red trail, go further down the grassy stretch along the river to the primitive boating campsites. You'll also see a 0.5-mile-long rock jetty on the banks of the river made from two or three layers of huge, quarried blocks. The jetty is a lot of fun to walk along as you dodge piles of flotsam and giant tree-trunks that have floated downstream and gotten stranded. On one side of the jetty is the river; on the other, a small tidal cove. The views up and down the river are tremendous, and any block is a great spot to sit and watch the river flow past.

Retrace your steps back to Hurd Brook and the red-blazed River Trail. Cross the small stream over a stone slab, then climb the trail to your left away from the river. Soon you'll pass the orange trail on your right. Note that this is a new mountain-biking trail not shown on the park map; avoid it by continuing on the red trail. You'll then come to a three-way trail junction at which you'll see a RIVER VISTA sign, turn right on the yellow trail, and continue climbing. At the top of your climb, turn right at a T-Junction toward Split Rock. Head

SPLIT ROCK, A 25-FOOT-DEEP CREVASSE

ROCK JETTY ALONG THE CONNECTICUT RIVER

downhill past a great white glacial boulder. Continue downhill to open ledges overlooking the Connecticut River—a far more dramatic scene than that of our earlier riverside ramble. Enjoy the view, and then keep going on the yellow trail until you reach Split Rock, a ledge bearing a narrow crevasse 25 feet deep. The US Geological Survey Benchmark confirms your location on the map at an elevation of 266 feet. This is a fine, sunny spot for lunch, with a good view of the Connecticut River 200 feet below.

After the respite, retrace your steps and climb back uphill, parallel to the ledge. You'll reach the junction with the RIVER VISTA sign; continue straight on the yellow trail, meandering over a well-worn path dotted with mountain laurel. The hike will then climb to the peak of White Mountain. Summer foliage

obscures your view, but the bare summit is impressive with its one massive, lichen-covered, granite stone.

At about 0.6 mile from the RIVER VISTA sign, you'll reach a yellow-gate and the paved park road. Turn right onto this road and then take your first left uphill towards the Picnic Pavilion. You'll pass another yellow gate; stay on the road to the parking lot and enter a large open field with the pavilion. Behind the pavilion, you'll see a gigantic white oak with large, gnarled, extended branches. This is a perfect example of white oak growth in an open field, complete with said field. Many hikes in Connecticut pass similar trees growing in the forest. These trees matured in open fields before the forest grew around them. Foresters know these trees as wolf trees. A white oak growing with other trees around it will grow straight and tall. To compete for sunlight it will channel all its energy into growing upward, rather than broad. The tree here did not have competition and thus grew wide and massive.

Passing the white oak, head toward the forest and turn on the leftmost green-blazed trail (formerly white on the state trail map). Follow a woods road past some intriguing stone ravines. A close inspection reveals a series of these carved into the hillside, all former mining quarries. Bear right behind the quarries to climb uphill, following the green blazes. There is quite a maze of paths throughout this section of the hike, all mountain bike trails. Keep following green blazes even though they are spray-painted on the trees and appear somewhat unofficial. You'll cross many impressive and robust stone walls while hiking this section, which is also covered with young hardwood trees sprinkled with the occasional evergreen eastern red cedar. You'll soon see what appears to be a clearing on your right, just beyond two stone walls—an curious rectangular bit of private land that juts into the park from Hurd Park Road. Continue following the green blazes, and you'll come to a clearing with tall grasses and wildflowers. In midsummer you'll observe bunches of red berries on your right. If you investigate more closely, you will find clusters of ripe, red raspberries. Enjoy this free, end-of-the hike snack. Continue a short distance further, and you will meet up with a woods road. Turn right and you'll quickly end up back at the parking lot and your car.

## OTHER HIKING OPTIONS

**Additional Resources:** A state park trail map can be found at www.ct.gov /deep/hurd. **A biker's trail map** shows the extensive trails that have been unofficially added to the park system (visit bikerag.net/images/MAPS/ct_hurd _review.htm#map).

**Short & Sweet:** This 3-mile option takes you on the river walk (but not to the ledges at Split Rock) and starts similarly to the original hike. However, when you reach the three-way trail junction with the RIVER VISTA sign, turn left and stay on the red-blazed River Trail. After 0.1 mile, you'll reach the paved park road. Turn left and head northwest toward Carlson Pond. Beyond the pond and the paved loop, turn right on the first woods road (there are two woods roads, both blazed in white) and head back to your car.

**Side Trip Option:** Early in the hike, just before you turn right onto the red-blazed River Trail, you can continue on the paved park road along the circular loop. Follow the road, crossing the earthen dam by Carlson Pond. Observe the 75-year-old stonework left behind by the Civilian Conservation Corps. A small quarrying operation also left a cleft in a ledge along the road. Retrace your steps along the road, and then continue with the hike along the red-blazed River Vista Trail.

# Northern Metacomet

This hike along a northern stretch of Connecticut's blue-blazed Metacomet Trail combines natural beauty with sites of historical interest. Traprock ridge-walking and Peck Mountain's volcanic cliffs offer great vistas on cool, clear days, while a visit to the environs of the infamous Newgate Prison offers an encounter with some of the more disturbing episodes of Connecticut's state history.

| | |
|---|---|
| **LOCATION**: Granby | |
| **DISTANCE**: 4 miles | |
| **VERTICAL RISE**: 500 feet | |
| **TIME**: 2.5 hours | |
| **RATING**: C | |
| **MAP**: USGS 7.5-minute Windsor Locks | |

## GETTING THERE

To reach the hike's start, from I-91 follow CT 20 west toward Bradley International Airport. As this divided highway ends, stay on CT 20 west. In approximately 2 miles, you'll reach the junction with CT 187. Continue west on CT 20, and in 0.7 mile turn right onto Newgate Road. Park immediately on your right—the shoulder of the road is wider here for parking, and you'll see the blue-blazed Metacomet Trail enter the woods on your right.

## THE HIKE

This hike follows the blue-blazed Metacomet Trail (part of the newly designated New England National Scenic Trail) along the ridge of Peck Mountain for 2 miles, after which you'll retrace your steps to return to the car.

The trail ascends steeply onto the traprock ridge and then bears left along its top. On leafless, winter days, the views here are particularly nice, but even in summer you'll catch glimpses of the countryside below through occasional breaks in the trees. After 0.5 mile, you'll pass beneath a utility line near a utility shed. These service three beacons on the ridge for planes approaching Bradley International Airport, just

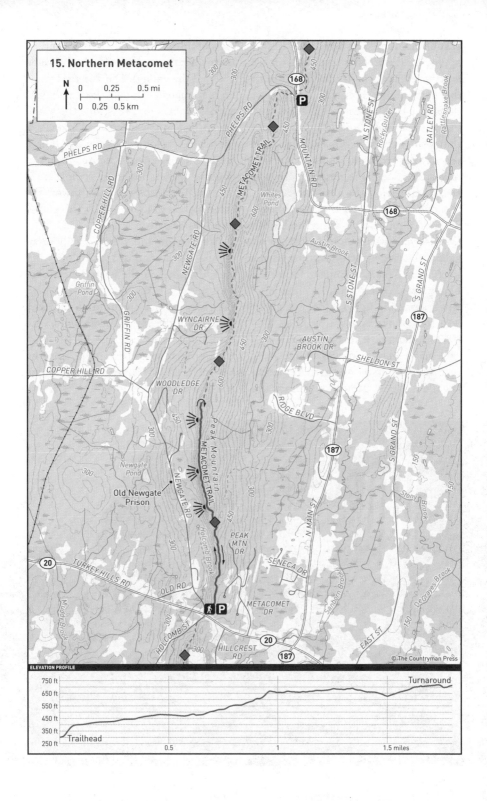

## 15. Northern Metacomet

N

0        0.25        0.5 mi
0     0.25    0.5 km

**ELEVATION PROFILE**

750 ft
650 ft
550 ft
450 ft
350 ft
250 ft

Trailhead

Turnaround

0.5          1          1.5 miles

© The Countryman Press

east of the ridge. The airplane buff will appreciate the procession of jet airliners and the myriad, smaller, private aircraft that come and go overhead. For the rest of us, the exhilarating cliff edges and views offset the aircraft noise. (Note that your experience may vary: on a recent afternoon hike, after about half-mile on the ridge, we heard no more road sounds and very little aircraft noise).

Continue to follow the blue blazes, and in 0.8 mile you'll see a red-blazed trail descend to your right down the east side of the ridge to East Granby Farms Recreation Area. Continue to follow the blue blazes. After a little over a mile, you'll scramble up to a lookout about 300 feet above the valley floor. The USGS benchmark reads COPPER MOUNTAIN. (The whole ridge is called Peck Mountain, while its southern highpoint is called Copper Mountain.) Enjoy the view at this lookout. There is a traprock ridge directly across from you (between you and the valley). The Tunxis Trail is on that opposite ridge. Look southward at the sinuous curve of ridge the Metacomet Trail follows. Penwood State Park (hike #21) straddles the nearest hump; Heublein Tower on Talcott Mountain (hike #47) stands out prominently behind it; and beyond the tower, the tilted slabs of Mount Higby (hike #20) rise on the horizon.

Staying on the ridge, you'll reenter the woods and descend slowly but steadily, passing the first airport beacon on your right. As you hike along the ridge in the spring and summer, look for wildflowers, especially the wild columbine—recognizable by its long, trailing nectar spurs extending from the base of its petals. These spurs tempt the taste buds of pollinators.

THE WALLS OF OLD NEWGATE PRISON

In another tenth of a mile, you'll pass the second airport beacon on your right. You will also continue to see ample evidence of traprock, also known as basalt, which forms the spine of the Metacomet Ridge. Basalt is a darkly colored rock, but the iron within it weathers to a rusty brown when exposed to air. Most of the ledges and rocks you'll see here have a distinct reddish appearance. You'll also come upon clusters of rock posts thrust upwards from the earth. This is also basalt, which frequently breaks into columns—you'll see many of these formations as you hike along the ridge. As basalt erodes further, it creates small, loose rocks called scree—which are especially evident along the base of basalt ridges.

The third airport beacon welcomes you into the woods on your right after another tenth of a mile. Continue following blue blazes, and in 0.2 more miles you'll come to a small, striking, columnar rock formation of basalt and a lookout with limited views. From here, you'll walk a short distance on the blue trail and come to a grassy spot that overlooks a scree slope on your left. This is the turnaround spot for the hike. If you were to continue further, the trail dips down a bit into the woods and follows the ridge until it descends (see *Other Hiking Options* for those wishing for a longer hike or to continue along this ridge).

Retrace the steps to your car, and then drive north on Newgate Road for 1.1 miles. Before long, you'll reach the impressive ruins of Newgate Prison on your left. The site became one of the first commercial mines in the British Colonies; copper mining began there in 1705. Alas, it was never profitable, and by the early 1770s, the mine's deep tunnels were converted into Connecticut's first prison. The prison originally housed hardened criminals, but during the Revolutionary War it was used for political prisoners. After independence, Newgate became America's first state prison; women were first incarcerated here in 1824. By 1827, the prison was closed as it was considered inhumane and too costly to run. Nowadays, this national historic landmark is a Connecticut state archaeological preserve; it went through an extensive restoration and stabilization process from 2015 to 2018. The prison's brick guardhouse still

FOLLOWING THE METACOMET TRAIL ALONG THE RIDGE

VIEW FROM COPPER MOUNTAIN ALONG THE METACOMET TRAIL

stands and houses exhibits and a gift shop. Of the other prison buildings, only ruins remain. Across the street from the prison is Viets' Tavern, the unrestored, mid-eighteenth century home of the first prison warden, Captain John Viets.

## OTHER HIKING OPTIONS

If traveling with two cars, you can leave a second vehicle at the end point at a parking area off Mountain Road (at the intersection of Mountain and Phelps Roads in Suffield). Start the hike at our same starting point (Newgate Road). Continue on the blue-blazed Meta-comet trail past the turnaround point. After 2 miles, you'll reach another lookout at the East Granby–Suffield town line. A tenth of a mile later, you'll come to Chimney Point, another example of Metacomet basalt eroding into columnar spires along the cliff's edge. After another half-mile, you will cross a feeder stream for Austin Brook, and 0.3 mile further will take you past a chimney off the east side of the trail (on your right) marking the site of a nineteenth century cottage. You'll keep following the blue blazes north, soon descending via switchbacks to the parking area where you left your second car. This option runs 5.2 miles with 1500 feet of vertical rise. For a real leg-stretcher, you can do this route with one car and retrace your steps from Mountain Road back to Newgate Road for an athletic 10.4-mile hike.

# 16

# Wolf Den

**LOCATION**: Pomfret

**DISTANCE**: 4.5 miles

**VERTICAL RISE**: 600 feet

**TIME**: 2.75 hours

**RATING**: C

**MAP**: USGS 7.5-minute Danielson

Once the domain of the Mohegan Chief Uncas, Mashamoquet (pronounced mash-muk-it; an Indian word for "stream of good fishing") Brook State Park is arguably one of the oldest in Connecticut. A combination of three state parks, Mashamoquet Brook, Wolf Den, and Saptree, a large portion of the now merged park was public domain even before the creation of the State Park and Forest Commission in 1914. The foresight of the Daughters of the American Revolution resulted in the purchase of the Wolf Den portion in 1899. That combined with the first Mashamoquet Brook parcel, a gift of former Pomfret resident Sarah Fay, along with other gifts—such as the 148-acres Hotchkins Wolf Den Farm parcel—as well as state purchases together form the present day park of over a thousand acres.

Among the varied attractions of this hike, you will find nestled the legendary Wolf Den where in 1742 Israel Putnam, of Revolutionary War fame, reputedly shot the last wolf in Connecticut, who had preyed on local sheep for some years. (Legends aside, the last wolf in the state was probably killed near Bridgeport circa 1840.) After tracking the wolf for several days from the Connecticut River, some 35 miles to the west, the intrepid Putnam crawled into the den with a lantern, saw the burning eyes of the trapped beast, backed out, grabbed his musket, crawled in again, and fired. Temporarily deafened, he left the smoke-filled hole, paused, went in a third time, and hauled out the carcass.

Near the Wolf Den are other interesting geologic formations—Table Rock and Indian Chair. These as well as the rock outcroppings and glacial boulders that dominate the hillsides are all made up of a metamorphic rock called Canterbury gneiss. Natural fractures in the rock,

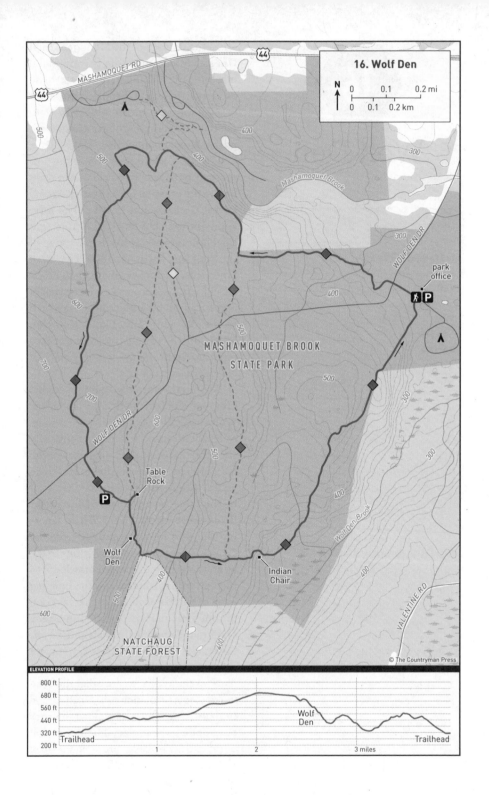

### 16. Wolf Den

N
| 0 | 0.1 | 0.2 mi |
| 0 | 0.1 | 0.2 km |

MASHAMOQUET RD

44

44

500

400

400

300

Mashamoquet Brook

WOLF DEN DR

park office

300

MASHAMOQUET BROOK
STATE PARK

400

500

600

500

700

700

WOLF DEN DR

600

500

300

400

Table
Rock

P

Wolf
Den

Indian
Chair

Wolf Den Brook

VALENTINE RD

400

600

500

400

400

NATCHAUG
STATE FOREST

© The Countryman Press

**ELEVATION PROFILE**

| 800 ft | | | |
| 680 ft | | | |
| 560 ft | | | |
| 440 ft | | | |
| 320 ft | | | |
| 200 ft | | | |

Trailhead

Wolf
Den

Trailhead

1        2        3 miles

from frost and weather, created openings and caves such as seen at Wolf Den.

In the section that is now the entrance to Mashamoquet Brook State Park, there once operated a cider mill, a grist mill, and a wagon shop. The old Brayton Grist Mill is now a museum maintained by the Pomfret Historical Society. It is open on a regular basis.

The Park offers a variety of outdoor pursuits to visitors including hiking, camping, fishing, swimming, and cross-country skiing.

## GETTING THERE

The hike begins at the Wolf Den camping area entrance off US 44, approximately 0.5 mile east of Mashamoquet Brook State Park's main entrance.

Coming from the west (Hartford area), take US 44 W (passing Mashamoquet Brook State Park) until you reach CT 101 where you turn left on CT 101 instead of right to stay on US 44. Once on CT 101, take a quick right onto Wolf Den Drive, heading south. And after 0.7 mile, turn left into the Wolf Den camping area, where you'll find parking by the campground office.

Coming from the east (Providence, RI) take US 6 west onto CT 101 west. Just before CT 101 ends at US 44 in Pomfret, you take a quick left onto Wolf Den Drive, heading south. Then follow the directions above.

Coming from the north (Worcester, MA) take US 395 south, exit 41. At the end of the ramp, go right on CT 101 west. Just before CT 101 ends at US 44 in Pomfret, you take a quick left onto Wolf Den Drive, heading south. Then follow the directions above.

Coming from the south (Norwich

LUSH FERN UNDERSTORY

area) take US 395 north, exit 41. At the end of the ramp, take a left onto CT 101 west. Just before CT 101 ends at US 44 in Pomfret, you take a quick left onto Wolf Den Drive, heading south. Then follow the directions above.

## THE HIKE

Today's route circles the park, mostly following the blue-blazed trail (with some sections both blue-blazed and red-blazed). The trails are very well maintained—comfortable wide paths, well signed, and blazed. Deciding on the difficulty rating for this hike was tricky. The first half of the loop is mostly a D—easy terrain with little or no elevation gain and easy footing, with some C-level sections of moderate ups and downs. The second half of the hike (especially starting at the Wolf Den) presents B-level difficulty with some steep climbs and poor footing. Overall, the hike averages to a C rating, but be aware of the more strenuous, scrambly bits on the blue- and red-blazed trail.

TABLE ROCK

Start your hike by walking back up the park road and crossing Wolf Den Drive. The trail begins through an opening in a stone wall where MASHAMOQUET has been painted in yellow on a rock. The blue blazes lead you through a wooded area and over a small footbridge before angling downhill to the right. You'll pass a small, wet area on your right where skunk cabbage spreads its large, aromatic leaves across the swampy, shaded ground.

The trail passes through another opening in a stone wall. You'll then cross another, more elaborate footbridge by a large old maple tree (on your left). The gentle path continues through a wooded area, paralleling a beautiful old stone wall on your right. Occasionally, other stone walls jut out perpendicular to

the first, and the trail will pass through openings. The land was clearly well used by early colonists, as evidenced by these property dividers. The wooded area through which you are now wandering soon becomes heavily carpeted with ferns on either side of the trail.

The stone wall that has been parallel to the trail changes direction and veers left, crossing your path. After walking through an opening in that wall, you'll come to a T-junction with a tote road marked by a sign displaying a weather-protected map. These helpful reproductions of the state park's trail map are placed at major junctions.

Turn right onto the level, blue-and-red-blazed tote road, and continue through maturing oak, maple, beech, and hemlock woods. Stay on the blue- and red-blazed trail until you come to another junction where the red blazes go left. Follow the blue blazes straight ahead. Shortly thereafter, a yellow-blazed trail veers right to the campground, picnic, and swimming area. The trail curves around and through a depression in the terrain. You'll angle left, following the blue blazes and keeping the brook on your right.

Your path will now level and meet a gravel road (Wolf Den Drive). Turn right and then left almost immediately onto another gravel road, passing between a pair of stone cairns. Each cairn contains a large stone with WOLF DEN ENTRANCE chiseled into it and highlighted with yellow paint (see *Other Hiking Options* for a shorter hike that starts here).

Follow the dirt road past thick clumps of laurel to a parking area with a few picnic tables nearby. Continue through the lot to the back of a small, circular drive where the trail entrance is marked by a rock painted with the words WOLF DEN. Proceed downhill on an eroded path blazed in blue. Soon the red-blazed

trail enters from your left. Directional arrows to Table Rock (left) and Wolf Den (right) are chiseled into a nearby rock. Take a detour here to your left to visit Table Rock. This trail is a short, downhill scramble to an impressively large, flat slab sitting in a wooded area. Retrace your steps back to the junction, and follow the red and blue-blazed trails steeply down on stone stairs into the valley below. Less than halfway down, you'll reach the fabled Wolf Den on your right. As you peek inside, note the weathered initials on the sides of the den entrance. This graffiti was etched onto the rocks over the past century.

When you finish examining the den, continue down the slope on the red- and blue-blazed trail. You'll enter a swampy area and then cross a brook on a long, simple footbridge. From here the trail climbs the sloping ledges on the other side. Note that the trail does have some poor footing over loose rocks and dirt. Just over the crest of the next rounded hill, the red-blazed trail breaks off to your left. You'll continue straight,

THE FABLED OLD WOLF DEN

following the blue blazes. A short distance beyond, the trail bears left on the slope; here, walk to the right a few feet to a ledge overlook and the Indian Chair. An appropriately shaped boulder, the chair commands a fine late-fall to early-spring view of the countryside.

Return to the blue-blazed trail and bear right, descending steeply before crossing through an opening in a stone wall, which then runs along the trail to your right for a short distance. You'll soon see the Equestrian Trail veer off on your left; continue straight on the blue trail. Here the trail meanders through rock-strewn woods. Shining club mosses perch on some of the fern-framed boulders; wood, polypody, and Christmas ferns thrive in these shady environs. You'll soon come to a muddy stretch of the trail and eventually cross a footbridge.

Now, you'll climb the boulder-strewn hill ahead, but be cautious of the steep root-covered trail, as roots can be quite slippery when wet. The slope is softened near the top by a carpet of white-pine needles. At this point, the path leads you through a pine forest with a few spectral hemlocks slowly joining the debris on the forest floor. You may notice the woods around you are now scattered with great slabs of rock formations that were not so prevalent in the first half of the hike. These boulders and slabs are all composed of Canterbury gneiss, a granite-based metamorphic rock found in the eastern part of Connecticut.

The trail begins a gentle, then insistent, downward course as you enter the valley. As you near the end of the hike, the path flattens and widens. You'll then pass through a stone wall before reaching the field that borders the camping area where you began. Pause to admire the vegetation around the borders of the forest. Nature, with all her diversity, loves edges. Edges provide habitat for plants that can stand neither full sun nor full shade. Wild animals use the woods for cover, and feed on the nearby field plants and border shrubs.

In the nearby woods is a backed-up pond where we once flushed a great blue heron. This long-necked bird with a six-foot wing-span uses its long legs to keep its plumage dry while wading in the shallow water. The sharp, pointed beak unerringly spears small fish, frogs, and other aquatic creatures that form the heron's diet.

When you're ready, cross the field to your waiting car.

## OTHER HIKING OPTIONS

**Additional Resources:** A state park trail map can be found at www.ct.gov /deep/mashamoquetbrook.

**Short & Sweet:** You can significantly shorten your hike (to approximately 1.5 miles) and still enjoy two of the popular geologic formations of the park. Continue driving down Wolf Den Drive without turning left into the camping area. Turn left onto a gravel road that passes between a pair of stone cairns, each with WOLF DEN ENTRANCE chiseled and highlighted with yellow paint. Follow the dirt road past thick clumps of laurel to a parking area with a few picnic tables nearby. You'll find the blue trail entrance at the back of the small, circular drive marked by a rock painted with the words WOLF DEN pointing the way. Follow the main hike narrative visiting first Table Rock and then the Wolf Den. Enjoy this fabled spot and then retrace your steps back to your car.

# Gay City State Park

**LOCATION**: Hebron

**DISTANCE**: 5 miles

**VERTICAL RISE 250 FEET**

**TIME**: 2.75 hours

**RATING**: C/D

**MAP**: USGS 7.5-minute Marlborough

Gay City was founded in 1796 by a religious group led by Elijah Andrus. For reasons unknown, Andrus left the town, and in 1800 John Gay was appointed president of the remaining 25 families, while Methodist minister Rev. Henry Sumner took Andrus' place as spiritual leader.

Even for those times, the villagers were an unsociable group; an itinerant peddler was robbed, murdered, and thrown into a town charcoal pit, and a blacksmith's assistant was slain by his employer for failing to show up for work. A nasty rivalry likewise soon developed between the town's Gay and Sumner families. The Gays called it Gay City, and the Sumners called it Sumner, although the settlement was locally known as Factory Hollow—undoubtedly for the wool mill with which the villagers unsuccessfully tried to make a living. Ironically, when the Foster sisters, descendants of the Sumners, deeded the 1,500-acre area to the state in the 1940s, they stipulated that it be called Gay City.

The community's decline, well under way before the Civil War, followed the usual pattern of hardscrabble areas: the old died, and the young left. The town had a difficult time maintaining successful businesses. A sawmill was built on Blackledge River, and a wool mill in the hollow. Both suffered fires. Later, a paper mill was built, but then that too burned to the ground. The village may have survived longer if it weren't for the terrible murders that led many to claim that Gay City was haunted. Hikers now enjoy the empty dirt roads of this New England ghost town.

In addition to trails, the park offers swimming and picnicking. Facilities include outhouses, bathhouses, picnic

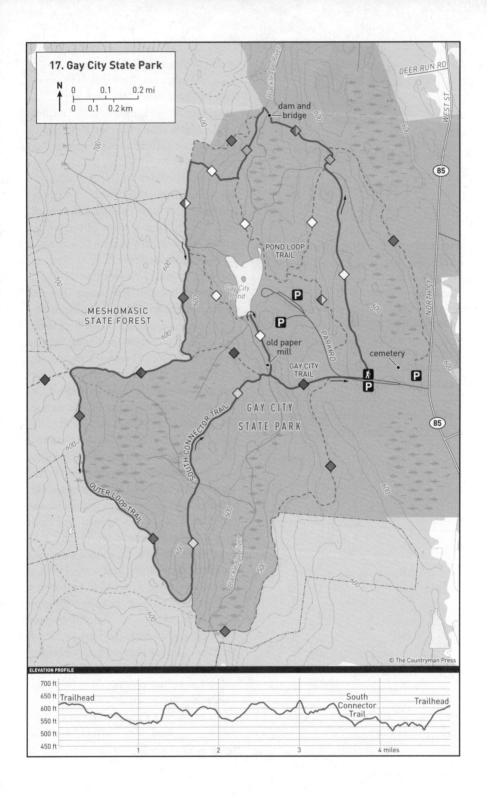

## 17. Gay City State Park

N

| 0 | 0.1 | 0.2 mi |
| 0 | 0.1 | 0.2 km |

DEER RUN RD

WEST ST

85

dam and
bridge

POND LOOP
TRAIL

Gay City
Pond

MESHOMASIC
STATE FOREST

P

P

PARK RD

cemetery

old paper
mill

GAY CITY
TRAIL

P

85

SOUTH CONNECTOR TRAIL

GAY CITY
STATE PARK

NORTH ST

OUTER LOOP TRAIL

Blackledge River

© The Countryman Press

**ELEVATION PROFILE**

700 ft
650 ft — Trailhead
600 ft
550 ft
500 ft
450 ft

South
Connector
Trail

Trailhead

1    2    3    4 miles

BLACKLEDGE RIVER IN WINTER

tables, and outdoor charcoal grills. Due to state budget cuts there were no state employees at the entrance kiosk in summer 2017, nor was there a lifeguard on the beach.

## GETTING THERE

Gay City State Park is located off CT 85, just south of the Bolton-Hebron town line. Take CT 384 east when traveling on CT 84 east. Exit 5 takes you to CT 85. Head south to the entrance of Gay City State Park (on your right in 4.7 miles). Drive past the entrance kiosk. Note the small graveyard in the woods to your right—save a visit here for the end of your hike. For now, continue a short ways on the park road and turn right into the parking area. There is a bulletin board in the far corner where we start our hike.

## THE HIKE

Our route will be a 5-mile loop that follows the white (Pond Loop Trail) to the orange, orange/red, red, orange, white, red/white, red (Outer Loop Trail), red/blue, red, yellow (Connector Trail), white, and blue (Gay City Trail) trails. This may sound pretty confusing, but the route is quite clear as you hike it around the park.

Just past the bulletin board you will begin on the white-blazed Pond Loop Trail. After three-quarters of a mile, the Pond Loop Trail veers left. Continue on the woods road, which veers slightly right, now blazed with orange paint. You'll see a trail map on a post at this junction. Next, bear left at a fork to stay on the orange-blazed trail. Soon you'll see the red trail merge from the right, at which point you'll follow the orange- and red-blazed trail through a woody swamp.

After about another quarter-mile, you'll reach a fork where orange goes left and red goes right. Follow the red-blazed trail to the right (the orange is the old red trail, rerouted due to the growth of the swamp). You'll cross an earthen dam and a wooden footbridge over the Blackledge River. The red trail now veers left. Soon you'll reach a four-way intersection, at which you'll continue straight onto the orange-blazed trail.

Proceed on orange for a quarter-mile. On your left, you'll soon see the Blackledge River; sharp eyes will reward you with a view of a beaver lodge as the stream widens out into a marshy pond. The orange trail comes to a T-junction with the white trail, adorned with trail map on a post. Take a right onto the white trail. Notice on your left the old stone wall, evidence of the community that once dwelled in this area.

You soon reach another T-junction. At this point, turn left onto the red- and white-blazed old woods road. Pass a white-blazed trail leading left to the pond (an option for shortening this hike). Further along the woods road, bear left to follow the red blazes over a rise, and then continue downhill to a T-junction with the Gay City Trail. Go to your right, following red and blue blazes. This trail was the old Gay City Road, the main route to Glastonbury and the Connecticut River. Before setting out on the old road, take a moment to enjoy the view of the swampland spread out before you.

The old road climbs gradually. Alert ears may hear noises in the brush: the dash and chirp of the chipmunk, the heavy-bodied bouncing of the gray squirrel, or the "drink your tea" call of the towhee, a common woodland bird with a black back, reddish sides, and a white belly.

Just after crossing a brook with a small earthen bridge, turn left onto the red-blazed Outer Loop Trail. Along this section in spring, you may here the low-pitched drumming of the male ruffed grouse. The bird perches on a log

ONE OF MANY CELLAR HOLES AT GAY CITY, EVIDENCE OF EARLIER INHABITANTS

GAY CITY POND

that gives its wings freedom to move, and then beats them faster and faster until they become a blur. The resulting thumping attracts females and warns away other males. The first time you hear this sound you may think it's a distant motor running, or wonder if you are really hearing anything at all. We like to think of this soft buffeting as the heartbeat of the New England woods.

In just under a mile after turning left, you'll reach the junction with the yellow-blazed South Connector Trail. Bear left, and begin the final leg of your circuit. Continue following the yellow blazes to the spot where a boardwalk crosses a swampy area and a brook. The trail then climbs gently to overlook another beaver pond below and to your left. The familiar stick-and-mud lodge is on the near bank of the pond. Rest here

a bit, and enjoy the chorus of birdsong and frog calls.

Proceed downhill until you reach the blue-blazed Gay City Trail. Just before this junction, note the old cellar hole to your left; it is one of the many in the park. Turn right, and cross the bridge over the Blackledge River. Look out over the bridge to the right: it may appear that the water is flowing uphill. This, at least, is how it appeared to laborers hired from nearby towns to assist Gay City in constructing the old mill: local legend has it that many threw down their tools at such an "un-natural" sight, refusing to aid what was surely "the Devil's work."

Over the bridge, you'll now take a 0.2-mile detour left onto a white-blazed trail to view the remnants of the old paper mill and the pond beyond it. So far, the trails have taken you around the outskirts of Gay City, through former pastureland and homesteads marked by stone walls and cellar holes. Now, at the very end of the hike, take time to visit the economic heart of this former settlement. A bit past the old cutstone foundation on your right is a ditch separated from the river by an artificial ridge. The small, now dry canal diverted water from the pond to power the mill downstream. The pond and the canal assured an even flow; the system dumped out the high water and accumulated water for controlled periods of operation during droughts. Just under three-quarters of a mile from the dam, the trail drops to your right off the canal and crosses a bridge over the mill's sluiceway. The squared blocks of the building's foundation and the square hole that diverted flow from the canal over the waterwheel to the sluiceway are both very prominent. The canal was reputed to be 10 feet deep in its heyday. A bit further along the canal is the pond. Feel free to enjoy a swim or a picnic lunch at this spot.

Head back on the white trail the way you just came until you return to the blue trail. Proceed to your left uphill, noting another old cellar hole on your right. Pass the red-blazed Outer Loop Trail entering on your right, and then bear right onto the paved park road.

We've reached the starting point of our hike, but before leaving Gay City, take a moment to visit this ghost town's small graveyard. You'll find it if you continue on the paved road past your car—on the left between the parking lot and the entrance kiosk. The cemetery tells a poignant story of the dour little settlement. It is a small plot—in stark contrast to the large, well-maintained historic graveyards you'll find in colonial-era towns across the state. You may also note that the rival Gays and Sumners are buried at opposite ends. The outlook and character of this vanished town may be best reflected in the harsh epitaph on a seven-year-old girl's grave: "Com pritty youth behold and see / The place where you must shortly be."

## OTHER HIKING OPTIONS

**Additional Resources:** A state park trail map can be found at www.ct.gov /deep/gaycity.

**Short & Sweet:** As noted in the write-up, you can shorten the hike to about 3.5 miles if when on the red-and-white-blazed trail you take the left onto the white trail. Follow this trail past the pond until you meet up with the blue-blazed Gay City Trail. Turn left, and continue along until you reach the paved road and then your car.

**Extending Your Hike:** Continue on the red Outer Loop trail—do *not* turn left onto the yellow trail near the end of the hike, but instead continue following red until the trail reconnects with blue just before the parking lot.

# 18

# Hartman Park

| | |
|---|---|
| **LOCATION**: Lyme | |
| **DISTANCE**: 5 miles | |
| **VERTICAL RISE**: 600 feet | |
| **TIME**: 3 hours | |
| **RATING**: C | |
| **MAP**: USGS 7.5-minute Hamburg | |

This delightful woods ramble takes the hiker through three centuries of Connecticut history. A result of the generous donation of 300 acres to the town by John and Kelly Hartman, Hartman Park has a diverse topography that includes old woods roads, steep hillsides, marshy wetlands, and miles of rolling trail through beautiful hardwood forest. There are wooden walkways and bridges over most water crossings and through especially mucky wetland stretches. One feature you will notice, no matter which part of the park you are in, is the lovely old stone walls and rock foundations that seem to be everywhere.

The nearly 10 miles of trails are the work of local volunteer hikers and are maintained by the Lyme Land Conservation Trust. There are numerous colored trails and some, such as the red and white, are found in more than one location throughout the park. Fortunately, all the trails are well blazed, and there are bulletin boards posted with large trail maps in a few locations throughout the park.

## GETTING THERE

You will find Hartman Park by taking CT 156 for 1.5 miles south from its junction with CT 82 (east of the Connecticut River and CT 9). Turn left onto Beaverbrook Road, just past Lyme School. After 2.7 miles, turn left again onto Gungy Road. The park entrance is 1 mile down this road on your right. You'll find ample parking near the gated road into the park. Take care not to block the road, which may be needed for emergency access.

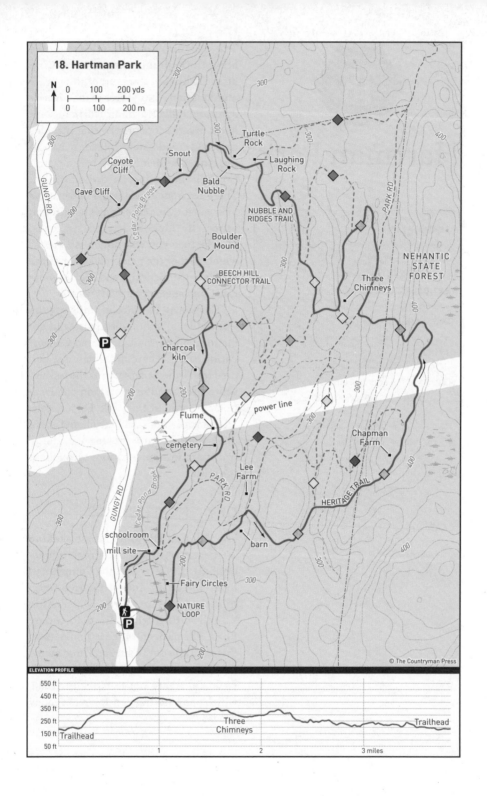

## 18. Hartman Park

N

| 0 | 100 | 200 yds |
| 0 | 100 | 200 m |

300

300

300

400

Turtle
Rock

Snout

Laughing
Rock

Coyote
Cliff

Cave Cliff

Bald
Nubble

NUBBLE AND
RIDGES TRAIL

Cedar Pond Brook

GUNGY RD

300

Boulder
Mound

BEECH HILL
CONNECTOR TRAIL

300

PARK RD

Three
Chimneys

NEHANTIC
STATE
FOREST

P

charcoal
kiln

300

200

Flume

power line

cemetery

Chapman
Farm

400

Lee
Farm

PARK RD

HERITAGE TRAIL

schoolroom

Cedar Pond Brook

mill site

200

barn

300

Fairy Circles

300

NATURE
LOOP

P

200

200

© The Countryman Press

### ELEVATION PROFILE

| 550 ft |
| 450 ft |
| 350 ft |
| 250 ft |
| 150 ft |
| 50 ft |

Trailhead

Three
Chimneys

Trailhead

1          2          3 miles

## THE HIKE

The trails are marked with painted aluminum rectangles. A vertical rectangle is used to mark the trails, with various arrow shapes used to mark turns. A horizontal rectangle indicates the end of the trail. Previously, small aluminum discs were used as blazes, and you'll see old ones in evidence. In general, any white-blazed trails you see are short side trails taking you to interesting sites. These are not shown on the maps. The only exception is the Three Pines Loop Trail (blazed in white) off the Yellow Beech Hill Connector Trail. The yellow-blazed trails are likewise connector trails (joining the main orange, red, and blue trails with one another). There are a number of yellow trails, each with its own name, that do not necessarily connect to each other.

This hike is a pleasant 5-mile loop that takes you to most of the interesting sights the park has to offer. The trails proceed in this order—orange, green, orange, yellow (Ridges Cut-Off Trail), red, yellow (Beech Hill Connector Trail), orange, yellow, red, and once again orange. Use the map to help you as you enjoy this meandering hike.

You'll begin by following the orange-blazed Heritage Trail into the woods just before the metal gate. Very soon, you'll reach a junction on your right with the Nature Loop, blazed with green rectangles. Bear right on the green trail. (You can also pick up the green trail loop 25 feet before the gate without first taking the orange trail.) This nature trail loop crosses two simple boardwalk-style bridges and passes a junction with the yellow-blazed Lee Farm Road trail, but continue here on the green Nature Loop. It then follows along the base of a hill and comes upon a children's area called Fairy Circles. You'll see painted stones, wooden mobiles, and hidden curios intended to surprise and delight.

After the Fairy Circles, the green

THE SNOUT IN HARTMAN PARK

LUSH UNDERSTORY ON THE TRAILS AT HARTMAN PARK

Nature Loop goes up a slight rise. The orange-blazed Heritage Trail links here on the right, passing between two boulders. Turn right to follow the orange blazes, soon passing through a stone wall and coming to another intersection with the yellow trail. Continue uphill on the orange, and observe an impressive stone foundation of a barn on your right. The orange trail briefly continues along an unpaved park road (blazed in purple), from which you'll see the stone foundation of the Lee Farm, also on your right. This house, burned after the Civil War, was probably built in the early seventeenth century.

Turn right up an old tote road opposite the foundation of the farmhouse (still following the orange blazes). Climb over the hill and descend into a wetland. The yellow-blazed Tween Brook Trail comes in on your left just before a bridge. Stay on the orange trail. Ascend Chapman Ridge via switchbacks through hedges of mountain laurel. Follow the ridgeline north, and on your left you'll pass the two-century-old remains of the Chapman Farm. Continue past the blue-blazed Chapman Path, and cross under a power line. After following the ridge a bit further, drop to the valley to the west and pass a stone fireplace. Then turn right onto the unpaved park road, again blazed in purple. Follow the road a short distance, and then take a left off the road, still following the orange trail. You'll soon see a ridge on your left as the trail drops down and crosses a muddy stream. The trail then circles around and climbs up onto Three Chimneys Ridge.

On this ridge, look along the sides of the trail to see the small, pointed evergreen leaves of the striped wintergreen stand out among the brown leaves of late March. These leaves have prominent white veins, striking regardless of the season.

The orange-blazed Heritage Trail links up with the red-blazed Nubble and Ridges Trails on your right. All three proceed together as you descend steeply toward a stone wall. On your left, you'll find a short, white-blazed side trail leading to the Three Chimneys: perhaps the most intriguing feature of the park. The chimneys may, as it is speculated, be the remains of an early colonial fort. In 1635, the governor of Saybrook Colony hired military engineer Lion Gardiner to construct a series of fortifications in order to protect local settlements from hostile indigenous peoples and Dutch colonists. The most famous of these was Saybrook Fort, which Gardiner designed and later personally commanded during the Pequot War of 1636. However, he designed several other forts whose locations have been lost to history. Here at Hartman park, the curious stone enclosures of the Three Chimneys are said to resemble the fortification engineering of the colonial period, and bear similarities to structures found at Plimoth Plantation. Could this be one of Gardiner's lost forts? If so, it would be one of the oldest standing stone structures in the eastern United States!

Follow the orange-blazed trail to your right soon after leaving the fort and descend to a woods road at the base of the hill. Here, you'll turn right to follow the yellow-blazed Ridges Cut-Off Trail through a wetland, crossing a simple bridge. Bear left onto the red-blazed Nubble and Ridges Trails and ascend Razorback Ridge. You'll then descend briefly to cross another bridge before climbing up to Jumbo Ridge. The trail passes a number of rock formations, including Laughing Rock, Turtle Rock, and the aptly named Snout. You'll then

CHAPMAN FARM RUINS IN HARTMAN PARK

cross another stream and then the trail climbs over both Coyote and Cave cliffs.

Follow the red-blazed trail south toward Hartman field. Turn left onto the yellow-blazed Beech Hill Connector Trail and circle around Boulder Mound. Cross over a bridge, and turn right onto the Orange Place Heritage Trail. Soon you'll pass a charcoal kiln on your right, marked with a small, yellow sign. The kiln is nothing more than a large, level, circular spot in the forest with no large trees growing in it. The local farmers would pile up wood and cover it with soil to permit a slow-burning fire, therein creating hot-burning charcoal for future use in blast furnaces.

Cross the power line clearing, bearing uphill and passing the flume, a cascade over moss-covered rock. Soon a yellow-blazed connector enters from your left and then exits to the right. Follow the yellow trail to your right, and turn right again into a small cemetery on a rise. The unmarked, vertical stones sticking out of the earth probably indicate graves of slaves and itinerant

gathering site on the Park Road with an informative bulletin board and visitors registrar. Please sign in and let the park manager and volunteers know about your visit. From the schoolroom, take the orange- and green-blazed trail south to the mill site just below an earth and stone dam. This structure was probably once a sawmill; however there is no positive identification in the records. It is only known that 50 years after the settling of Saybrook Colony, there were complaints from Lyme of overcutting of timber in the uplands. Much of this timber was exported as wood products to lumber-starved England.

Below the mill, come out onto the gravel park road (purple blazed), and then turn right to pass through the gate and return to your car.

## OTHER HIKING OPTIONS

**Additional Resources:** A map may be found at the Lyme Land Conservation Trust website (lymelandtrust. org). Large trail maps are posted on a number of bulletin boards at the park, and updated maps can be picked up at Lyme Town Hall on Route 156. There are over 10 miles of trails in the park. You can use the map to plan many different alternate routes. Some short but enjoyable hikes include:

**Nature Trail Loop:** Green-blazed trail, a total of 0.6 mile

**Beaver Pond Loop:** Pink-blazed trail, a half-mile loop is picked up at the schoolroom

workers. The only pertinent documentation in the Lyme records is that of a penniless man of partial Native American descent buried here by a white landowner, who then sought reimbursement from the town.

Turn left onto the red-blazed trail and follow it to the schoolroom, an open-air

**19**

# McLean Game Refuge

| | |
|---|---|
| **LOCATION**: Granby | |
| **DISTANCE**: 5 miles | |
| **VERTICAL RISE**: 600 feet | |
| **TIME**: 3 hours | |
| **RATING**: C | |
| **MAP**: USGS 7.5-minute Tariffville | |

Tucked away in north-central Connecticut, the privately endowed McLean Game Refuge was established in 1932 by George P. McLean, a former governor of Connecticut and US senator who in his will stated: "I want the game refuge to be a place where some of the things God made may be seen by those who love them, as I loved them, and who may find in them the peace of mind and body that I have found." Comprised of over 4,000 acres, the refuge is open to the public daily from 8 a.m. to dusk. Dogs are allowed in the park but must be on leash at all times.

Today, the refuge's excellent trail network provides access to acres of woodlands teeming with wildlife, just as McLean had hoped. Although it is hard to predict what you will see on any given hike, on a mid-February day we watched a fairly common, but rarely seen, brown creeper moving in fits and starts up a shagbark hickory; a flock of bustling chickadees; and a chipmunk breaking its hibernation in the above-freezing temperatures. A small, quick noise proved to be a ruffed grouse taking a few short steps before launching into flight with a thunderous roar.

## GETTING THERE

The main entrance to this refuge (Salmon Brook Street entrance) is located on US 202/CT 10 in Granby, 1 mile south of the highway's junction with CT 20. Year-round parking is available just off the highway in a gravel lot.

## THE HIKE

Today's route follows the blue loop trail to a well-worn woods road with a side trip up to the summit of East Barn Door Hill. From the woods road, we then

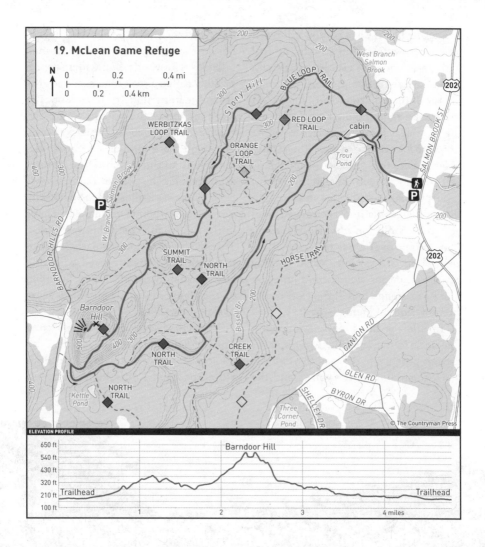

**19. McLean Game Refuge**

**ELEVATION PROFILE**

Barndoor Hill

Trailhead

Trailhead

© The Countryman Press

follow the purple-blazed North Trail along a ridge and back down to a woods road. We then take the woods roads back to Trout Pond to complete the loop.

From the parking lot, you will cross the field on a macadam road to the edge of the woods. To your left is a beautiful map giving a sense of the trail system ahead of you. Walk along the road a short distance to an old shelter on your left. Cross the bridge over Bissell Brook, which flows from the trout pond just beyond the shelter. The loop trail starts just beyond the bridge on your right.

Follow its blue, orange, and red blazes to ascend a small knoll.

The trail, which has been paralleling Salmon Brook (just out of sight to your right), bends away from the brook to the left. About a half-mile from the start, at the top of a small rise, the red-marked loop trail branches off to the left to return to the woods road west of the trout pond. Continue by following the blue and orange blazes.

After a level stretch, the blue- and orange-blazed trail tends gently upward, downward, then upward again.

In another half-mile or so, you will reach an overgrown clearing atop Stony Hill with Barndoor Hills visible to the south when the trees are bare. Shortly thereafter, the orange-blazed trail diverges left toward the valley below. Keep following the blue-blazed trail over a rise to a junction with a worn woods road. (See *Other Hiking Options* for a description of how you can shorten your hike at this point.) A purple-blazed path goes straight into the woods at this intersection, instead you turn right on the woods road. Then you go over a rise to a Y-junction, where you will go left. You'll shortly come to a larger woods road junction that has a bench and signs (left to the summit, right to Picnic Grove).

Turn left at this junction, following the signs to the summit. After a short ascent, pass a woods road to your left and resume climbing. As you ascend, the forest changes from the moisture-loving hemlocks to the oaks of well-drained hillsides. The woods road is more appropriately called a rock road as it hugs the steep, western slope of Barndoor Hill. Near the top of the rise on your right, you'll see a steep, rocky, unmarked trail. Turn right here for a short, perpendicular climb to the summit. The summit is an ideal lunch spot, with grand views (when trees are leafless) to the north and west. The viewpoints along the cliff have fairly well-trodden paths between them. Try not to wander off the path; the vegetation here is already stressed by the lack of moisture on this hilltop. Stepping on the plants can easily kill many years of slow growth.

When ready, retrace your steps to the woods road and turn right, descending steeply southwest toward Barndoor Hills Road and Kettle Pond. Turn left

TROUT POND WITH TROUT POND CABIN

A LOVELY WOODS ROAD AT McLEAN GAME REFUGE

50 yards before a wooden gate, and follow the worn path northeast toward the pond. You'll soon pass on your right the depression of Kettle Pond. Continue along the main path, passing a side trail to your right, through a mature pine forest with plenty of partridgeberry, a trailing shrub, on the forest floor. Bear right at a Y-junction to stay on level ground, and start following purple blazes along a narrow ridge. Turn left at a T-junction to leave the ridge.

Descend to another junction, and turn right onto a wide woods road. Continue along the unblazed woods road to a large open T-junction (with signs and a bench). Signs here tell you the road to your left leads to Trout Pond; to your right is the trail to Spring Lake. Turn left and follow the unblazed woods road north, keeping the ridge to your left and Bissell Brook to your right.

Near Trout Pond, you'll reach another signed woods road junction. Bear right on the trail to Route 10 Cabin, and soon you will pass the locked Trout Pond cabin to your right, and then Trout Pond. Spend a few minutes at the pond's edge. In the middle of the pond, you'll see some small islands. These were built by Senator McLean to create refuge for ground-nesting birds from foxes, raccoons, and other predators.

Also take some time to observe and identify fish swimming in the water. Tossing some small pieces of bread into the pond may attract some. Since fishing in the refuge is prohibited, the fish are quite tame. Watch for the flat ovals of the sunfish and bluegills, the former distinguished by sharper

coloration and a sunburst of yellow on their chests. Vertical-barred yellow perch, black bass with horizontal side stripes, and swarming shiners complete the list of the pond's bread-eating fish. You may also see, lurking in the weeds, a long, thin pickerel sliding in to make a quick meal out of one of the bread-eaters.

This fecund pond is also the annual breeding ground for Canada geese. If you look sharply to your right toward the pond's shallow end, you may notice a large brush pile—a beaver lodge. The beavers occasionally create trouble by damming up the pond's outlet.

Once you've enjoyed all the sights of the pond, follow the woods road to your right (passing the start of the loop trail), and hike back to your car.

## OTHER HIKING OPTIONS

**Additional Resources:** There is a map available on the refuge website, but it does not print well as it covers a large area (mcleangamerefuge.org). You can zoom into the section you need or view the map on your phone while you hike.

**Short & Sweet:** For an enjoyable 2-mile loop, start the hike as suggested, but when the blue loop trail meets the unmarked woods road, turn left to head back to the starting point. Just before you reach the junction with the loop trail, you'll come to Trout Pond and the Trout Pond Cabin. Be sure to take time to enjoy this peaceful spot (see the description at the end of the hike narrative above).

# Mount Higby

| | |
|---|---|
| **LOCATION**: Middlefield | |
| **DISTANCE**: 5 miles | |
| **VERTICAL RISE**: 1,100 feet | |
| **TIME**: 3.75 hours | |
| **RATING**: B | |
| **MAP**: USGS 7.5-minute Middletown | |

This is a hike that ancient volcanism built. Two miles long and 1.2 miles wide at its widest point, Mount Higby, like much of the Metacomet Ridge, is a traprock ridge. Its conspicuous, sharp cliff line is visible throughout the upper Quinnipiac River Valley and is a familiar landmark as you drive on I-91. This hike follows the blue-blazed Mattabesett Trail along the ridge with a sheer drop of 400 to 500 feet. The prominent, southern high point on the ridge, the Pinnacle, is just before a shallow gap called Preston Notch. At the summit, you'll stand near the edge of a geologic fault on a ridge of basalt dating from the Triassic Period some 200 million years ago. The Metacomet Ridge continues northwest with a gap between Mount Higby and Chauncey Peak (hike #32) and then south to Beseck Mountain.

## GETTING THERE

You start this hike west of the CT 66/ CT 147 junction, west of Middletown and just east of the I-91/CT 66 junction. The parking area (marked with a blue, elliptical MATTABESETT TRAIL sign) is on CT 66 and can only be accessed when traveling west on this divided highway. If you are traveling east, drive past the parking area and turn around in Guida's. From the parking area, a short, blue- and red-blazed side trail leads you to the actual Mattabesett Trail. There is also a side trail to Guida's, but hike parking is not permitted in the lot. Still, a short walk east for refreshments makes a nice reward after the hike.

## THE HIKE

Just into the woods, you'll see a covered bulletin board describing the New England Trail. Created in 2009

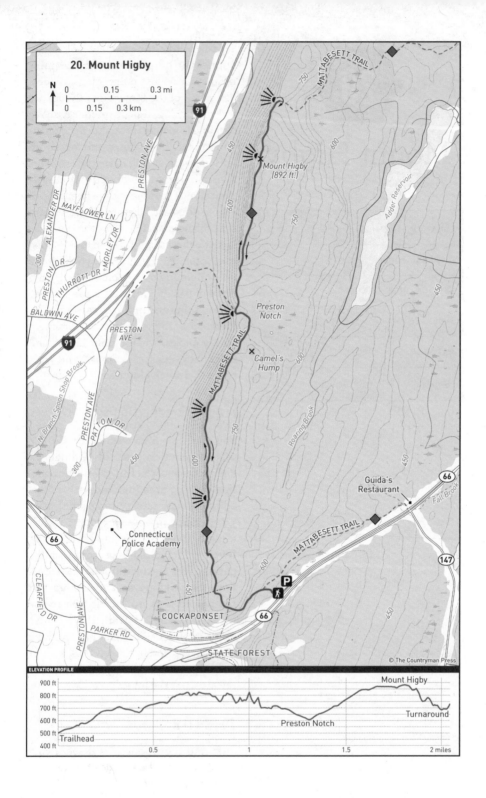

### 20. Mount Higby

**ELEVATION PROFILE**

VIEW OF THE CLIFFS FROM THE PINNACLE ALONG MOUNT HIGBY RIDGE

by the merging of the Mattabesett, Metacomet, and Monadnock systems, the New England Trail stretches from Connecticut to the New Hampshire border. From this point, you'll follow the blue- and red-blazed side trail about 100 yards up to the Mattabesett Trail, where you'll take the blue-blazed path uphill and away from the road. The trail threads through a hardwood forest and then begins to climb the mountain's loose traprock slopes. There are numerous unmarked side trails, so keep your eye out for blue blazes as you hike. After several switchbacks, a dip into a small ravine, and a steady climb, you'll come out of the stony woods at the open rock Pinnacle, a great viewpoint about a mile from your start.

Rest a bit, and enjoy the southern high point of the ridge. The mineral content, shape of the ridge, and exposure to sun result in a microclimate on the ridge that is quite different than that found in nearby lowland forests. It is a warmer microclimate that supports plants found more commonly quite south of here; thus many of the plants here are at the northern edge of their grow range. Also the harsh conditions and exposure of this microclimate result in plants growing here that you would find on other extreme mountain areas in New England. In the spring and summer months, enjoy the diversity of wildflowers from woodland sunflowers and blue harebells to yellow corydalis. At your feet, you may notice mats of a creeping evergreen shrub—bearberry. The white or pink, bell-shaped flowers and tasteless seedless berries are borne in terminal clusters. This plant is more typical of the summits of New Hampshire's White Mountains than Connecticut woodlands—another result of the soil of traprock ridges.

Continue along the ridge on the blue trail. You'll hike close to the cliffs, with excellent views to the west in a panorama that unfolds as you advance. West Peak and Castle Craig (hike #36) are visible in the middle distance; on your right is a traprock quarry taking a bite out of Chauncey Peak (hike #32). You'll also see the Connecticut Police Academy below you on Preston Avenue. You may hear the sound of recruits at target practice, an eerie intrusion upon the quiet of this gorgeous ridge. The land below provides excellent examples of the stages of forest succession. In one area, immature evergreen cedars are just rearing up above the field's pioneering weeds; in another, mature cedars completely obscure the former pastures; and in still others, the succeeding hardwoods are shading out the cedars. Forest succession silently continues.

At 1.7 miles the trail drops down into Preston Notch. As you descend, you'll notice an interesting rock outcropping to your right (away from the cliffs) with a small cave at its base. You'll then dip down to a small stream trickling over the traprock. Be sure to stay on the ridge by turning right at this stream crossing. A left turn will take you on the unmarked Nature Conservancy Trail down to the parking lot at the end of Old Preston Avenue (if you come across a power line, you've taken the wrong turn—retrace your steps back to the stream).

Out of the notch, you'll climb alongside a cliff with additional superb views. Near the top of your ascent, look for a natural-bridge formation. Soon you'll reach the summit of Mount Higby. Scanning the horizon on a clear day, you will see to your left Long Island Sound and the New Haven skyline. Further to the left are the long traprock ridges traversed by the Regicides Trail and the lumpy mass of the Sleeping Giant (hike #35). In front of you is the I-91 interchange; the large building on your right is the University of Connecticut Medical Center in Farmington.

As you hike along the summit ridge, you'll notice some small, pine-like plants. These are horsetails, diminutive descendants of ancient forests. Eons ago, they dominated the land towering more than 100 feet high. Run your hand along the length of one of the plants, and you'll find it feels very stiff. The silica content of horsetails not only betrays a story of the species' origin (from a time when carbon compounds in the soil were far less common), but is also suggestive of the plant's colonial use and name—scouring brush.

The summit is also an excellent spot from which to visually review the northern Mattabesett and southern Metacomet trails (all part of the scenic New England Trail). Ahead, at the end of the ridge you are hiking, the Mattabesett follows Country Club Road over 1-91, enters the woods, and climbs Chauncey Peak to the left of the large

SMALL WOODLAND SUNFLOWERS

traprock quarry. It continues back along that ridge over Mount Lamentation (partially hidden from view), ending on the Berlin Turnpike (CT 15/US 5). The Metacomet picks up where the Mattabesett ends, heading west from the Berlin Turnpike over Castle Craig and West Peak. It then proceeds north over Talcott Mountain (hike #47) past the Heublein Tower, and eventually reaches its terminus on the Massachusetts border at Rising Corner.

Leaving this cliff edge, your trail drops down and then climbs to another viewpoint. On a clear day, you can see the Hartford skyline on your right, with Mount Tom, north of Springfield, Massachusetts, to the east. To the right of Mount Tom, the Holyoke Range stretches like a roller coaster. The gap between the two is threaded by the Connecticut River, and the Massachusetts extension of the Metacomet Trail (the Metacomet-Monadnock Trail) traverses these two ridges. At this point, take time to contemplate what you have seen and implant it firmly in your mind; with time, these mountains and ridges will become old friends.

The trail soon bears right and descends away from the ridgeline to the east; here you can choose to hike farther, but this is the turnaround point of this hike. Retrace your steps back over the ridge to your car on CT 66.

## OTHER HIKING OPTIONS

**Additional Resources:** A map of Mount Higby and Beseck Mountain can be found online (meridenlandtrust .com/Higby_Beseck_tri.pdf).

**Nearby:** Curious about Beseck Mountain just south of Mount Higby?

PINNACLE CLIFF

Enjoy a 2- to 3-mile hike to Black Pond and the summit of this smaller, neighboring peak. You'll take the Black Pond Trail (black blazes), starting from a gate at the north end of the parking lot at Black Pond on CT 66. At the top of the hill, follow the blue blazed Mattabesett Trail to the right for about a mile to the summit, enjoying numerous views along the way.

# Penwood State Park

**LOCATION**: Bloomfield

**DISTANCE**: 5 miles

**VERTICAL RISE**: 600 feet

**TIME**: 3 hours

**RATING**: C

**MAP**: USGS 7.5-minute Avon

The traprock ridges flanking the Connecticut River Valley offer secluded hiking on the outskirts of the state's central cities. Penwood State Park sits atop one such ridge, along the northerly portion of the Talcott Mountain Range. Only a few minutes' drive from Hartford, the trails of Penwood carry you beyond the sights and sounds of the workaday world to a place where the most blatant intrusions are the blue blazes marking your route on the Metacomet Trail. This park's proximity to Hartford, along with its paved circular loop road, makes it very popular with joggers, fitness walkers, and dog owners year round.

In 1944, the industrialist, inventor, and outdoorsman Curtis H. Veeder gave the state the nearly 800 acres that now comprise this state park. Veeder and his wife Louise, ardent hikers, built numerous trails from which to more intimately observe the wildlife, woodland phenomena, and scenic vistas of this mountain. The Metacomet section of Connecticut's blue-blazed trail system (part of the New England Scenic Trail) traverses much of Penwood.

## GETTING THERE

From I-91 north or south, take exit 35B (the Bloomfield Route 218 exit). Route 218 is also known as Cottage Grove Road. Follow 218 west to CT 185, and then take CT 185 west toward Simsbury. The entrance to Penwood will be on your right.

From 1-84 east or west, take the CT 44 exit. Follow CT 44 west until the junction of CT 10 and CT 202 in Avon. Here take CT 10 north to CT 185 east toward Bloomfield. Penwood is on your left on CT 185. There is a large paved parking lot just to the right of the entrance.

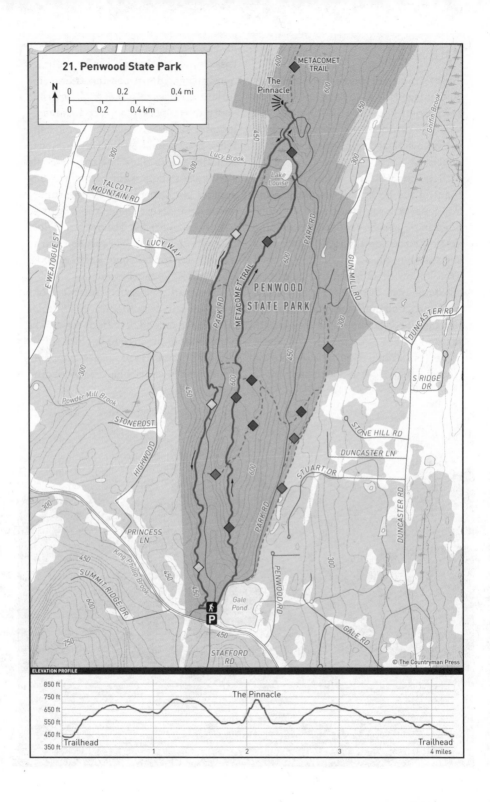

## 21. Penwood State Park

N

0        0.2        0.4 mi

0    0.2    0.4 km

METACOMET TRAIL

The Pinnacle

Lucy Brook

Lake Louise

TALCOTT MOUNTAIN RD

E WEATOGUE ST

LUCY WAY

PARK RD

PARK RD

METACOMET TRAIL

PENWOOD STATE PARK

GUN MILL RD

DUNCASTER RD

S RIDGE DR

STONE HILL RD

DUNCASTER LN

DUNCASTER RD

Powder Mill Brook

STONEPOST

HIGHWOOD

300

STUART DR

PRINCESS LN

King Philip Brook

PARK RD

PENWOOD RD

SUMMIT RIDGE DR

Gale Pond

STAFFORD RD

GALE RD

Griffin Brook

© The Countryman Press

**ELEVATION PROFILE**

| 850 ft |
| 750 ft | The Pinnacle |
| 650 ft |
| 550 ft |
| 450 ft | Trailhead | Trailhead |
| 350 ft |

1        2        3        4 miles

## THE HIKE

Today's hike will follow the Metacomet (blue-blazed) Trail to Lake Louise and a scenic vista known as the Pinnacle. You will then return to the lake and pick up the yellow-blazed ridge trail to return to your car.

Begin by heading to parallel, gated roads at the far end of the parking lot. You'll see a large stone with a plaque honoring Curtis H. Veeder. Start walking down the road on the right. You'll soon see the blue blazes of the Metacomet Trail; follow them along this path for a short distance. Just after passing a tote road and small outhouse, you'll bear left into the woods (along a blue-blazed path marked with a signpost for the Metacomet trail). You'll climb quickly onto the traprock ridge, forested with hardwoods and the skeletal remains of hemlock trees. Once at the top, the trail climbs gently up and down, passing a number of little-used side trails that lead north and south to the park's loop road. Salvage-logging to remove dead and dying hemlocks has opened up the forest floor to sunlight where once few shrubs could survive. You'll pass through a grove of spindly birch seedlings, a new primary succession forest under the scattered oak and maple trees. The dry forest floor is teaming with life—be sure to keep an eye out for toads, small snakes, and a wide variety of mushrooms.

The trail passes two intersections with the purple trail, and in 1.8 miles crosses the tar end of the loop road. Take a break from the hike to explore a little ridgetop pond. Head across the pavement onto a short boardwalk leading

LAKE LOUISE, A "KETTLE BOG" AT PENWOOD

VIEW OF TALCOTT MOUNTAIN FROM THE PINNACLE AT PENWOOD

through the thicket and onto the edge of the pond, grandiosely named Lake Louise for Mr. Veeder's wife. This lake is actually a "kettle bog," a body of water that forms when a glacier retreats and leaves behind a big chunk of ice. The teeming fecundity of life here makes the dry, forested ridge seem like a desert.

Notwithstanding the usual forest birds that are drawn to this cornucopia, we saw or heard more varieties of living things in just a few minutes of standing by the pond than in our total time spent on the ridge—dragonflies with outstretched wings, damselflies with folded wings, water striders miraculously skimming the pond's surface, circling whirligig beetles setting a dizzying, circular pace when disturbed, and water boatmen riding just under the water's surface. Gaily-colored butterflies displayed marked contrast with the mud perches on which they sat, absorbing moisture from their surroundings. Numerous, small fish were flitting into sight along the surface of the pond as they searched for food. Through the water flicked aquatic green newts, the adult form of the red

efts found on the springtime forest floor after a night of gentle rain. Here and there, small frogs sat propped up, half in and half out of the water, still exhibiting the rounded softness of their recent tadpole stage, and we saw two small water snakes sunbathing near the boardwalk.

Even the vegetation here is varied and lush. Lily pads adorned with their yellow flowers dot the surface. Marsh fern, swamp loosestrife, and buttonbush edge the pond, and a sour gum tree grows on your right. The white blossoms of the swamp azaleas perfume the air. Look for the few clumps of swamp Juneberry amid the numerous smooth alders. Their lustrous black berries, which resemble huge huckleberries, make a nice snack. If such a place fascinates you as it does us, read the book *Watchers at the Pond* by Franklin Russell.

When ready, return to the loop road. Just beyond the boardwalk bear left onto the blue-blazed trail that skirts around the pond and a swampy area on your left. The trail climbs steeply up the ridge, at one point clambering up some rough stone steps installed by

HIKING ALONG THE YELLOW TRAIL AT PENWOOD

a trail crew to make the loose traprock slope easier for hikers. Cross a paved circle where Mr. Veeder's chestnut-log cabin once stood, and pick up the blue-blazed Metacomet Trail again for the final ascent to the Pinnacle, a fine scenic lookout. Enjoy the view of the forested land below you. The ridge traversed by the Tunxis Trail lies to the west across the valley. To the south rises Heublein Tower on Talcott Mountain (hike #47), and further left the great, tilted volcanic slabs of Mount Higby (hike #20).

Return to the cabin clearing and retrace your steps on the blue trail back to Lake Louise. Bear right to follow the old woods road past the pond. You can continue on this road to your car or take our suggested route along the yellow-blazed ridge trail. Look for the first path to branch right from this road; it is a short, unblazed connector trail. Follow it; you'll meet up with the yellow-blazed trail in about 100 feet. Once you do so, turn left. Soon you'll pass another blue-blazed trail. This one is marked with blue plastic rectangles nailed onto trees; however, it is not the Metacomet trail. Ignore it and stay on the yellow-blazed trail. This lovely trail walks you along the western side of the ridge. As you hike along this section, you'll see the yellow trail and unblazed side trails crisscross each other. Be watchful of the yellow blazes throughout. After 0.4 mile you'll come to a viewpoint of the valley. Take some time to enjoy an alternate vista on the landscapes you enjoyed previously at the Pinnacle. After another 0.4 mile, the yellow trail takes a sharp left (not well blazed) and switchbacks down to a simple bridge crossing. Then the trail goes right back up the ridge (this strange detour helps bypass a deep gully). After another mile, the yellow-blazed trail empties onto a paved road just below the parking area where you'll find your car.

## OTHER HIKING OPTIONS

**Additional Resources:** A state park trail map can be found at www.ct.gov /deep/penwood.

**Short & Sweet:** Follow the blue trail as per our hike write-up to Lake Louise. Enjoy exploring this ridgetop pond and then retrace your steps back to the car. This trims the total mileage to a little over 3 miles.

As noted in the write-up you can take the paved park road back to your car from the pond instead of following the yellow-blazed trail.

# Soapstone Mountain

| | |
|---|---|
| **LOCATION**: Somers | |
| **DISTANCE**: 4 miles | |
| **VERTICAL RISE**: 700 feet | |
| **TIME**: 2.5 hours | |
| **RATING**: C | |
| **MAP**: USGS 7.5-minute Ellington | |

Soapstone Mountain sits in the midst of the 7,078-acre Shenipsit State Forest. A quarry on the east slope used by Native Americans and early settlers once yielded the soft, talc-like, greasy, lustered stone from which the mountain derives its name. In colonial times, this stone was valued for its high heat retention; flannel-wrapped, hot soapstones lessened the shock of icy bedclothes.

Soapstone Mountain was purchased by the state in 1927 so as to erect a fire tower for monitoring the forests of the eastern woodlands. Over time, more land was purchased, resulting in a state forest that covers portions of Ellington, Somers, and Stafford. The fire tower has since been removed, and an observation tower has been built in its place. Unfortunately, the observation tower is in disrepair and closed to the public. However, if you hike the mountain in late fall through early spring, when leaves are down, you will still have panoramic views.

## GETTING THERE

Soapstone Mountain is located east of the Connecticut River in Somers. From the junction of CT 140 and CT 83, drive north on CT 83 for 4 miles to Parker Road and turn right. After 1.3 miles (the last 0.4 mile are on a rough, three-season dirt road), you'll reach a four-way junction with Soapstone Road and Sykes Road. Park across the way to your left.

## THE HIKE

Today's route starts by following the gravel Soapstone Road east toward the mountain. Pass some logging yards to your left, and reach an old woods road flanked by large boulders, also to your left. Turn left onto the woods road and

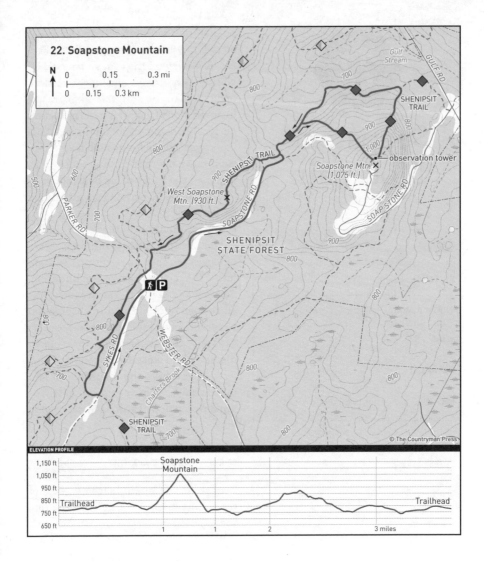

## 22. Soapstone Mountain

N

| 0 | 0.15 | 0.3 mi |
| 0 | 0.15 | 0.3 km |

Gulf Stream

GULF RD.

700

800

SHENIPSIT TRAIL

900

1,000

observation tower

SHENIPSIT TRAIL

Soapstone Mtn. (1,075 ft.) ✕

800

West Soapstone Mtn. (930 ft.) ✕

900

SOAPSTONE RD.

PARKER RD.

500

600

700

800

900

SHENIPSIT STATE FOREST

800

900

800

SYKES RD.

WEBSTER RD.

Charters Brook

800

800

800

700

700

SHENIPSIT TRAIL

700

© The Countryman Press

**ELEVATION PROFILE**

| | | | |
| 1,150 ft | | Soapstone Mountain | |
| 1,050 ft | | | |
| 950 ft | | | |
| 850 ft | Trailhead | | Trailhead |
| 750 ft | | | |
| 650 ft | | | |
| | 1 | 1 | 2 | 3 miles |

descend to where the blue-blazed Shenipsit trail bears right uphill. (If you miss this turn, follow the road to the summit of the mountain and then pick up these directions again from the tower.) The Shenipsit trail heads to the right up the main peak of Soapstone Mountain—a good, steady climb. You'll reach the top (elevation 1075 feet) about a half-mile after leaving the road. At the fork there, bear left toward the observation tower following the blue blazes. When

the trees are bare you have panoramic views. Off to the west from the summit is the flat countryside. To the northwest are the high-rise buildings of Spring-field, and Mount Tom and the Holyoke Range in Massachusetts. To the north and south is the well-wooded mountain ridge of which Soapstone is a prominent part.

The trail down the summit is just past the observation tower. You'll enter the woods just to the left of the telephone line. Follow the blue blazes. Your route threads down a rocky path through an attractive field of small glacial erratics. After 0.4 mile, turn left onto a tote road blazed in green and faded yellow. The green blazes start out being formed by duct tape. (The blue-blazed Shenipsit Trail continues to your right to the Massachusetts border about 6 miles further on.)

The trail is peppered with informative plaques, but many of these have fallen into disrepair. Gently ascend the yellow-blazed tote road around the north side of Soapstone Mountain. You'll see more prominent yellow blazes accompanied by faded green triangles once you leave the informational section of the trail. Continue climbing toward Soapstone Mountain Road, and bear right onto the blue-blazed trail to climb the steep hill to the west. At this right-hand turn, there is a white arrow on the tree to alert you. (Going left will return you to your car and is an option for a shorter hike.)

Bearing right, you will descend briefly and cross a muddy stream over a simple plank bridge. Then you will climb the steep hill to the west. On a leafless day, the tower on the summit of the main peak of Soapstone Mountain appears across the valley. Eventually, you'll stand on the rocky summit of West Soapstone Mountain (930 feet).

Near the top in spring, you may find the northern downy violet, an atypical species. Instead of the heart-shaped, smooth leaves of most violets, the northern downy violet's are long, oval, and fuzzy; however, its blue flowers are unmistakable. The trail proceeds downhill and passes another rocky outcropping over upward-tipped ledges; this is gneiss, the basic bedrock of much of Connecticut, laid down in flat layers

hundreds of millions of years ago. These protruding ledges were tilted by subsequent crystal deformations.

You will pass a vernal pond on your right. Then, as you approach a road crossing, you will pass through a swamp. The trail is made easily passable with stepping stones and wooden plank bridges. In the spring the swamp resonates with the high-pitched call of peepers. Many of us have heard these diminutive tree frogs with the big voices, but have you ever seen one in song? Cautious evening creeping with the subtle use of a flashlight may reward you with the sight of one of these small, tan frogs, whose throats swell into great, white, bubble-like sound boxes from bodies less than an inch long. Summer sightings are more a matter of quick eyes, quicker hands, and luck. Most of the woodland hoppers you'll encounter are black-masked wood frogs, but occasionally you will find a tiny frog with a faint contrasting X on its back—this is a Spring Peeper.

The trail is bordered by luscious undergrowth in this hardwood forest. In spring, fern fiddleheads pop up everywhere. Instead of growing gradually like most annuals, the fern uncoils like a New Year's Eve party favor—from a tightly curled mass into a fully-grown plant. In northern New England, the fiddleheads of the ostrich fern are considered a delicacy. We are told that our common cinnamon fern fiddlehead is also good to eat, but you have to remove all the light brown fuzz first.

Cross gravel Parker Road and continue east, following the blue-blazed trail. Carefully follow the blazes through here. You will also see a larger, white-circle blaze lower down on the trees with blue blazes. There are many paths and old tote roads in this forest. If you are

ON THE TRAIL UP WEST SOAPSTONE MOUNTAIN

daydreaming or taking the path of least resistance, it is very easy to miss a turn or two and find that the worn path you are traveling is devoid of blue blazes. In that event, retrace your steps to the last blaze and try again.

In late spring, there are at least two types of vegetation you may notice and wonder about. Plentiful clusters of star flowers are one. Spreading mostly by means of underground rhizomes, they are usually found in large stands or not at all. Secondly, you may think the compact masses of moss have grown hair. Actually, in late spring, moss sends up flowering stalks that allow the resulting spores to spread farther after they ripen.

The forest you're hiking through has a lovely, soothing sameness. An understory of maple and black birch struggle for sunlight in the gaps among large, red oak. The leaf-littered floor is carpeted with masses of ground pine and wild lily of the valley. Many of Connecticut's forests are like this one, with trees all of a similar size. The last great timber harvests were in the early part of the twentieth century, and since then cutting has been sporadic—far less than the annual growth—resulting in many trees across the state being about the same age. The logging that does occur, some of which you pass by on this hike, appears to leave the forests virtually untouched.

VERNAL POND ON THE SHENIPSIT TRAIL

THE UPWARD TIPPED LEDGES OF ROCK ALONG THE TRAIL ARE GNEISS

Soon you bear left cross Sykes Road. Turn left here to follow the road for about 0.4 mile back to your car.

## OTHER HIKING OPTIONS

**Additional Resources:** There are numerous options for shortening or lengthening your hike. Some are noted within the write-up. If you wish to explore further, consult the state park trail map found at www.ct.gov/deep /shenipsit. You'll see a network of hiking trails, horse paths, and snowmobile courses. A number of trails are multiuse so on your hike you may encounter mountain bikers as well.

**After Your Hike:** Visit the Civilian Conservation Corps (CCC) Museum in Stafford Springs on CT 190. The CCC was established in 1933 by President Franklin D. Roosevelt. He saw the need for environmental conservation work, and as the country was in the midst of the Great Depression, there was a large number of unemployed young men. The Corps ran until the bombing of Pearl Harbor in 1942 and America's entry into the Second World War. Workers were paid a dollar a day and lived in labor barracks. Many of the state parks and forests in Connecticut benefited from the labor of the CCC. The museum is located at the original site of Camp Conner and is the only remaining CCC barracks in the state. Call in advance to confirm the museum hours at 860-684-3430.

# Mount Misery

**LOCATION VOLUNTOWN**

**DISTANCE**: 5.25 miles

**VERTICAL RISE**: 380 feet

**TIME**: 2.75 hours

**RATING**: C/D

**MAPS**: USGS 7.5-minute Voluntown, Jewett City

Mount Misery is not a very appealing name for a mountain or a hike. Reportedly, the name comes from the fact that when the land was first being settled, it was found to be poor for farming—creating misery for all who tried to settle there. But for hikers, this prominent rocky mass within Pachaug State Forest is a delightful summit to scale. Set amid the flat pinelands of Pachaug State Forest, Mount Misery adds a nice, short climb to an otherwise level hike.

At over 27,000 acres, Pachaug State Forest is the largest state woodlands in Connecticut. Most trips to the park pass through Voluntown, a corruption of 'Volunteer Town' and a reference to English veterans who fought in the seventeenth-century American Indian Wars and afterward settled the area. Specifically, this borderland between modern-day Connecticut and Rhode Island saw heavy fighting in the largely forgotten King Philip's War from 1675 to 1678. This bloody conflict ranged over the whole of New England, pitting the early colonial states and their native allies against a coalition of local tribes. Over the course of three years, nearly half of New England's settlements would be raided by Native American warriors. More grievously, thousands of native people were killed or enslaved, with several tribes—including the Narragansett—completely destroyed. In terms of casualties relative to the population of the region, it may have been the deadliest war in New England's history. When passing through Voluntown, it's worth taking a moment to remember the unsavory aspects of Connecticut's colonial past, to which the volunteers of King Philip's War contributed just one small part.

Please note that hunting is allowed in Pachaug State Forest. Refer to the

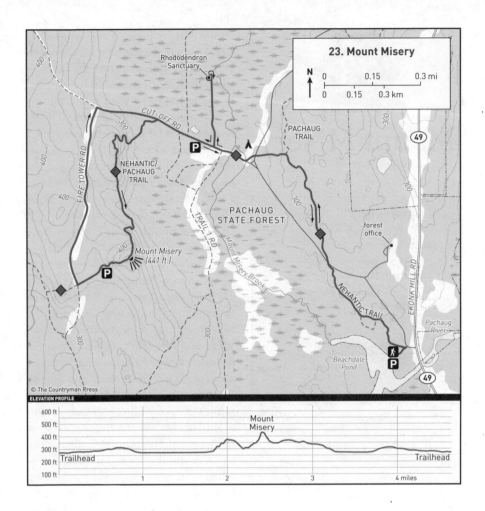

23. Mount Misery

ELEVATION PROFILE

Mount Misery

Trailhead

Trailhead

© The Countryman Press

book introduction section on Hunting for more information.

## GETTING THERE

From I-395 exit 85, you will take CT 138 east and follow it for 9 miles to Voluntown. Then take a left onto CT 49 north. The forest entrance and Doug's Place Picnic Area will be on the left, 1 mile from where the Nehantic Trail crosses CT 49. (On the opposite side of CT 49 is the Beachdale Pond parking lot.) Pull into the picnic area where you will find a viewing platform, with information plaques, overlooking Beachdale Pond.

## THE HIKE

Today's route goes along the blue-blazed Nehantic Trail, named for the Niantic or Nehantic people, an Algonquian speaking people who occupied the shoreline of Southern New England in the early colonial period. The hike continues through a forest harvesting area, intersecting and coinciding with the Pachaug trail that leads to Mount Misery Campground. You'll take a short detour to

WHITE PINES IN THE FOREST HARVESTING AREA AT THE START OF THE HIKE

the Rhododendron Sanctuary and then return to the blue-blazed trail, traveling up to the summit of Mount Misery. On the return, you'll take a small loop on forest roads and then retrace your steps along the blue-blazed Nehantic Trail back to your car. Most of the route is easy walking along level trail. Be aware that the short climb and descent of Mount Misery can be steep with some poor footing.

After crossing CT 49, the blue blazes lead you toward the picnic area and then veer off right into the woods. As you enter the woods, uniform rows of tall, straight white pines stretch away on either side of the trail. Your footfalls are softened by the lush pine needles that cushion the path. It's a beautiful stretch of trail on which to begin today's hike. Look down at your feet, and you'll see partridgeberry—a white-veined, leafy ground-cover with red berries. This woodland is forest harvest area called a shelterwood. Informative signs on the trees detail how the area is managed, in order to create a new generation of healthy trees.

Eventually, still following the blue blazes, you'll cross the paved access road. The trail widens here into an old forest road softened by a carpet of pine needles. Next, you'll walk under and then along utility lines before bearing right off this forest road into the woods. The blue-blazed trail here is well worn and not difficult to follow.

About a mile from the start, the Pachaug Trail enters from the right and merges with the Nehantic Trail on which you are hiking. The route bears left downhill, goes under a utility line and into an open campground field to the stone-gated campground road. Cross the road and go through a picnic site, shortly crossing Mount Misery

MOUNT MISERY BROOK

Brook on Cut-Off Road. Follow the blue-blazed gravel road, and as you pass a large playing field to your left, you'll see a side trail to the Rhododendron Sanctuary.

This handicapped-accessible trail is less than a half-mile long. The path takes you through a rare and impressive colony of giant native rhododendrons within an Atlantic white cedar swamp. You'll immediately appreciate the dry, raised, crushed-stone pathway through the swamp. At first the trail is bordered by mountain laurel and sweet pepper-bush, but soon you'll come to large, jungle-like rhododendrons flanking the trail. This native evergreen can grow surprisingly tall—to 40 feet—and its leathery leaves can reach eight inches in length. The combined effect of all that green is impressive. In July, these huge shrubs are dotted with white or pink bell-shaped flowers, reportedly one of the showiest displays of rhododendron blooms to be seen in any natural area in the state. Generously scattered among the rhododendrons are the straight, even trunks of tall white cedars. These are much statelier than the wizened, old red cedars usually seen along fields in the process of reverting back to forest. Atlantic white cedars grow upwards to 75 feet tall. Their bark is soft and flaky; the greenish tint you see is algae growing on the tree's damp surfaces. The durability of this tree's wood was so highly valued that fallen and submerged cedars were once mined from beneath swamps and put to use in making shingles, tubs, pails, and casks. Continue through the sanctuary. The path will turn into a short boardwalk leading to an observation platform in the middle of the swamp. When ready, retrace your steps to the campground road.

Before you return, stop and listen. On one mid-March hike here, despite a light coating of snow from a recent flurry, the sun beating down on the swamp had aroused the resident wood frogs. Their full, guttural chorus was broken only by the plaintive peep of a solitary spring peeper too groggy to give the second half of his familiar call.

Return to the gravel road and turn right, once again following the blue blazes. You'll pass a campground road on your left, and soon after on your left you'll see a MM OVERLOOK sign. Here, the blue-blazed trail veers left into woods (if you decide to take the first of the shorter options, you'll start here). You'll be following this trail to the summit of Mount Misery. The level path passes through oaks, hemlocks, and large white pines.

The trail then zigzags as it climbs to the top of the ridge. These switchbacks not only make the slope easier to surmount, but also reduce the trail's susceptibility to erosion by avoiding the fall line of the slope. The trail then turns left and soon emerges on open rock. You'll walk along a ridge and then descend into a cull through a small swampy area. Climbing steeply for a short distance,

GIANT NATIVE RHODODENDRONS WITHIN AN ATLANTIC WHITE CEDAR SWAMP

you'll then make your final assault on Mount Misery. The bolts you see as you emerge onto the ledges at the top were used to support an abandoned fire tower. The more efficient, but far less romantic, small spotter planes have now replaced the picturesque fire towers dotting the woods of old. Although Mount Misery, at 441 feet, is not very high, the summit provides a fine view of Voluntown, which lies to your far right, while Beachdale Pond is dead center.

On a calm day, the open summit ledges make a fine picnic spot. Be sure to carry out your garbage with you—even fruit scraps such as peels and cores should be taken. The forest's animals should not be exposed to such popular throwaway items lest they become dependent on them.

As you begin your descent along the rocky trail, notice the misshapen pine trees along the path. At one point they form a canopy over your head. These are pitch pines, a common sight on the dry, rocky ridgetops in Connecticut. Often twisted by the prevailing winds, they are easy to identify as Connecticut's only three-needled pine. The pitch pine's wood contains so much resin, or pitch, that it is easily lit and was often used as a torch (before our modern flashlights)—resulting in its common name, candlewood.

Keep following the blue blazes down the backside of Mount Misery: the trail soon curves left, joining a dirt fire road and cul-de-sac. Follow the blue-blazed road until the trail reenters the woods (as it continues northwest toward Griswold and Hopeville Pond State Park). Here you'll leave the blue blazes and instead bear right to follow another gravel road north. Continue on this road for another half-mile or so to a T-junction with Cut-Off Road. Turn right again, heading back toward the Rhododendron Sanctuary.

As you pass the sanctuary, consider one more side trip to visit this beautiful natural state landmark. Continue past the playing field to your right. After crossing the brook, bear left onto the paved road to the campground field. Turn right into the field and reenter the woods at the near corner across the field. At the junction of the Nehantic and Pachaug Trails, be careful to follow the Nehantic Trail to your right back to your car.

## OTHER HIKING OPTIONS

**Additional Resources:** A state park trail map can be found at www.ct.gov /deep/pachaug.

**Short & Sweet #1:** A 2-mile loop to the summit of Mount Misery. You will start at Mount Misery Campground. Instead of pulling into the parking area at Doug's Place Picnic Area, turn right on the forest road into the park. At the fork, bear left and you'll come to a playing field on your left and sanctuary trail on your right. Continue along the road (now Cut-Off Road) through a gate, and you'll see the trail on your left. You can park back at the playing field or park alongside the road near the trailhead. Follow the hike directions as noted.

**Short & Sweet #2:** This one is very short—about a tenth of a mile up to the summit, and only 0.2 mile round trip. Following the driving directions in option #1 above, go past the playing field and continue along the dirt Cut-Off Road. Turn left onto Fire Tower Road, and then bear left onto a gravel road following it to the cul-de-sac. (If you try to continue on Fire Tower Road,

PINE PITCH CANOPY NEAR THE SUMMIT OF MOUNT MISERY

you'll find it gated closed). Park your car and follow the blue blazes on a short but steep climb to the summit. Retrace your steps on the same trail to return to your car.

**Very Short & Sweet:** It's worth a mention here that the short (less than a half-mile) trail through the Rhododendron Sanctuary is a delightful hike on its own. Not only does it take you through a beautiful white cedar swamp with jungle-like rhododendron bushes throughout, the trail is also a handicapped-accessible trail allowing persons with differing abilities to enjoy this site. To get to the sanctuary, follow the initial directions for this hike but then instead of pulling into the parking area at Doug's Place Picnic Area, turn right onto the forest road into the park. At the fork, bear left and you'll come to a playing field on your left and sanctuary trail on your right. There is parking next to the field.

**Nearby:** Two other hikes in this book (#27 Green Fall Pond and #31 Bullet and High Ledges) also explore Pachaug State Forest, which at over 27,000 acres is the largest state forest in Connecticut.

# Chatfield Hollow State Park

| | |
|---|---|
| **LOCATION**: Killingworth | |
| **DISTANCE**: 5.5 miles | |
| **VERTICAL RISE**: 500 feet | |
| **TIME**: 3 hours | |
| **RATING**: B/C | |
| **MAPS**: USGS 7.5-minute Clinton, Haddam | |

Hikers may complain about the overuse of a few select areas, but Connecticut's trails are for the most part underutilized. As elsewhere, Connecticut's portion of the Appalachian Trail is heavily traveled, while other trails are often practically deserted. If you feel that one of the joys of hiking is temporarily leaving behind the clamor of fellow human beings, consider Chatfield Hollow State Park. Despite several hundred carloads of people swimming and picnicking in the park on summer weekends, we've met very few folks on our visits to this park's well-maintained trails.

Chatfield Hollow lies within that wide band of woodland separating the overdeveloped shore from the inland tier of cities. Chatfield Hollow Brook flows toward Long Island Sound between two ridges covered with hardwood forest of beech, oak, and maple. In 1934, the Civilian Conversation Corps built an earth and stone dam across the brook, creating the seven-acre Schreeder Pond. Pines planted at the same time create a peaceful setting around the pond. Chatfield Hollow was designated as a state park in 1949.

## GETTING THERE

Chatfield Hollow is on CT 80. Arriving from the east, the trail entrance is 3 miles past the junction of CT 80 and CT 79 on the left. Arriving from the west, the trail entrance is 1 mile from the junction of CT 80 and CT 81 on the right. Park in either parking lot found to the right and left of the park gate (before the entrance kiosk). There is no fee for these parking lots, but they fill up early.

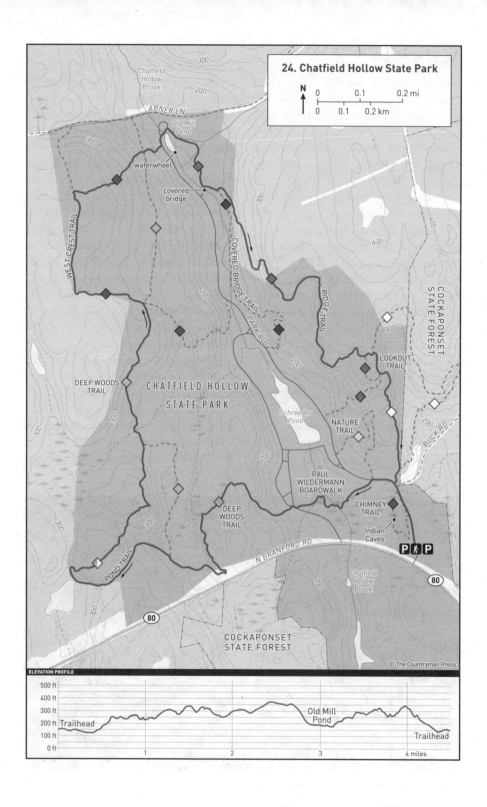

**24. Chatfield Hollow State Park**

N

| 0 | | 0.1 | | 0.2 mi |
| 0 | 0.1 | | 0.2 km | |

Chatfield Hollow Brook

ABNER LN

Old Mill Pond

waterwheel

covered bridge

WEST CREST TRAIL

COVERED BRIDGE TRAIL

PARK RD

RIDGE TRAIL

LOOKOUT TRAIL

COCKAPONSET STATE FOREST

DEEP WOODS TRAIL

CHATFIELD HOLLOW STATE PARK

Schreeder Pond

NATURE TRAIL

BUCK RD

DEEP WOODS TRAIL

POND TRAIL

PAUL WILDERMANN BOARDWALK

CHIMNEY TRAIL

Indian Caves

P 🚶 P

N BRANFORD RD

Chatfield Hollow Brook

80

80

COCKAPONSET STATE FOREST

© The Countryman Press

**ELEVATION PROFILE**

| | |
|---|---|
| 500 ft | |
| 400 ft | |
| 300 ft | |
| 200 ft | Trailhead |
| 100 ft | |
| 0 ft | |

Old Mill Pond

Trailhead

1    2    3    4 miles

## THE HIKE

Our trail will be a loop that goes over the Paul Wildermann Boardwalk and then continues in this order on the following trails: orange (Deep Woods Trail), orange/white (Pond Trail), blue (Crest Trail), red (Ridge Trail), and white (Lookout Trail).

Follow the paved park road. Take your first left, following signs for the boardwalk. Bear left in the parking lot to arrive at the beginning of the Paul Wildermann Boardwalk. This 825-foot boardwalk takes you through a beautiful, red-maple swamp with numerous informative plaques. The boardwalk was built in 1988, and sections were rebuilt in 2006. Caution, the boardwalk can be slippery when wet.

Continue straight from the boardwalk and cross the park road. A little to the right, you will see two posts and the beginning of the orange-blazed Deep Woods Trail (marked with a small sign). You'll start by going up a rise and then descend with a vernal pond on your left. The trail is generally well-blazed but be on the lookout for turns throughout the hike. You will be walking along a typical, fern-bordered, rock-strewn path through a hardwood forest of beech, oak, maple, and hickory. The trail climbs up a rocky slope and continues along open rock ledges. Mountain laurel are abundant alongside the trail (the Connecticut state flower which blooms mid-June). A half-mile from the start, you'll begin to descend with a bit of a scramble. The trail bears sharp right off the ledges and passes under and around them. We found this portion to be lacking in blazes. This section of the trail is very close to CT 80; you'll see it through the trees and hear cars on the road.

The ledge's rock faces are covered with mosses and lichens, and trees sprout from great cracks. You can use lichens an indicator to measure air quality—sensitive to pollution, an abundance of them signifies clean air. At 0.61 mile from the start of the orange

PAUL WILDERMANN BOARDWALK AT THE START OF THE HIKE

THE RED TRAIL ALONG CHATFIELD HOLLOW BROOK

OLD MILL POND AT CHATFIELD HOLLOW

trail, you'll turn left onto the orange-and-white-blazed Pond Trail. This turn-off is marked with a wooden sign. This trail has orange blazes with cut-out open circles in the center. This approximately 0.7-mile trail travels along an old stone wall, evidence of a farm at one time. Descend gently down to a pond (on private property). Notice that the pond is slowly being reclaimed by aquatic grasses and water lilies.

Leaving the pond area, the trail soon intersects and follows another stone wall. The trail then ascends and meanders along a grassy path. Be mindful of blazes as the trail turns sharply left (the blaze is obscured by lichen on a dying cedar tree). Descend down to the main orange trail marked with a wooden sign. Bear left to continue on the orange-blazed Deep Woods Trail. In a

short distance, you will come to a gentle brook-crossing on a simple wooden bridge.

You'll then come to the East Woods and West Crest Trail. Go left on this blue-blazed trail. The trail follows the eastern boundary of the park abutting water supply land. After 0.2 mile, the path turns sharply right, with a metal WATER COMPANY SUPPLY LAND sign high up on a tree. After another 0.2 mile, the route again turns sharp right on the well-blazed blue trail. You'll pass two large, old beech trees on your left, one with numerous holes made by birds foraging for insects. Descend gently, passing an old foundation on your left and drop to the paved park road.

Proceed to your left along the road, across the bridge, and around the east side of the dammed Old Mill Pond to pick up the red-blazed Ridge Trail. This is a good time to take a mid-hike rest at Old Mill Pond. There are picnic tables under the shade of the old white pine trees. Notice the restored waterwheel across the pond. This is an undershot wheel, wherein the water strikes the middle of the wheel and its falling weight turns the wheel. You can get a closer look at this waterwheel if you take the purple trail (see *Other Hiking Options*).

Initially the red-blazed trail parallels the stream and then bears uphill just before reaching a covered bridge (again the purple trail will bring you across the bridge, see *Other Hiking Options*).

Follow the red-blazed Ridge Trail generally uphill, passing beside and over several ledges. Finally, the trail winds left steadily uphill. Then after a few yards, the trail curves back on itself. The park's trail system does a marvelous job of twisting and winding through the most interesting areas, passing numerous glacial erratics. After passing around the left end of a large, almost perpendicular rock wall, you'll level off a bit, climb steeply again, and emerge on top of a ledge.

At a T-junction turn left, following an unblazed trail that shortly leads to the white-blazed Lookout Trail. Turn right when you reach this trail (turning left uphill will add almost a mile to this hike and will still bring you back to the park road). After turning right, you'll walk downhill until you reach a junction at which point you'll turn right to reach the paved park road (0.4 mile). Turn left on the park road, and follow to the parking lot where you left the car.

## OTHER HIKING OPTIONS

**Additional Resources:** A state park trail map can be found at www.ct.gov /deep/chatfieldhollow.

**Short & Sweet:** Do you have less than an hour? Follow the beginning trail information and take a walk on the boardwalk. This well-maintained 825-foot trek through a red maple swamp makes a wonderful short walk. Once you've hiked the full boardwalk, turn around and retrace your steps back to the car.

**Extending Your Hike:** You can also add on to the hike by including the green-blazed Chimney Trail found near the parking lot on the west side of the road. This 0.22-mile trail offers wonderful examples of the interesting geology of the park. Almost immediately, the trail encounters a large outcrop of monson gneiss. This large outcropping contains a number of small rock-fall caves, one with two entrances. The park map describes these as "Indian Caves," as they may have been used as shelters by Native Americans. The trail climbs over the south end of the outcrop then runs along its eastern side before returning to the road.

The purple-blazed Covered Bridge Trail starts soon after our route on the red Ridge Trail. This half-mile trail brings you across a covered-bridge reproduction spanning Chatfield Hollow Brook. The gentle route eventually exits further down the park road. You can take this trail to shorten the hike (not completing the red or white trails) and walk back to the car on the park road.

# Collis P. Huntington State Park

| | |
|---|---|
| **LOCATION**: Redding | |
| **DISTANCE**: 5.5 miles | |
| **VERTICAL RISE**: 350 feet | |
| **TIME**: 3 hours | |
| **RATING**: C/D | |
| **MAP**: USGS 7.5-minute Botsford | |

The casual seeker easily finds many of Connecticut's trails. However, Collis P. Huntington State Park in Redding is off the beaten path and frequented primarily by locals. Opened to the public in 1973, this park of over a thousand acres is a delightful hidden treasure. Most of its trails are on old woods roads that meander through fields, dense woodlands, and around manmade ponds. The trails are used for hiking, running, mountain biking, horseback riding, and cross-country skiing.

The land was a gift from Archer M. Huntington, the stepson of the railroad magnate and philanthropist for whom the area was named. Archer was a noted poet and Spanish scholar in his own right. Two striking sculptures by the world-renowned Anna Hyatt Huntington (Archer's second wife) welcome visitors to this park. Among the most famous of her sculptures are Joan of Arc in New York City; El Cid Campeador in Seville, Spain; and the heroic statue of General Israel Putnam at the Putnam Memorial State Park entrance in Redding. Mrs. Huntington was a hard-working artist all her life, finding recognition and respect in an era when very few women found success. She continued working up to a venerable age; her monument to Israel Putnam was created when the artist was in her 90s!

Please note that the park is open to archery-only deer hunting from September 15th through December 31st. The area near Old Dodgingtown Road, however, is closed to hunting due to high public use. Refer to the book introduction section on Hunting for more information.

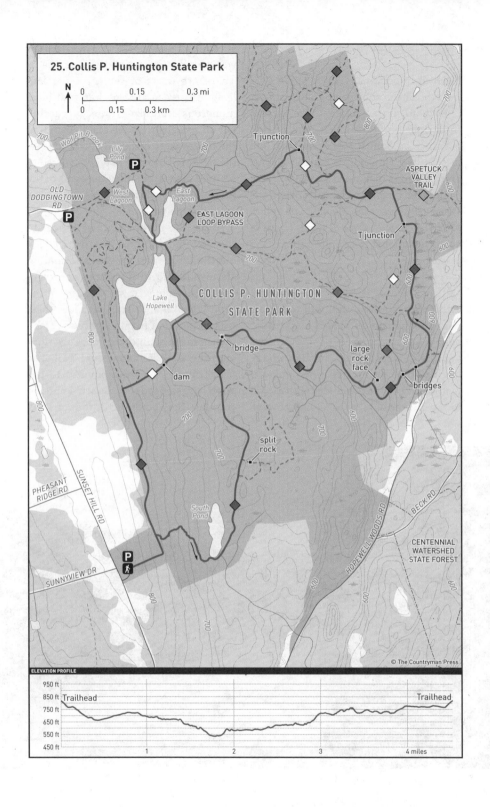

## 25. Collis P. Huntington State Park

N

0 — 0.15 — 0.3 mi
0 — 0.15 — 0.3 km

Wolf Pit Brook

Lily Pond

P

OLD DODGINGTOWN RD

P

West Lagoon

East Lagoon

EAST LAGOON LOOP BYPASS

T junction

ASPETUCK VALLEY TRAIL

T junction

COLLIS P. HUNTINGTON STATE PARK

Lake Hopewell

bridge

dam

large rock face

bridges

split rock

South Pond

PHEASANT RIDGE RD

SUNSET HILL RD

P

SUNNYVIEW DR

HOPEWELL WOODS RD

BECK RD

CENTENNIAL WATERSHED STATE FOREST

© The Countryman Press

**ELEVATION PROFILE**

950 ft
850 ft — Trailhead — Trailhead
750 ft
650 ft
550 ft
450 ft

1 — 2 — 3 — 4 miles

## GETTING THERE

From the junction of CT 302 and CT 58 in Bethel, head south on CT 58 (Putnam Park Road) for 1.3 miles. Bear left and then right on Sunset Hill Road. After 2.2 miles on Sunset Hill Road, turn left into Collis P. Huntington State Park. The entrance road is flanked by two wildlife sculptures by Anna Hyatt Huntington: *Wolves Baying at the Moon* at left and *A Mother Bear with Cubs* at right. There is a parking lot just inside the gate.

## THE HIKE

This route is a loop that will take you past South Pond on blue-blazed trails, and then follows a series of blue-, white-, and green-blazed trails through woodlands dotted with interesting geologic features. The hike concludes with a visit to the cluster of lakes at the southwest section of the park. We will follow well-trodden paths and woods roads. There are parts of the hike, particularly in the eastern section, that have numerous unmarked trails (be careful: not all are given on the map). Note that the blazes were originally colored plastic markers but have been converted to painted blazes. You may see some of the formerly used, plastic blazes on trees as you hike the park.

From the parking lot, walk over to the covered bulletin board to check out the large map and for information about hunting in the park. Go downhill on an unblazed woods road on the right side of a large, open meadow (thick with vegetation in late summer). You'll then come to an intersection. Turn right onto the well-defined gravel trail. The trail travels downhill, coming to the open, grass-bordered South Pond on your left. Stay on the well-trodden trail,

EAST LAGOON AT HUNTINGTON STATE PARK

SPLIT ROCK AT HUNTINGTON STATE PARK

which after the pond is marked with blue blazes (previously blazed in white).

You'll now walk through a well-managed woodlot. Selective harvesting has been used to eliminate junk species such as black oak, to remove wolf trees (oddly shaped trees that have grown in ungainly configurations, do not produce good timber, and shade out potentially valuable trees), and to create optimum conditions for the growth of usable trees. You'll also pass several scarred beech trees. The beech's smooth, gray bark grows with the tree—it doesn't flake off with time, so marks or initials decades old still retain their shape. Legend has it that Daniel Boone carved his name into a beech tree where he once "cilled a bar" in Tennessee. The carving lasted for more than 150 years before the tree finally toppled.

Proceed past an unmarked trail at right by a huge split rock. Pause here to enjoy this interesting geologic feature. How many thousands of years ago did

water seep into a fissure in the original large boulder? Over time the water accumulated and froze. The power of the expanding ice was strong enough to actually split the large boulder, leaving us with this interesting feature to explore.

Continue straight on the blue-blazed wide trail, passing numerous unmarked trails on either side of your path. Cross a bridge that spans Lake Hopewell's outlet stream. About 1.75 miles from the start, take a right at the junction following the rectangular blazes (now painted blue and red). A stream comes in and soon parallels the trail on your right.

In about a half-mile, reach a Y-junction below a large rock face—follow the now blue blazes to your right. If you are interested in a brief detour, a short side trail here leads left to the top of the rock. Otherwise, your route goes downhill, reaching a small stream below still more rocks. Cross the stream on a wooden plank bridge, and soon you will cross another stream running under yet another wooden plank bridge. Pass through an area of old blowdowns within a narrow stream valley. You can see Hopewell Road (the old Newtown Turnpike) to your right through the trees in the distance. You'll pass another park entrance on your right; continue straight on the trail you have been following.

Next you'll parallel the turnpike, climb uphill, bear left, and cross a stream on a small plank footbridge with a large boulder on your right. The boulder's source, a ledge, is on your left. Pause here to consider the tremendous commotion this mighty boulder made as it fell from the ledge to its current location along the trail. Soon after passing through these boulders, you'll turn right at a trail junction. You'll be following a flat, somewhat muddy trail blazed in blue. There will be a rocky hillside on your left and a swamp on your right. In August, you'll see numerous, striking, red cardinal flowers in the swamp.

After another 0.3 mile, you will come to another T-junction. Stay with the blue blazes, and go right—the swamp will now be on both sides of the trail.

You'll arrive at another T-junction with a generic park trail sign. This is the junction with the Aspetuck Valley Trail. Turn left here, following darker blue blazes (light-blue blazes go right on the Aspetuck Valley Trail, heading out of the park). The next stretch of the hike has you passing two junctions with white-blazed trails (they are different trails, both blazed in white). Note that you will be turning on the second of the two white-blazed trails. About a tenth of a mile from the Aspetuck Valley Trail junction, you'll pass a white-blazed trail on your left—do not turn here, and instead continue on the blue-blazed trail. After another tenth of a mile, you'll

WOLVES BAYING AT THE MOON, A SCULPTURE BY ANNA HYATT HUNTINGTON AT THE PARK ENTRANCE

come to a Y-junction. Here turn left on the white-blazed trail. (If you miss this second white trail junction, you'll come to another white trail junction in a quarter-mile, where you can turn left and then left again on the green trail. You'll mirror the directions below and be back on track, having incurred only slightly longer mileage.)

Next, in about a quarter-mile, you'll reach a T-junction marked with a wooden post adorned with blazes. Turn left here, now following the green-blazed trail. You'll cross a culverted stream. This area has a large number of tulip trees, a southern species that is more dominant in the Great Smoky Mountains National Park.

The trail climbs then levels out. You'll pass a stone wall on your right about halfway up the hill. Continue through a rusted gate. Immediately turn right onto a less-used, white-blazed path, away from the wide old woods road. This white-blazed trail will take you around East Lagoon on a somewhat steep, rocky trail that does have some poor footing. (If you wish, you may eliminate the loop around East Lagoon by staying on the main, green-blazed trail, which shortly crosses the lagoon's outlet via a wooden bridge and then rejoins this path at the bridge between East Lagoon and Lake Hopewell.)

The white-blazed trail parallels a rusted fence, and then heads uphill around East Lagoon. Adjacent to the lagoon, you'll come to a grassy area—head across it to follow the white blazes. Continue uphill, then down to a junction. You'll see a parking area downhill to your right. Turn left onto a narrow path through mountain laurel before going down toward the lot. Descend steeply over ledges to the shore of West Lagoon and follow the trail to the bridge over its outlet. Cross between East and West Lagoons on the footbridge. Immediately at the junction, go left over still another bridge with East Lagoon to your left and Lake Hopewell to your right.

At the junction just past this bridge, proceed to your right uphill on a red-blazed (previously orange-blazed) gravel road that continues along and above Lake Hopewell. At the junction at the lake's end, turn right onto the white-marked path and walk across an earthen dam. At the end of the dam, the road curves left to follow from above the outlet stream's valley below.

You'll pass a small stand of rhododendron bushes as you hike around the lake. This shrub is less common on our hikes than the ever-present mountain laurel. Rhododendron and mountain laurel are similar in they are both evergreen with oval dark green leaves, but they are each of a different genus (family). You'll find rhododendron has a longer leaf with a brown fuzz on its underside and it blooms in July/August, while Mountain Laurel blooms in May/June.

The trail parallels a fence, and then reaches a T-junction—turn left to follow blue blazes. Shortly thereafter, you will pass through a gateless, pole-flanked opening in the wire fence. Continue on the old road through seemingly impenetrable vine and brush thickets. In a half-mile or so, you'll reach the trail that leads uphill through the field to your car. Ascend along the edge of the field to the parking lot.

## OTHER HIKING OPTIONS

**Additional Resources:** A state park trail map can be found at www.ct.gov/deep/collisphuntington.

**Short & Sweet:** For a shorter hike (about 2 miles) that travels through the area closed to hunting, park at the Old Dodgingtown Road entrance—found north of the main park entrance on Sunset Hill Road. Take the blue-blazed trail to the white trail between West and East Lagoon then go right on the red trail and right again on the white trail to go around Lake Hopewell. You can then take an unmarked, twisty trail on your right back to the parking lot or continue a little further to go right on the blue-blazed trail back to your car.

## 26

# Northern Nipmuck

**LOCATION**: Ashford

**DISTANCE**: 5.5 miles

**VERTICAL RISE**: 550 feet

**TIME**: 3 hours

**RATING**: B/C

**MAP**: USGS 7.5-minute Westford

The Nipmuck Trail extends over 35 miles from the town of Mansfield north to the Massachusetts border. It is shaped roughly like an upside-down fork. It is part of the blue-blazed trail system that is maintained by the Connecticut Forest and Park Association.

The Nipmuck people are descendants of the indigenous Algonquian peoples of Nippenet, "the freshwater pond place," which corresponds to central Massachusetts and parts of Connecticut and Rhode Island.

The entire 14-mile section of the northern Nipmuck Trail, opened in 1976, offers delightful woods walking. The northern section passes through the Yale-Myers Forest, a 7,800-acre forested tract that runs through northeastern Connecticut and is owned and managed by the Yale School of Forestry and Environmental Studies. The forest is managed for multiple uses, from scientific research and teaching to commercial timber production. The Nipmuck Trail is the only public access to this forest (except for permitted hunting in season).

## GETTING THERE

Follow CT 89 north for 4 miles from junction of US 44 and CT 89 in Warrenville. Bear right at the Westford blinking traffic light. In 0.3 mile, where the tar road bends right, stay straight on gravel Boston Hollow Road. The blue-blazed trail crosses the road in another 1.3 miles with a small parking area on your left. Watch carefully for this, as there is no Nipmuck Trail sign. Note that there is enough room for three cars to park.

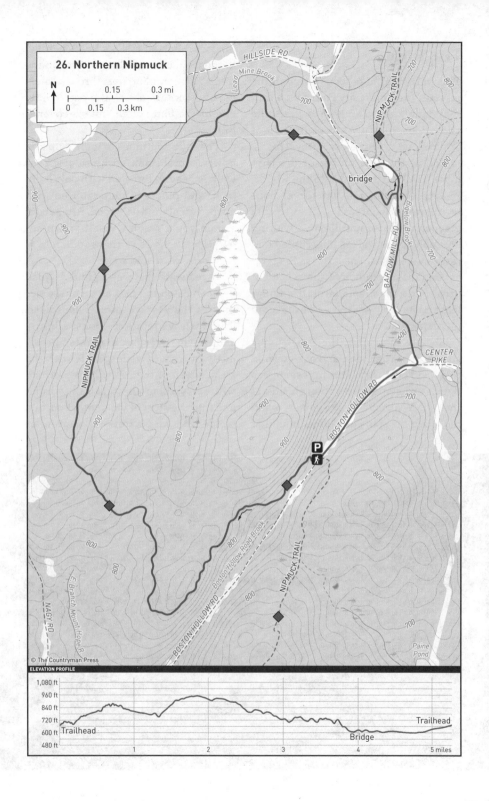

## 26. Northern Nipmuck

N

| 0 | 0.15 | 0.3 mi |
| 0 | 0.15 | 0.3 km |

HILLSIDE RD

Lead Mine Brook

NIPMUCK TRAIL

700

800

700

800

700

bridge

BARLOW MILL RD

Bigelow Brook

NIPMUCK TRAIL

900

900

900

800

800

900

900

800

800

600

CENTER PIKE

700

BOSTON HOLLOW RD

800

P

800

Boston Hollow Road Brook

BOSTON HOLLOW RD

NIPMUCK TRAIL

800

800

800

E. Branch Mount Hope R.

NAGY RD

700

Paine Pond

© The Countryman Press

**ELEVATION PROFILE**

| 1,080 ft |
| 960 ft |
| 840 ft |
| 720 ft |
| 600 ft |
| 480 ft |

Trailhead

Trailhead

Bridge

1    2    3    4    5 miles

## THE HIKE

This particular hike loops through the private Yale University Forest on a trail that undulates up and down over hills and ridges. It returns to your point of origin along two little-used gravel roads.

Follow the blue blazes of the Nipmuck Trail north (left) into the woods. In late summer, the flat forest floor is liberally decorated with Virginia creeper, wild sarsaparilla, and fruiting blue cohosh, as well as interrupted and rattlesnake ferns. The latter is the largest and most common of the succulent grape ferns; the simple, large, triangular leaf and its early-season spore stalk are unmistakable.

Shortly thereafter, the trail climbs steeply onto a hemlock- and oak-covered ridge and bears left. This first ridge has downward slopes close to each side of the trail. You may feel like you are walking along the spine of a large animal or dinosaur! Boston Hollow Road, parallel to the trail, is visible below through the trees. Then, winding west through thickets of mountain laurel, the path gently climbs the flank of a hemlock-covered hillside.

The hike continues to jounce up and down several small, rocky ridges. Your walk is heavily forested with oak, hemlock, and pine and understoried with striped maple and dogwood. After about a mile you'll reach a small viewpoint with lovely views of the woodlands to the north, west, and south.

If you walk this way in mid-August, you can catch the first signs of the tipping of the year's seasonal hourglass. The lush vegetation looks slightly shopworn. Evergreen plants, previously overshadowed, sparkle with the fresh sheen of their new leaves, which will carry them through fall, winter, and into the start of yet another spring. Goldenrod and aster—fall's premier

MARSHLAND ALONG BIGELOW BROOK

flowers—are prominent. The autumn spate of mushrooms has started: white and yellow fungi litter the trail. The ghostly Indian pipes here have become blackened skeletons, although they are just erupting through the forest litter in the mountains in the north. An admirer of a particular flower can often prolong the viewing season by moving north with the blooms.

In about 2 miles, you'll cross a private forest road. You may see signs of logging and perhaps some cleared areas with small orange flags. These are all evidence of the Yale forestry school at work. You'll find that after descending a number of the ridges, you'll cross small muddy streams with moss-covered rocks and logs. Your route will twist, climb, and fall over hemlock-covered hills and ridges, but the well-maintained blue-blazes will be easy to follow.

THE BLUE-BLAZED NIPMUCK TRAIL

After about 4 miles, you'll see a sign alerting you that you have entered Bigelow Brook Forest, a small tract of private forestland. Soon the trail winds back through the Yale Forest, ascending again and then descending along a hillside. The path will take a sharp right and you will then descend, before emerging on the gravel Barlow Mill Road.

This hike will turn right onto the road, but take a short detour first to your left. A short walk will take you to a bridge with beautiful views of a marshy stream trickling underneath. Minnows and pickerel play a deadly game of hide-and-seek amid the waterweeds. Although the wood's vegetation has faded, late summer brings a riotous flowering in open fields and meadows. Great purple-crowned stalks of Joe-Pye weed, white-flowering boneset (an herbal fever remedy), goldenrod, Saint John's wort, the three-leafed hog peanut vine, and pea-like clusters of groundnuts are everywhere. Blackberries invite you to snack, bumblebees engage in a final orgy of nectar gathering, and the sweet smell of pepperbush pervades the air.

After enjoying the view, retrace your steps on the road pass the trail you emerged on. You are just less than 1.25 miles from your car. You'll follow Barlow Mill Road with a stream-fed meadow on your left. The road passes through both private land and Yale Forest. Soon you'll see the Axe Factory Farm on your left. As you walk along, private lots with houses have carved small, sunny spaces out of the woods on your route. You'll come to an intersection; turn right onto Boston Hollow Road. Continue on this gravel road through the Yale Forest, and soon you'll see your car on the right where you entered the woods at the start of this relaxing hike through the countryside.

# Green Fall Pond

| |
|---|
| **LOCATION**: Voluntown |
| **DISTANCE**: 5.7 miles |
| **VERTICAL RISE**: 540 feet |
| **TIME**: 3 hours |
| **RATING**: B/C |
| **MAP**: USGS 7.5-minute Voluntown |

Far eastern Connecticut seems to have been forgotten by the twentieth century—let alone the twenty-first. Roads change from tar to dirt, and stone walls are strikingly square and straight, evidence that they are not the trappings of gentlemen farmers but carefully maintained, functional components of working farms. Except for occasional fields and farmhouses, this untenanted, overgrown area is much as the westward-bound pioneers left it. Your hike on the Narragansett Trail to Green Fall Pond in Pachaug State Forest takes you through this secluded region.

Please note that hunting is allowed in Pachaug State Forest. Refer to the book introduction section on Hunting for more information.

## GETTING THERE

From the junction of CT 49, CT 138, and CT 165 in Voluntown, drive south on CT 49 (Pendleton Hill Road) for 4 miles, and then turn left onto Sand Hill Road. In about a mile, turn right onto Tom Wheeler Road and go a half-mile, where you will see the blue blazes of the Narragansett Trail marking a telephone pole to your left. Park near the blazes, pulling off the road as far as possible; the traffic here is minimal.

## THE HIKE

Enter the woods on the east side of the road (to your left as you drove down Tom Wheeler Road from Sand Hill Road). The blue trail system marks trail changes with double blazes, usually offsetting the upper blaze in the direction of the turn. In May, the flowering dogwoods punctuate the springtime greens with their white bracts. Their flowers are

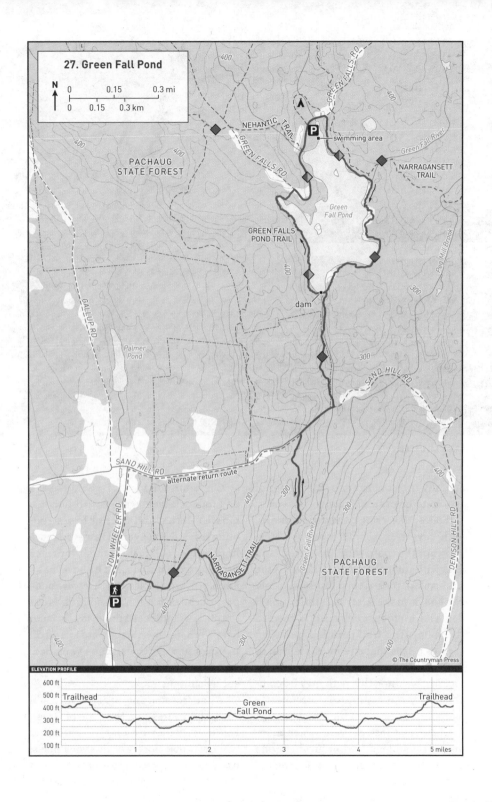

## 27. Green Fall Pond

N

0    0.15    0.3 mi
0    0.15    0.3 km

PACHAUG STATE FOREST

NEHANTIC TRAIL

GREEN FALLS RD.

P

swimming area

Green Fall River

NARRAGANSETT TRAIL

GREEN FALLS POND TRAIL

Green Fall Pond

dam

Peg Mill Brook

SAND HILL RD.

GALLUP RD.

Palmer Pond

SAND HILL RD.

alternate return route

TOM WHEELER RD.

NARRAGANSETT TRAIL

Green Fall River

PACHAUG STATE FOREST

DENISON HILL RD.

P

© The Countryman Press

**ELEVATION PROFILE**

600 ft
500 ft — Trailhead
400 ft
300 ft
200 ft
100 ft

Green Fall Pond

Trailhead

1    2    3    4    5 miles

GREEN FALL POND

actually green clusters in the center of the white-colored, specialized leaves.

Follow the trail gently downward, with several seasonal streams interrupting the path and soothing the soul with their melodious chatter. This thin-soiled, rock-ribbed land is largely clothed in oak. After 0.4 mile, you'll descend a steep, rocky slope toward the valley. The trail parallels and then crosses a seasonal stream. Note that at the height of summer or in especially parched weather, this path may be completely dry. Navigating this infrequently maintained section of the Narragansett Trail during these periods—when man-made trails blend into natural runoffs and the blazes are few and far between—can be difficult.

On your left, you'll soon pass a 25-foot rock face graced with lichens, mosses, ferns, and even a few struggling trees. Just beyond is an even more impressive rock face, with larger trees growing from its sides. At its base, lies a jumble of large rock slabs that were once part of the cliff but have split off since the glaciers bulldozed their way through here. Perhaps these slabs were forced off in years past by trees, since vanished, whose incessant growth slowly but surely split the rock.

After crossing another stream, you'll soon find yourself on the edge of Green Fall River Valley by a large, crumbling boulder. Look closely at this rock mass; its shade, moisture retention, and slant toward the sun create miniature ecosystems. While the stark, drier sides are gray with lichens, the shaded areas with pockets of soil hold a soft cushion of mosses. In wet seasons, the surface of a moist, crumbly hollow is colored with light green algae. The thin soil of its horizontal surfaces supports clumps of polypody fern. Large birches buttress the sides of the boulder, which is crowned with an unexpected juniper; the rock's sunny, well-drained top provides the conditions the juniper needs. An early settler of untended, tired fields, this prickly evergreen is ordinarily shaded out by the forest canopy as taller trees eventually grow above it.

Bear left, crossing two rocky, seasonal streams. Step carefully—the smooth rocks become very slippery when their covering of mosses and lichens swells with moisture. After the second stream, proceed gradually uphill and along the valley rim to Green Fall Road, a dirt road 1.4 miles from your start. This road is an eastern extension of Sand Hill Road.

Turn right, and follow the road downhill for a tenth of a mile. Just before crossing the bridge, turn left off the road and follow the blue-blazed trail along the river, which is now on your right. The path climbs a rocky ridge and passes a large cairn before descending to follow the bottom of a narrow ravine that speeds the river over boulders and ledges. About midway to the pond you'll cross the river. Depending on the time of year, this may be easiest at a shallow rocky spot along the trail or over one of several ad hoc log bridges. Be careful, the logs can be slippery when wet.

The trail clambers over boulders where root-hung hemlocks cling to a steep, eroding slope. The inward-pressing rock walls are thickly covered with mosses and lichens. Soon the trail climbs steadily and steeply up the side

of the ravine to avoid a sharp drop into the river. Pay attention here—the thin, poor soil on these eroding sides can make footholds difficult and have left exposed roots on which it's quite easy to trip. A recent hike up this trail found a wooden bridge built into the side of the ravine where the trail had become dangerously eroded.

You'll reach the base of Green Fall Pond Dam 1.9 miles from the start. Climb up the embankment to the right of the dam, and turn left to cross over

INLET TO GREEN FALL POND BY THE CAMPING AREA

EAGLE SCOUT BRIDGE AT GREEN FALL POND

The trail hugs a shore thickly grown with laurel, oak, birch, and hemlock. About 0.2 mile from the dam, the path crosses a feeder stream and continues rounding the pond. If you lose the trail here, head toward the pond—in most places the trail edges the shore. A ledge-tipped point across the bay to your right soon comes into view.

After ascending a wide, wooden-stepped path, you'll reach the paved road that services the campground; turn right. Continue following the orange/blue blazes along the road. This is the main access point for most visitors to the pond, and here you'll see many of its other amenities: parking, camping, and a boat launch. Most notable is a small swimming area, replete with picnic tables and grills. From here on summer afternoons, you'll see families picnicking, children swimming, and kayakers exploring the pond's inlets and islands. While the buoy-marked beach has no lifeguard on duty, we definitely recommend bringing sandals, or even a swimsuit—this halfway spot on the pond makes a great place for lunch and a mid-hike dip.

After you decide to continue along the paved road, you'll pass the blue blazes of the Nehantic Trail to your left. Shortly after passing the campground and crossing the major inlet to the pond, the trail turns right at a sign for the Green Fall Trail. Many of the large outcroppings on your left bear patches of a large, thick-fleshed, curling lichen called rock tripe, which is considered nourishing in case of dire emergency. Canadian voyageurs reputedly used it to thicken their soups.

The trail is now in sight of the pond. The orange/blue trail links up with the blue-blazed Narragansett Trail 1.2 miles from the dam; turn right to follow these

the top of the dam on a wooden footbridge with handrails. Follow the route, now marked by blue blazes with orange spots (referred to as orange/blue blazes for simplicity), around the west side of Green Fall Pond. The Narragansett Trail goes around the east side of the pond—you will return that way.

Follow the orange/blue blazes, first on a gravel road, then onto a footpath, keeping Green Fall Pond always on your right. This trout-stocked pond is one of Connecticut's nicest—it has lovely ledges dropping into the water, small islands, fully wooded shores, and no cottages.

double blazes along the edge of the pond. A small brook here is crossed by an impressive wooden bridge, a recent Eagle Scout project.

The trail climbs a rocky ridge, affording the view of the nearby rolling hills, then drops down and visits a rocky point. Enjoy these meanderings—a well-laid-out trail lets you explore all points of interest. The trail goes over an earth-filled auxiliary dam. The underwater face of the dam to your right is covered with rock riprap to minimize erosion.

The trail enters the woods just beyond the auxiliary dam. Follow the ridge overlooking the pond before descending diagonally down to the shore. Pass the dam to your right and descend the embankment. Retrace your steps down the ravine and back to your starting point.

## OTHER HIKING OPTIONS

For those averse to backtracking on the trail, one can finish the hike on a quiet country road instead of rehiking the last stretch of the Narragansett. After leaving the pond and passing through the ravine, instead of reentering the woods on the other side of Green Fall Road, you may choose to continue along the gravel road, passing a farm, to the junction with Wheeler Road. Turn left onto Wheeler Road; your car will be a half-mile down the quiet road.

For those especially drawn to all the aquatic activities that Green Fall Pond has to offer (swimming, kayaking, fishing), one option is to skip the southern Wheeler Road entrance and instead park at the main lot off of Green Falls Road. You'll be right at the swimming and picnic area here. Several loops can be constructed from the blue-blazed Narragansett, Nehantic, and Pachaug Trails along with their connectors, all of which are easily supplemented by a leisurely lunch or swim.

**Additional Resources:** A state park trail map can be found at www.ct.gov /deep/pachaug and follow link on left to Green Falls Area. This brings you to a page where you can access the map: Pachaug State Forest (Green Falls Area) Forest Map. Note that the starting point of the hike is covered by the key on this map. Always check the map date before using to be sure it is a recent update (otherwise be aware there may be inaccuracies).

Two other hikes in this book (#23 Mount Misery and #31 Bullet and High Ledges) also explore Pachaug State Forest, which at over 27,000 acres is the largest state forest in Connecticut.

## 28

# Great Hill

**LOCATION**: East Hampton

**DISTANCE**: 6 miles

**VERTICAL RISE**: 800 feet

**TIME**: 3.5 hours

**RATING**: C

**MAP**: USGS 7.5-minute Middle Haddam

This hike begins on the Shenipsit Trail near a long-abandoned cobalt mine in the small town of Cobalt. From there you climb a rocky ridge to Great Hill, which rewards you with a panoramic view over the Connecticut River. A short hike along the ridge brings you past an old abandoned quarry and then to a beautiful, secluded cascade at the foot of Bald Hill.

## GETTING THERE

From the junction of CT 66 and CT 151 in Cobalt, drive north on Depot Hill Road. At the first fork, keep right up a steep hill. After almost 0.9 mile, turn right onto Gadpouch Road, the first right after Stage Coach Run. The blue-blazed trail starts on your left in a half-mile, soon after the road turns to dirt. Park on your right, opposite the trailhead. Parking is limited, with room for only three cars at most.

Before you start your hike, walk down the ravine next to the parking spaces. Once down the hill, bear left (there is somewhat of a trail), and you'll see the abandoned mine—an impressive stone façade built into the hillside. The entrance to the cobalt mine (now sealed up) is down the hill in the shaded ravine. Deep pits on the top of the hill, farther up the road to your right, tell of the collapse of the mine roof. Originally opened by Connecticut Governor John Winthrop (son of colonial Massachusetts's John Winthrop) in 1661, the mine was active until the mid-1800s. The cobalt extracted was shipped as far away as England and China for use in the manufacture of a deep blue paint and porcelain glaze.

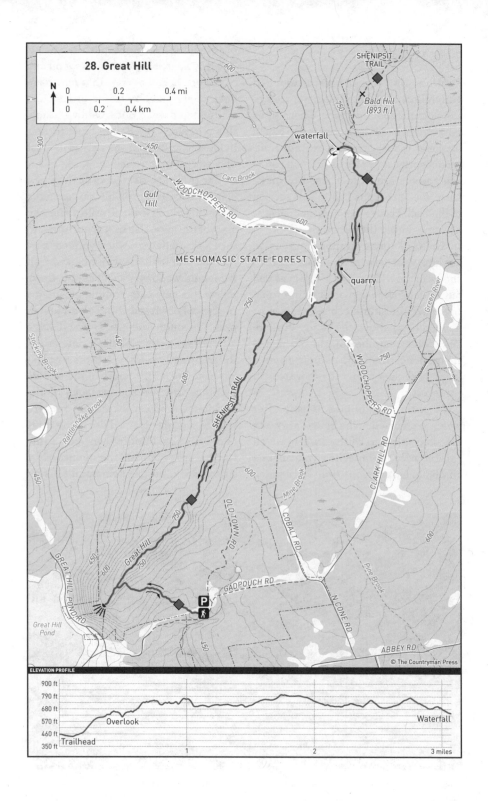

### 28. Great Hill

N

| 0 | 0.2 | 0.4 mi |
| 0 | 0.2 | 0.4 km |

SHENIPSIT
TRAIL

Bald Hill
(893 ft.)

waterfall

MESHOMASIC STATE FOREST

Gulf
Hill

WOODCHOPPERS RD

Carr Brook

quarry

SHENIPSIT TRAIL

WOODCHOPPERS RD

Stocking Brook

Rattlesnake Brook

Great Hill

GREAT HILL POND RD

Great Hill
Pond

OLD TOWN RD

GADPOUCH RD

COBALT RD

Mine Brook

CLARK HILL RD

Green River

Pine Brook

N. CONE RD

ABBEY RD

© The Countryman Press

**ELEVATION PROFILE**

| 900 ft | | | |
| 790 ft | | | |
| 680 ft | | | |
| 570 ft | Overlook | | Waterfall |
| 460 ft | | | |
| 350 ft | Trailhead | | |
| | 1 | 2 | 3 miles |

## THE HIKE

Return to the trailhead across the road and follow the blue blazes through ash-dominated hardwoods. These trees range from mature specimens two feet in diameter to fast-growing, strong, light-weight sprouts the size of baseball bats—ash sprouts are in fact, used to make most wooden baseball bats! This section of the trail, always wet and muddy, is at its worst during the spring thaw.

The trail starts climbing gradually. Look to your left for the round-leafed shoots of the wide onion. The leaves and bulb can provide a sharp-tasting treat. In spring, the skunk cabbage raises its hooded head above the soggy ground. You'll see a number of big old maple trees along this trail as you ascend, larger and older than the other trees in the forest.

Soon the trail climbs steeply after leveling off briefly. The blazes are quite faded on this part of the trail so watch carefully for them. When you resume climbing, look to your right for a patch

of a creeping evergreen: partridgeberry. The tiny heart-shaped leaves set off any of the bright red berries that may have been overlooked by ruffed grouse and white-footed wood mice. Oddly enough, this relative of the dainty bluet thrives in Mexico and Japan, as well as in most of eastern North America.

The trail zigzags steeply up the rocky side of Great Hill. You'll soon reach the hillcrest, about half a mile from the start of the hike. Use this opportunity to take a small detour: when you reach an intersection with the white-blazed trail (which now appears as a faded-yellow), follow this new path straight ahead to a rocky lookout treed with oak and pitch pine. Through the trees, you'll have a panoramic view of the Connecticut River. Directly below you is the cottage-rimmed Great Hill Pond. In the middle distance are the smokestacks of the Middletown power plant. To your left, next to a girder-framed dock, the Pratt and Whitney Middletown jet engine facility sprawls over the countryside. At the dock, barges and small tankers

RUINS OF THE OLD COBALT MINES—IN USE FROM THE 1660s TO THE MID-1800s

VIEW FROM GREAT HILL

off-load their cargoes of jet fuel. Continuing southward, the river's wanderings become lost to your eye amid the horizon's low rolling hills. The Mattabesett Trail follows the western horizon ridge. Northwest of the power plant, the bare slopes of the Powder Ridge Ski Area punctuate the hillside. The old colonial seaport of Middletown lies on the western side of the river.

After taking in the view, retrace your steps to the blue trail. The trail climbs for a short distance and then continues north-northeast along a straight, narrow ridge punctuated by very faded blue blazes.

About 1.5 miles into the hike, look for an attractive rock-jumbled hill on your right. Several of the larger, flatter rocks have masses of the evergreen polypody fern on them. The deep green leaves of this shade-loving fern arise from creeping rootstocks. It grows on rocks, cliff edges, and even downed trees where acidic humus has accumulated. In midsummer, the undersides of the upper leaflets are decorated with double rows of red-brown spore bodies—the next generation.

The trail descends the ridge gradually and joins a tote road about 2.25 miles from the start. These abandoned roadways are a staple of Connecticut's woodlands. Used mostly before World War I, tote roads were cut to tote logs from the woods. The soil became so compacted from this use that many of these old lanes are still virtually free of vegetation.

After another 0.2 mile of branching onto several tote roads, the trail crosses a hard-packed dirt forest road (Woodchopper Road). Large rocks have been placed at the trailhead on either side of this road to discourage all-terrain vehicles from riding through.

GENTLE WOODLAND CASCADE AT THE TURN-AROUND POINT OF THE GREAT HILL HIKE

As you cross to the west-facing slope along this dirt and gravel road, notice the scattered, straight, tall tulip trees that were absent from the east-facing slope. Here, near the northern limit of the tulip trees, minor differences of soil or exposure can create distinct demarcation lines. The large, tulip-like orange and green flowers and distinctive, four-pointed leaves with notched tips are unmistakable in summer. The numerous flower husks clinging to the upper branches make for certain winter identification.

Continue uphill on the blue-blazed trail, and you'll soon begin to observe sparkly flat fragments on the trail, evidence of a small quarry that you'll see on your right about 0.3 mile from Woodchopper Road. The quarry is quite old and abandoned and looks more like a white rock face with a small cave at the bottom. Quartz, mica, and pegmatite were most likely mined at this quarry.

Continue to follow the blue blazes along this muddy tote road. You'll leave the road and follow the trail to your left downhill, crossing a small brook about 1 mile from Woodchopper Road. After crossing a second, larger brook, you'll reach a cascade, which is at its best during the early spring runoff. However, be warned that crossing the brook can be problematic in these early months.

This is one of Gerry and Sue's favorite places. In spring the sheet of water flowing evenly down the steep face of the moss-covered rock ledge creates a soothing sound. Bubbles formed in the turbulence glide merrily across the pool at the base of the cascade, accumulating in windrows of pollution-free foam. This is a fine place for a quiet picnic, a good book, or simply a restful interlude.

When you are ready, retrace your steps, taking care to follow the blazes through the maze of tote roads back to Woodchopper Road. As you are coming down Great Hill (about 2.5 miles from the cascade), don't miss your left turn onto the blue trail; the blazes are very faded in this area. If you miss the turn and continue straight, the trail will bring you back to the Great Hill lookout—a place you might want to revisit anyway before returning to your car.

## OTHER HIKING OPTIONS

**Short & Sweet:** If you want to see the view on top of Great Hill just take the blue-blazed trail up and follow the white/faded yellow-blazed side trail to the view of the Connecticut River. Then retrace your steps back to the car.

**Extending Your Hike:** Continue along the blue-blazed Shenipsit Trail to the summit of Bald Hill (893 feet). From the cascade and in about in 50 yards, bear right and begin to ascend Bald Hill. Continue climbing, and reach the summit about 0.5 mile from the cascade. Once you reach the summit, enjoy the western view and then retrace your steps back to the car.

# Northwest Park

| | |
|---|---|
| **LOCATION**: Windsor | |
| **DISTANCE**: 6 miles | |
| **VERTICAL RISE**: 200 feet | |
| **TIME**: 3.25 hours | |
| **RATING**: C/D | |
| **MAP**: USGS 7.5-minute Windsor Locks | |

Northwest Park and Nature Preserve is a 473-acre municipal park owned and operated by the town of Windsor. Established in 1972, much of what once was tobacco farmland has been converted to biologically diverse forests and fields embedded with streams, bogs, and protected grasslands. Northwest Park's mission is to provide an accessible living classroom with a diverse habitat that ties Windsor's past to the present. The park has many educational opportunities (summer camp programs, etc.) and offers passive recreational pursuits for the public with 12 miles of hiking and cross-country skiing trails.

Northwest Park preserves the history of the region by highlighting the role of shade-grown tobacco, once the most valuable agricultural crop in the country. In the late 1930s, Windsor alone had 3,000 acres of shade-grown tobacco. More than 1,600 square miles of tobacco, under its head-high cover of shade-cloth, were located in the Connecticut River Valley and dominated the landscape long after World War II. Cheaper tobacco from other countries, a reduction in the number of smokers, and the astronomical increase in the value of the land for housing have all contributed to the near extinction of our shade-grown tobacco.

Most of the state's thousands of imposing tobacco barns, where the crop was dried for use as top-quality cigar wrappers, were torn down for the weathered lumber, which, ironically, was extensively used in the same houses that contributed to the decline of this valuable crop. One of the special features of this hike is the still-looming presence of tobacco barns. A generation ago these barns were everywhere. These days they are almost gone, but here you will pass several of these reminders of bygone days.

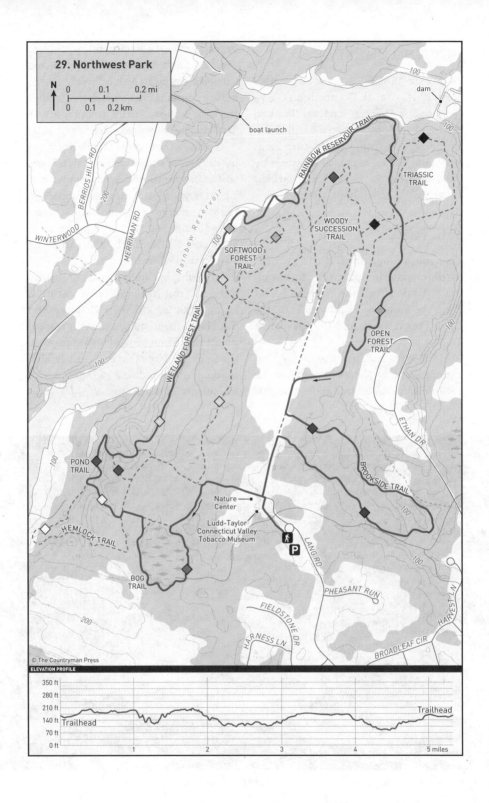

## 29. Northwest Park

N

| 0 | 0.1 | 0.2 mi |
| 0 | 0.1 | 0.2 km |

boat launch

RAINBOW RESERVOIR TRAIL

dam

100

100

TRIASSIC TRAIL

BERRIOS HILL RD

200

MERRIMAN RD

WINTERWOOD

Rainbow Reservoir

WOODY SUCCESSION TRAIL

SOFTWOOD FOREST TRAIL

100

WETLAND FOREST TRAIL

OPEN FOREST TRAIL

100

100

ETHAN DR

POND TRAIL

BROOKSIDE TRAIL

100

HEMLOCK TRAIL

Nature Center

Ludd-Taylor Connecticut Valley Tobacco Museum

P

LANG RD

BOG TRAIL

200

PHEASANT RUN

HARVEST LN

FIELDSTONE DR

BROADLEAF CIR

HARNESS LN

© The Countryman Press

**ELEVATION PROFILE**

| 350 ft |
| 280 ft |
| 210 ft |
| 140 ft | Trailhead |
| 70 ft |
| 0 ft |

Trailhead

1    2    3    4    5 miles

## GETTING THERE

Take exit 38 off I-91 (about 7 miles north of Hartford). Go north on CT 75 (Poquonock Avenue) for 1.2 miles, and then turn left onto Prospect Hill Road. At the second traffic circle, turn right onto Lang Road. This road leads directly into Northwest Park. You'll find parking on your right after about 0.4 mile.

## THE HIKE

This route loops around the perimeter of the park including the following trails: the Bog Trail, the Wetland Forest Trail, the Rainbow Reservoir Trail, the Open Forest Trail, and the Brookside Trail.

Head to the northern end of the parking lot toward the Nature Center. Pass the covered bulletin board, and follow the gravel path past a small pond on your left. Stop a bit and enjoy the fish, frogs, and turtles swimming around. Walk by the nature center (save a visit there for after the hike—it's especially great for kids!). Trail maps are available near the door.

Go down the dirt road to the left of the nature center and continue past it. There will be tobacco barns, a playground, and a field to your left. Enter the woods, and follow the signs that indicate straight ahead leads you to the Bog, Hemlock, and Pond Trails. Shortly thereafter, the Pond (and Wetland Forest) Trail will go straight, but go left instead toward the Bog Trail (the sign reads NATURE & BRAILLE TRAILS, which is what the Bog Trail is) as the marsh overlook is toward your right. Then turn left again to go on the Bog trail. Note that the blaze symbol is rather unorthodox: a red square with a black dot in the center.

BOARDWALK-STYLE BRIDGE ON THE BROOKSIDE TRAIL AT NORTHWEST PARK

OLD TOBACCO BARN AT NORTHWEST PARK

The Bog Trail is a 0.6-mile braille trail, dedicated to the memory of Merlin W. Sargent in appreciation of his many years of service to the American Youth Hostels Yankee Council. The guide rope will conduct you around the bog and return you to the starting point. There are information plaques around the path that have nature facts in both text and braille. On hot and humid days, this trail can be very buggy, but otherwise is quite easy and fun to walk along.

A little more than halfway around the Bog Trail you'll pass through a chain-link fence associated with the landfill on your left. Go straight at an upcoming fork, not right (continuing right keeps you on the Bog trail). You'll pass on your left a junction with the white-blazed Hemlock Trail; stay on the wide path following signs to the Pond Trail. There will be a boggy field on your right that is covered with invasive, purple loosestrife. Soon you'll come to a junction with the Pond Trail, marked with blue-hourglass blazes. Turn right onto the Pond Trail. This slightly hilly trail goes through a hardwood forest, passing an overgrown pond on your left; in deep summer, vegetation all but obscures any view of the water. The trail turns sharply right just before reaching a gravel road.

You'll next turn right onto the yellow-blazed Wetland Forest Trail. Continue downhill on the yellow-blazed trail, soon crossing an old gravel road as the trail levels out. After this, you'll start to catch glimpses of the Farmington River below at left. You'll soon parallel the edge of a field to your right. After about 0.8 mile, you will come to a junction with the Rainbow Reservoir trail blazed in dark-pink circle blazes. Rainbow Reservoir encompasses 234 acres and is a section of the Farmington River that lies below the Rainbow Dam in Windsor. You will continue straight to hike the Rainbow Reservoir Trail (turning right continues onto the Wetland Forest Trail back to the Nature Center: see *Other Hiking Options*). This trail hugs the reservoir on your left but is thickly forested, obscuring any full views until you reach the boat launch after 0.6 mile. Note that the

RAINBOW RESERVOIR PEAKS THROUGH THE TREES AT NORTHWEST PARK

trail before the boat launch twice veers away from the reservoir to avoid stream gullies, taking you over a footbridge each time and then back to the reservoir.

About 0.2 mile after the boat launch, you'll see the dam at the end of the reservoir and the Rainbow Reservoir trail will turn away from the dam to the right. The trail follows a deep gully with a small stream running through it. Soon you'll come to an intersection: the official start of the Rainbow Reservoir Trail (our route started at the end of this trail). Continue straight and you'll soon cross the Triassic Trail (black-square-blazes). Continue straight following a sign that says TO THE NATURE CENTER as you walk along an unblazed old farm road. You will cross another old farm road with a sign that indicates the nature center is to your right. Keep straight on the trail

without turning, following signs toward the Open Forest Trail.

Soon you'll come to the Open Forest Trail, blazed in light-green, crescent-moon blazes. Turn right. This section of Northwest Park was deliberately disturbed by cutting and clearing some areas. These openings within a forest provide wildlife with a diverse assemblage of plants that are important to the overall ecology of a forest system.

At the end of this trail, turn left on another old farm road with large, overgrown fields on your right that are part of a Grassland Restoration Project. This area was deliberately cleared and planted with specific grasses and plants in 2002. The United States Fish and Wildlife Service wanted to create the grassy, upland habitat essential for the endangered grasshopper sparrow. As you pass this field, also note the large, narrow barns that were once full of cutting tobacco leaves.

Within sight of the Nature Center, turn left to follow the purple-hexagon-blazed Brookside Trail. This 1.1-mile-long nature trail with interpretive plaques was an Eagle Scout project from July 2000. About halfway around this loop, you will come to a lovely moss-lined brook with a footbridge—a final, peaceful rest stop before you end your hike. Upon returning to the gravel road, turn left back to the Nature Center and to your car.

## OTHER HIKING OPTIONS

There are multiple ways to shorten or lengthen your hike. You may wish to omit the Bog/Braille Trail if you find it too buggy. Or for a shorter (2.5-mile) loop, continue past the Bog Trail entrance until you read the Pond Trail. Then follow that to the Wetland Forest Trail as instructed, but instead of continuing straight on the Rainbow Reservoir, turn right on the Wetland Forest Trail back toward the Nature Center.

**Additional Resources:** You can print a full-color map from the Friends of Northwest Park website (northwest park.org). They also provide black-and-white copies near the nature center. Use the map to personalize your hike.

**After the Hike:** Visit the Luddy-Taylor Connecticut Valley Tobacco Museum on the grounds of Northwest Park. This museum preserves the history of cigar-tobacco agriculture to educate future generations. There are two large buildings in Northwest Park housing the museum. The refurbished tobacco shed (a barn modified for tobacco drying) houses large antique farming equipment. In the archive, you will find a library and an art gallery. The museum is open Thursday through Saturday. Check their website for hours (northwestpark.org).

# 30

# Devil's Den Preserve

| | |
|---|---|
| **LOCATION**: Weston | |
| **DISTANCE**: 7 miles | |
| **VERTICAL RISE**: 750 feet | |
| **TIME**: 3.75 hours | |
| **RATING**: C | |
| **MAPS**: USGS 7.5 minute Norwalk North and Bethel | |

The devil was busy in old Connecticut. It may be hard to envision the awe and fear inspired by the deep, dark forest of seventeenth- and eighteenth-century New England. However, this Nature Conservancy preserve combines enough acreage, rugged terrain, and an impressive spiderweb of roads and trails that today's hiker can imagine themselves in a very different time.

Nestled in the heavily populated New York–New Haven corridor, Devil's Den's 1,746 acres provide sanctuary from the bustle of urban life as well as a home for birds, mammals, trees, and plants that require large, unbroken tracts of forest. The preserve is part of the watershed of the West Branch of the Saugatuck River and part of the extended 70-mile Saugatuck Valley Trails System.

Devil's Den also has a rich human history. Archaeological evidence indicates human use of the area, mostly for hunting, as far back as 5,000 years ago. The remains of a sawmill can be found below Godfrey Pond, as well as a second portable sawmill deeper in the park. These attest to the importance of lumbering and charcoal burning in the 1800s. Local lore has it that the name of the park came from the charcoal makers who worked in this hilly, rocky area: a hoof-like mark made in the side of a boulder caught their eye and imagination, and the tale arose that this was a footprint of the devil.

Throughout the mid-1960s, Katharine Ordway of Weston donated the land to the Nature Conservancy. Devil's Den is also known as the Lucius Pond Ordway Preserve in memory of Katharine's father. This huge preserve guaranteed that much of the northern portion of Weston would remain without buildings or human habitation.

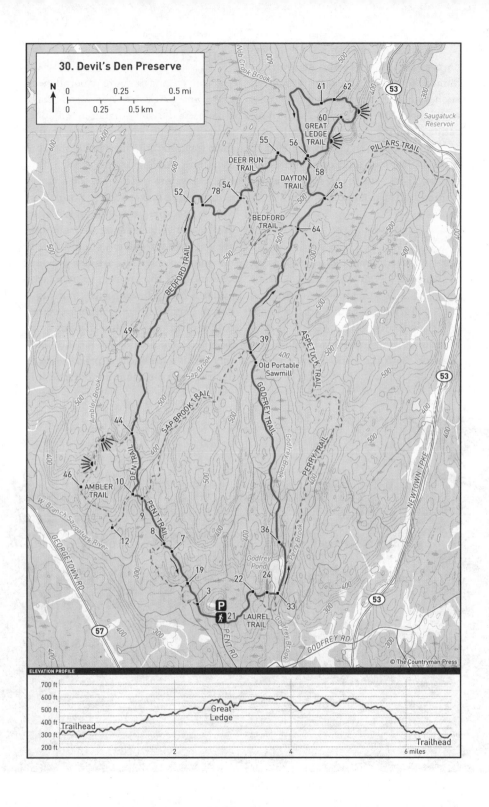

30. Devil's Den Preserve

N

0          0.25          0.5 mi
0     0.25     0.5 km

ELEVATION PROFILE

700 ft
600 ft
500 ft                    Great
400 ft  Trailhead         Ledge                    Trailhead
300 ft
200 ft
            2              4          6 miles

© The Countryman Press

The Nature Conservancy preserves natural communities and so restricts human activity to passive recreation such as hiking, birding, nature study, and cross-country skiing. The organization prohibits walking the trails with pets or using mechanized vehicles or bicycles. Devil's Den is open sunrise to sunset. There are over 20 miles of intersecting trails throughout the park.

## GETTING THERE

Take the Merritt Parkway (CT 15) to exit 42. Follow CT 57 north for about 5 miles (after 3.5 miles turning left to stay on CT 57). Turn right onto Godfrey Road. After a half-mile, take a sharp left onto Pent Road. Pent Road dead-ends at the preserve with the parking lot on your right.

## THE HIKE

The trails in the park are generally well worn, and many are wide woods road. Hikers use the well-numbered trail junctions, found on wooden posts, to find their way around. There are blazes, but they indicate the purpose of each trail. Red blazes are good for cross-country skiing; white blazes indicate trails that are connectors to Saugatuck Valley Trails; and yellow blazes are trails that are just good for walking. (Implied is the fact that red and white are also good for walking!) At the parking lot is a large bulletin board listing rules and regulations, and displaying a large, hand-painted trail map with trail names but no junction numbers. The most reliable way to hike around the preserve is to use the trail junction numbers, so it is

VIEW OF SAUGATUCK RESERVOIR FROM THE GREAT LEDGE TRAIL

recommended you use a map with the junction numbers clearly marked.

Today's hike will be a large loop through the preserve that takes you to a beautiful lookout over the Saugatuck Valley Reservoir. The hike begins at junction 21 found at the northeastern edge of the parking lot. This is the start of the Laurel trail. Follow this up and down gentle hills though mountain laurel amid numerous glacial erratics and stone walls. When snow conditions allow, this is a lovely cross-country skiing trail to Godfrey Pond.

Bear right at junction 22, and then left at junction 23, following the trail downhill in the direction of Godfrey Pond. Cross a bridge and stay right at junction 24, and then bear right again at junction 25. You'll then go downhill, cross over a dam, and pass a mill foundation on your right. Millponds were common in the early days of the industrial revolution, requiring only a stone-and-earth dam that forced water through a sluiceway to turn the wheel that powered the mill. Waterpower is still an important source of electricity today.

After crossing the dam, turn left uphill and you will come to junction 33. Turn left again at junction 33, staying on the tote road past junction 36. Remain on the route as it takes you north, away from the pond and its profusion of trails. You are now on the Godfrey Trail leading to the heart of the den.

The alternately rocky and swampy ground likely protected this land from the development that surrounds it. The hardwood forest around you has regenerated numerous times after supplying charcoal and lumber for the nearby towns. The road is periodically hardened with corduroys, a road and trail building technique in which logs are laid on wet ground perpendicular to the

HIKING ALONG THE GREAT LEDGE TRAIL

route to provide a solid, if not slip-proof, surface. In fact, if the corduroy remains damp year-round, it is likely to last for years: The moist ground retards the rotting process by preventing oxygen from accelerating the growth of molds and fungi.

The road winds through a forest of oaks and tulip trees, and you may see the dark-green, variegated leaves of the evergreen Pipsissewa, also called stripped wintergreen, growing close to the ground along the way. You'll pass a portable sawmill on your right—all that remains is the old boiler and flywheel. The portability of the steam-powered mill allowed the sawyer to take the saw

WET TRAILS ARE PERIODICALLY HARDENED WITH CORDUROYS—LOGS THAT CREATE A SOLID SURFACE

the trail). These blazes are most likely boundary blazes but do not correspond to the boundary seen on the map. A little later on, you'll see a second set of blazes extending through the woods on trees (again perpendicular to the trail) that results in your crossing briefly onto private property. You'll turn left at junction 63, and reenter the preserve on the Dayton Trail.

Ascend alongside a great outcropping of rock to enter an overgrown pasture at junction 58. Bear right, and then immediately right again, at junction 56 to descend to Great Ledge. Here you'll walk along a stone-covered vista with a view mostly obscured by the forest treetops. For a better view, follow the ledges (yellow blazes), and descend to junction 59. Then at junction 60, turn right onto a white-blazed trail. You'll briefly be hiking in the Centennial Watershed State Forest for this loop. You will soon come to a more impressive vista with a view of the Saugatuck Reservoir. This is a great place to stop for lunch—there are large log seats in place for you to sit and enjoy the view. To complete the loop, continue off the ridge following the white blazes. Go straight at junction 62, and then left at junction 83. You'll continue on the trail, passing junction 61, before coming back around to junction 56 and 58. Turn right at junction 58.

We found a leopard frog on this highland route. This frog is frequently confused with the similarly marked pickerel frog. The leopard frog, which is the larger of the two species, has round spots, while the pickerel frog has square or blocky spots.

You'll come to a T-junction with 55, turn left. You will now be on the Deer Run Trail. Turn right at junction 54, onto the Bedford Trail. Stay straight uphill at junction 78 to follow the long downhill

to the logs, since it was much easier to tote boards out of the forest.

Continue along the road bearing right at junction 39. Later, you will pass the Saw Mill Trail on your right. Continue straight on the trail, following it downhill to cross a small stone bridge. At junction 64, hike straight through a four-way intersection (follow PILLAR signs) to stay on the Godfrey Trail. You'll cross through an opening in a stone wall that appears to be blazed yellow in both directions (perpendicular to

on the Bedford Trail back to the Devil's Den entrance. You'll pass junction 52. Bear left at junction 49, walking over more corduroy trail work on your route. Then pass junction 44 (bypassing a nice loop through Ambler Gorge, noted in *Other Hiking Options*). Cross a long boardwalk-style bridge over Ambler brook, and then turn left at junction 10 to cross another bridge over Sap Brook. At junction 9, remain on the main road: you are now on the Pent Trail. Pass straight through junctions 8 and 7 continuing on the Pent Trail. You'll pass junctions 19, 5, 4, and 3 in fairly quick succession as you near the Den entrance. Continue following this woods road; come out on Pent Road just below the trailhead parking.

On a recent visit here we were following a large woodpecker down the last couple of yards of our hike. From a distance its size hinted that it was a pileated woodpecker, and as we slowly drew closer the red crest and white wing flashes confirmed our sighting. No doubt the maturing forest of Devil's Den will continue to provide an island of habitat for this bird as well as many others that require a large, unbroken forested landscape.

## OTHER HIKING OPTIONS

**Additional Resources:** There are numerous ways to lengthen or shorten your hike. You can find a detailed trail map via the Nature Conservancy's website (nature.org) and search for Devil's Den trail map.

**Extending the Hike:** A worthwhile addition/modification to today's hike is to take a right at junction 44 while coming downhill on the Bedford trail (after junctions 52 and 49); this trail will take you through Ambler Gorge and has some nice vistas. When you reach junction 46 continue straight until you reach junction 12. Then turn left and come to junction 10 at which you turn right getting back on to our route along the Pent Trail to head back to the car.

# Bullet and High Ledges

**LOCATION**: North Stonington

**DISTANCE**: 6 miles

**VERTICAL RISE**: 600 feet

**TIME**: 3.5 hours

**RATING**: C

**MAPS**: USGS 7.5-minute Voluntown, Ashaway

The Bullet and High Ledges section of the Pachaug State Forest is a beautiful enclave with its own character and points of interest, yet is seldom visited. Reportedly, it is one of the least travelled portions of the Narragansett Trail within the largest state forest in Connecticut. Pachaug State Forest boasts over 28,000 acres with numerous opportunities for outdoor activities with many miles of trails available for hiking, mountain biking, horseback riding, and more.

The first ledge, Bullet Ledge, does not have much of a view but has impressive caves that you will see as you descend. The second ledge is High Ledge at the end of a ridge. This has a much better view of the surrounding forest and Wyassup Lake. Much of this hike has extensive woods roads and stone walls. These markers indicate that much of the land was used for settlements and farms up until the early twentieth century, after which the land was allowed to return to forest. Some old stone foundations can still be found off the trail in the Legend Woods area.

Please note that hunting is allowed in Pachaug State Forest. Refer to the book introduction section on *Hunting in Connecticut* for more information.

## GETTING THERE

The Narragansett Trail to Bullet and High Ledges crosses and goes along CT 49, south of CT 138 in Voluntown. Coming from the center of Voluntown, travel south on CT 49. After about 4 miles, you'll pass Sand Hill Road on your left and then after that take your first right onto the Johnson Road. You'll come to a T-junction with Legendwood Road (where you'll see a dead end sign) where you turn right. After about 0.2 mile, you'll park in a small parking area on

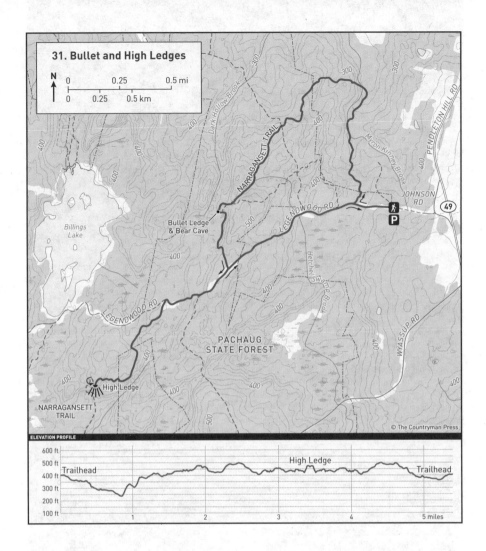

**ELEVATION PROFILE**

your left. Coming from the south from the junction of CT 184 and CT 49, follow CT 49 north for about 6 miles, and turn left onto Johnston Road (0.3 mile after Wyassup Road). Veer left onto Legendwood Road (where you'll see a dead end sign) and follow the directions above.

## THE HIKE

Today's route follows the blue-blazed Narragansett Trail through beautiful woodlands, crisscrossing numerous woods roads and stone walls. The hike ends at High Ledge where you'll retrace your steps until reaching a well-worn woods road (an extension of Legendwood Road), at which point this hike departs from the Narragansett Trail until rejoining it again in the final leg. Most of the hike is C-rated terrain, average terrain with moderate ups and downs. Note, however, that the ascent and descent of both ledges has some poor footing, and for a short stretch in those places the trail could be rated B.

From your car follow the paved road left, away from where you drove from. It

MYRON KINNEY BROOK DURING A SOFT RAIN

soon turns into hard-packed gravel. In 0.3 mile, turn right off the road following the blue blazes. Here the forest floor is carpeted with club mosses: first ground cedar alone (many capped with candelabrum-like spore stalks), then mixed with ground pine, until finally the ground pine predominates. Beyond the club mosses, you may find rounded masses of gray-green reindeer moss. The winter mainstay of the caribou herds of the North, this "moss" is in fact lichen.

Roll with the terrain, crossing and paralleling several finely constructed stone walls and walking along numerous woods roads. You'll then bear right along a seasonal stream and over another stone wall to Myron Kinney Brook—a river in microcosm. Nature's immutable laws are more easily observed when the familiar is seen on a different scale. Spring runoff forms the seasonal headwaters of this small brook. Within a few tenths of a mile, small tributaries entering from both sides swell the brook many times. The water volume increases further from hidden springs where the stream cuts into the permanent water table. Walk slowly along the stream with an alert eye—the forms darting across gravel riffles and through deep pools are native brook trout. Since these char need an unending supply of ice-cold water, you will see them in abundance only when you have passed the point where the brook has cut into the permanent water table. While you are looking for trout, notice how the current rushes around the outer curves of the stream, undermining its banks. Sediment carved from these areas is carried downstream and deposited as sandbars on inside curves, where the current is slower.

You'll leave the brook in about a quarter-mile and turn left to walk uphill. The trail then dips to cross a small stream. After the stream, the path hugs a stone wall going up the hillside. With posted land on your right and Pachaug State Forest land on your left, follow the blue blazes carefully through another

A STONE WALL ALONG THE NARRAGANSETT TRAIL

THE MASSIVE ROCKY UNDERSIDE AND CAVES OF BULLET LEDGE

network of interlocking stone walls and tote roads.

You'll then enter an area of prominent boulders and ledges jutting out of the forest floor; bear left at a fork still following the blue blazes. After a quarter-mile merge left with an old, eroded road. Follow the blue blazes as the undulating footpath passes through cozy-cornered stone walls and a partially cutover area with mountain laurel stems as thick as a person's arm.

You'll soon reach your first woods road junction; keep straight to remain on the trail. Bear right at another woods road junction, and continue generally upward with a rocky ridge to your right. Pass through a compacted-dirt clearing in the woods. Just beyond this clearing, when the trail takes a steep right turn downward, continue instead straight ahead to the Bullet Ledge Lookout. The view is somewhat overgrown, offering you a nice look at the forest foliage.

Before you start feeling under-whelmed by this ledge, return to the trail and descend steeply to the rocky valley floor. The unimpressive view at the top leads to a massive rocky ledge underneath. Enjoy the beauty of this rock formation with all its mini-canyons and caves. Look for the Bear Cave soon after you descend the ledge (facing southeast, on your right). The cave has two openings that can be crawled into and explored by flashlight. Before investigating, do note that black bears have returned to Connecticut and Rhode Island, so there is always the possibility that the cave could be inhabited.

After descending Bullet Ledge the trail veers right along a swampy stretch. When you reach the tote road set between a rock ridge and a swamp, turn left. Following the blue blazes at succeeding junctions, you'll finally emerge onto a well-defined old town road flanked by stone walls. To your left is an extension of Legendwoods road leading back to your car. You'll take that route when you return this way after visiting High Ledge. Instead turn right for now, continuing on the blue-blazed Narragansett Trail. You'll notice this abandoned road has stone walls on either side, indicating a old main town road leading from one place to another, rather than a wood-gathering tote road that goes nowhere.

The road will climb a bit and then veer left, at which point you'll follow the blue-blazed trail left off the road. After about 0.2 mile, the trail dips into a small notch and then ascends. Then, after another 0.2 mile, it dips slightly into the valley before quickly rising to the edge of a steep hill. You'll wind through ledges before dropping into a narrow, rocky valley, which in summer is full of stinging nettle plants. Unlike poison ivy, the nettle's sting is short lived. Cross the stream and climb steeply, bearing left toward High Ledge.

A rocky point perched above the valley, High Ledge affords a bird's-eye view of nearby treetops. Island-dotted Wyassup Lake sparkles in the middle distance. On a clear day, the faint line of Long Island Sound can be seen beyond the lake against the horizon. On your right, you can pick out the fire tower on Wyassup Lake Road.

Retrace your steps along the blue-blazed trail back to the well-worn woods road you walked along earlier (the extension of Legendwoods Road). Do not turn left off this road toward the blue blazes; instead continue along the woods road. As you walk along this route, you'll once again see well-constructed stone walls on either side. Notice how the landowners used the natural boulders and ridges to help in the construction of their boundaries.

After a half-mile, another well-worn woods road comes in on your left. Continue straight ahead. After another 0.2 mile, you'll see boulders placed by people to mark an old gravel pit/dump on your left. Soon after that, the woods road is joined by the blue-blazed Narragansett Trail coming in on your right, and in 0.2 mile you'll be back at your car.

## OTHER HIKING OPTIONS

**Additional Resources:** There is no state park map available online of this area. We provide a good map, but one can also be found through the Connecticut Forest and Parks Association in their Connecticut Walk Book.

**For a Different Route:** You can park at the Wyassup Lake Boat Launch on Wyassup Lake Road. This has you hike the Narragansett Trail in the opposite direction. Follow the blue blazes carefully. After 0.8 mile, you'll reach High Ledge, then after another 1.6 miles you reach Bullet Ledge (look for the Bear Cave on your left before you climb). After enjoying the view, retrace your steps back to the car at the Wyassup Lake Boat Launch. This route is about 5.6 miles.

**Nearby:** Two other hikes in this book (#23 Mount Misery and #27 Green Fall Pond) also explore Pachaug State Forest, which at over 27,000 acres is the largest state forest in Connecticut.

# Chauncey Peak and Mount Lamentation

**LOCATION**: Meriden

**DISTANCE**: 6 miles

**VERTICAL RISE**: 800 feet

**TIME 3.5 HOURS**

**RATING**: B

**MAP**: USGS 7.5-minute Meriden

The traprock ridges of the Connecticut River Valley are a hiker's paradise. Ascents are steep and rugged, but the views from the cliff edges are superb. This hike along a section of the Mattabesett Trail in Giuffrida Park has some of our best traprock cliffs and offers a panoramic view within its first half a mile. Climb Chauncey Peak and Mount Lamentation on a cool, clear day and you won't be disappointed.

## GETTING THERE

From I-91 near Meriden, take exit 20 to Country Club road. Follow this road west 2.7 miles. Where the road takes a sharp left turn, turn right into Giuffrida Park.

## THE HIKE

Our route will follow the blue trail up to the Chauncey Peak and then across the ridge and down to a stream that feeds Crescent Lake. Crossing that we take the red trail up to the ridge of Mount Lamentation and then continue to follow blue across the ridge. Once we reach the last high point on the ridge we retrace our steps on blue and continue to follow blue down to Crescent Lake and return to our car. Please note that there is a short very strenuous climb up to the first summit. You'll encounter other ups and downs but none as rigorous as this initial ascent.

Follow the blue-blazed Mattabesett Trail as it leads just below the dam to the right of the parking lot. Ascend through the woods on the far side of the dam, following the blue-blazed to your right. You soon begin to climb as the trail becomes steadily steeper and rockier. Just before the summit (0.7 mile from car), you'll see the blue/red trail on your left. Bear right to stay on the blue (blue/red will bypass the summit). It is a steadily ascending

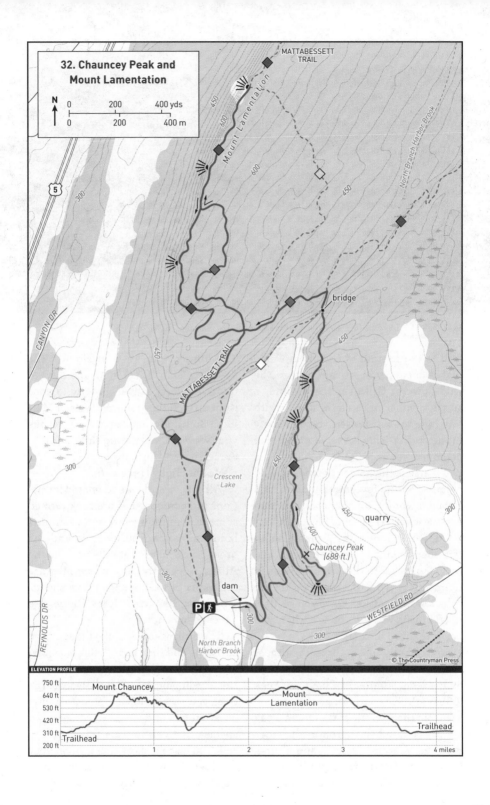

## 32. Chauncey Peak and Mount Lamentation

N

| 0 | 200 | 400 yds |
| 0 | 200 | 400 m |

MATTABESSETT
TRAIL

Mount Lamentation

MATTABESSETT TRAIL

bridge

CANYON DR

North Branch Harbor Brook

Crescent
Lake

quarry

Chauncey Peak
(688 ft.)

dam

REYNOLDS DR

WESTFIELD RD

North Branch
Harbor Brook

© The Countryman Press

**ELEVATION PROFILE**

| 750 ft |
| 640 ft |
| 530 ft |
| 420 ft |
| 310 ft |
| 200 ft |

Mount Chauncey

Mount
Lamentation

Trailhead

Trailhead

1      2      3      4 miles

AN EXPANSIVE VIEW FROM THE SUMMIT OF CHAUNCEY PEAK

trail to the summit of Chauncey Peak; rest a bit as you go and enjoy the wild-flowers. Gill-over-the-ground, a small member of the mint family with tiny blue tubular flowers, blooms early in the spring. This invasive non-native perennial was once used to ferment beer. You'll also come across patches of wild onion—a spring favorite that provides a strong flavor for your sandwiches—and silverweed. Gerry first identified silverweed, which looks like a many-leafed strawberry plant, in Newfoundland, and we've since spotted it several times in Connecticut. This illustrates one of the values of recognition: Once you've identified a plant, you will notice it where you never realized it existed.

You finally pass through almost sheer traprock ramparts and emerge on the level summit of Chauncey Peak (688 feet). The southern panorama you see from the summit of Chauncey Peak features a number of prominent ridges between you and Long Island Sound. New Haven and the faint blue line of the Sound lie straight ahead to the south.

The lumpy mass to your right is the Sleeping Giant (hike #35), and next to it is West Rock ridge. Directly to your right stretch the Hanging Hills of Meriden. South Mountain partially blocks your view of Castle Craig (hike #36). To our left across the highway rise the cliffs of Mount Higby (hike #20).

All of these ridges and related formations are composed of traprock formed some 200 million years ago when this land was volcanically active and the great crack that eventually became the Atlantic Ocean was expanding. Most are remnants of vast upended lava sheets, but a few, like West Rock Ridge, are exposed lava dikes.

The trail tacks east along the southern cliff edge and then turns left to meander across the top to the western cliffs, occasionally dipping down into the woods. The trees you pass on top are predominantly chestnut oak and staghorn sumac—two species that can tolerate this thin, dry soil. You'll see a short side trail on your right, leading to views looking down on a traprock quarry (this hard stone is, when crushed, an ideal highway base). Unfortunately, a little farther on the quarry has expanded to eat away the mountain. You'll see the quarry again as the trail again climbs out of the woods to your right.

The vistas from these cliffs are among the finest in the state; as you work your way along the edge, rocky outcroppings provide unobstructed views of Crescent Lake (Bradley Hubbard reservoir) 400 feet directly beneath you. From the final outcrop, the vista sweeps from New Haven west past the Hanging Hills and north past the Hartford skyline to the hills crossed by the northern section of the Shenipsit Trail (hike #22). Notice the bench on the shore opposite from where you are standing; you'll soon reach that at the end of today's hike. As you leave the summit you'll see the blue/red trail come in on your left. You will stay on the blue-blazed trail.

The trail drops off Chauncey Peak, leads you down into the woods, and crosses a footbridge over an old canal. After crossing the bridge, follow the blue blazes to the right. In a short distance, turn left to follow the red blazes up a ravine. Over the next mile as you hike on the red trail you'll hit junctions with both the yellow and blue trails, but continue on red through both (the yellow-blazed trail is an alternate route to the summit, and we'll be heading down the mountain on the blue-blazed trail). Once you reach the ridge line of Mount Lamentation, we'll encounter blue once more—this time, turn right on the blue trail and follow it for a half-mile walk. You'll enjoy a particularly fine view as you walk parallel to the cliff that extends from New Haven to Hartford and beyond. Enjoy a snack of blueberries from the bushes that line your path along this ridge. On a clear day you can identify the traprock ridges north of Springfield, Massachusetts. From left to right, the eastern facing cliffs of Mount Tom are followed by the gap cut by the Connecticut River, the multi-summited Holyoke Range, and finally Mount Norwottuck. This last peak marks the spot where the emergent traprock disappears into the valley's older red sandstone.

CRESCENT LAKE AS SEEN FROM THE CLIFFS ALONG MOUNT LAMENTATION

EXCELLENT TRAIL WORK UP CHAUNCEY PEAK

When you reach the yellow-blazed trail again the blue trail will begin to head down off the peak of Mount Lamentation. Instead, turn around on the blue trail to head back to your car. You'll follow the blue-blazed trail descending quickly at times. Take care to watch your footing in these steep sections, as there is a lot of loose traprock. After a steady downhill walk the blue trail will go left on a woods road and then soon turn left again back into the woods. At this point the blue trail

goes straight to Crescent Lake (the former Bradley Hubbard Reservoir). Rest a bit on the lakeshore bench that you saw earlier from the top of Chauncey Peak. The trail continues to the right alongside the lake on a peaceful trail cushioned by pine needles. Follow this a short distance to the parking lot and your car.

## OTHER HIKING OPTIONS

The Meriden Land Trust suggests a number of further hiking options.

**Chauncey Peak Loop:** Blue/Black/White trails, about 2.5 miles. This involves following the blue-blazed trail up to Chauncey Peak as noted in our hike. Climb down Chauncey Peak using the blue trail. At the bottom, cross the footbridge and turn left to leave the blue-blazed trail and follow the unblazed and white-blazed trails back to the parking area

**Mount Lamentation Loop:** White/Yellow/Blue/Red trails, about 4 miles. Start at the picnic area and follow the white-blazed trail along the western shoreline. Bear left at the fork to follow the yellow blazes. When you intersect with the red-blazed trail turn and follow it to the top of Mount Lamentation as noted in our hike. Continue with our hike description in exploring the ridge and then returning to the car on the blue trail.

There are other hikes they suggest, these and a full color map can be found online (meridenlandtrust.com).

# Mohawk Mountain

**LOCATION**: Cornwall

**DISTANCE**: 7 miles

**VERTICAL RISE**: 1000 feet

**TIME**: 4 hours

**RATING**: B/C

**MAP**: USGS 7.5-minute Cornwall

Mohawk Mountain rises 1,683 feet above its surroundings, offering a nearly 360-degree view from its summit tower. Colonial historians noted that the summit was used by the Tunxis and Paugussett Indians to produce smoke signals warning local tribes of the approach of the Mohawk Indians from the north and west.

Mohawk State Forest began with a 250-acre gift to the state from Alain C. White (who also founded White Memorial Foundation with his sister, May W. White—hike #42), in 1921. In total, the White Memorial Foundation contributed over 2,900 acres to the acquisition of the forest. The park has since grown to over 2,900 acres in the towns of Cornwall and Goshen. In the 1930s the Civilian Conservation Corps established Camp Toumey, located near the current Forest Headquarters. You can now find a memorial plaque and the remnants of buildings and fireplace chimneys in the area.

Mohawk Mountain also boasts a popular downhill ski area which first opened in the 1950s with a rope tow and has since expanded to a multi-trailed system through the beautiful woods.

Mohawk State Forest contains sections of the Blue Trail System's Mohawk (formerly Appalachian) and Mattatuck Trails within its boundaries. These trails, coming from divergent directions, meet near the summit and provide delightful alternatives to the summit road.

## GETTING THERE

Take CT 4 west from Goshen approximately 4 miles to the entrance on the left for Mohawk State Forest. Alternatively from the east, the entrance is 1.3 miles from the junction of CT 4 and CT 43. The

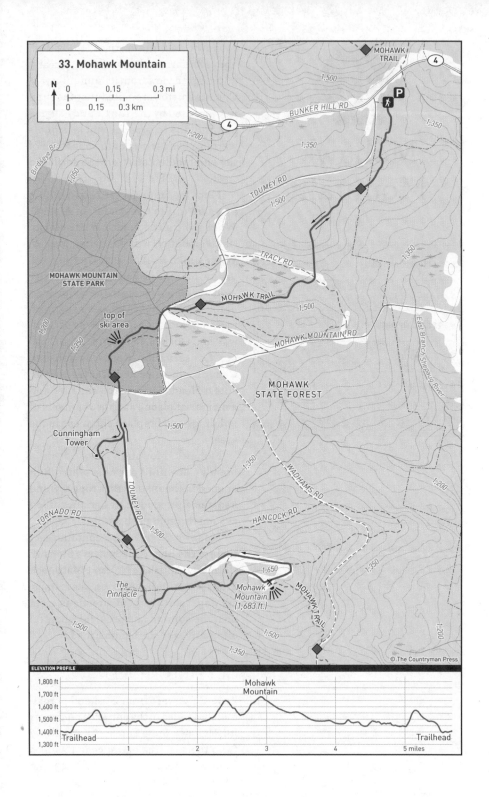

## 33. Mohawk Mountain

N

| 0 | | 0.15 | | 0.3 mi |
| 0 | 0.15 | | 0.3 km | |

MOHAWK
TRAIL

4

P

BUNKER HILL RD

4

TOUMEY RD

1,200

1,350

1,500

1,350

Birdseye Br.

1,050

1,200

TRACY RD

MOHAWK MOUNTAIN
STATE PARK

MOHAWK TRAIL

1,500

MOHAWK MOUNTAIN RD

top of
ski area

East Branch Shepaug River

1,200

MOHAWK
STATE FOREST

1,350

Cunningham
Tower

WADHAMS RD

1,500

TOUMEY RD

TORNADO RD

1,500

HANCOCK RD

1,350

1,200

1,500

The
Pinnacle

1,650

Mohawk
Mountain
(1,683 ft.)

MOHAWK TRAIL

1,350

1,500

1,500

1,350

1,200

© The Countryman Press

### ELEVATION PROFILE

| | Mohawk Mountain |
| 1,800 ft | |
| 1,700 ft | |
| 1,600 ft | |
| 1,500 ft | |
| 1,400 ft | |
| 1,300 ft | Trailhead ... Trailhead |
| | 1   2   3   4   5 miles |

BIRCH GROVE ON MOHAWK MOUNTAIN

parking lot is immediately on your left as you turn off.

## THE HIKE

Today's route will wind along the northern section of the forest to Mohawk Mountain first using the Mohawk Trail and then on the Mattabesett Trail. All trails are blazed in blue and are very well maintained with clearly signed trail junctions.

From the parking area you'll go left on the gravel road just past the gated entrance. About 150 feet on your right you'll see a sign for the blue-blazed Mohawk Trail (with the Mattatuck junction 1.8 miles ahead). Follow this blue-blazed path. You'll immediately come upon a shelter for trail hikers only, a remnant of the since re-routed Appalachian Trail (AT). Bear left into the woods past the shelter and walk upon a trail cushioned with fallen pine needles and fringed with lush green ferns. You'll reach a large rock slab with a daunting vertical face. Don't worry: you turn right to bypass this imposing rock ledge. Take time to admire the bounteous lettuce lichen all over the rock as you walk past. The trail has periods of up, down, and level in this first section and can be swampy and damp. Keep your eyes out for a bright orange salamander with spots called Red Efts. This is the terrestrial stage of the red-spotted newt, which is ubiquitous throughout eastern North America. The usual life cycle of this species includes three distinct post-hatching stages: from aquatic larva, to terrestrial (juvenile) eft, and finally aquatic adult.

CUNNINGHAM TOWER

You'll see this second stage along the damp swampy Mohawk Trail and many other trails in Connecticut.

After 0.9 mile you'll cross Tracey Road, a forest road. The trail will be fairly level, followed by a steady but gentle climb and then a descent past another shelter. Here you reach Toumey Road and a scenic vista of the Catskill Mountains in New York. Walk along the road a short distance and turn right back into the woods. You'll cross the top of the ski slope, bearing left around a ski trail sign and a chair lift. After walking through a stand of pine and hemlocks you'll soon pass more ski trails and chair lifts. The top of the ski trails gives you a good view of the Riga Plateau in the northwest corner of Connecticut. In early April there may be remnants of human-made snow here. Snowmaking is necessary at Connecticut ski slopes to supplement our unreliable snowfall. Just northwest of the lift is a small stone lookout tower that predates both the ski area and, judging by its low height, the forest that surrounds it.

Follow the blue blazes south into the woods, descending on a forest road to the junction of the Mohawk and Mattatuck trails. Turn left at this well-signed junction onto the blue-blazed Mattatuck; soon you reach Toumey Road once more. Follow it straight (south) and soon bear right onto the blazed path opposite a small picnic area. The trail curves up onto the extensive flat ledges, covered with a lush pine forest. The ruins of a great stone tower (Cunningham Tower) dominate this rocky stretch. While the Civilian Conservation Corps built much of Connecticut's forest stonework in the late 1930s, Seymour Cunningham built this steel-braced tower, with its magnificent fireplace, in 1915, before the state began to acquire the surrounding land.

You soon cross a field being reclaimed by the forest, as evidenced by the numerous white birch trees. Then enter some pine woods and pass an abandoned well and hand pump. Follow the trail through a swampy area where you will find several large bull pines and scattered spruce and black cherry trees.

On the far side of the swamp you cross a stone wall and soon the trail curves left to follow beside it. Pass a piped spring; a small cement cistern protects the source, and an adjacent pipe runs with cold, clear water. Caution: untreated water, even from a spring, may be contaminated with microscopic Giardia cysts. Even a small drink may cause illness (see Introduction).

Climb up to and across the gravel Tornado Road and continue a steady ascent up the north side of the Pinnacle. Near the top the trail skirts some small boulders. During seasons when the trees are leafless, Mohawk's summit towers are visible across the valley. Descend along the forested blue-blazed trail. Level out and cross a beautiful glade with ferns and a view southeast to Mohawk Pond. Cross a stone wall and a tote road before climbing steadily to the gravel summit road.

Head to your right up the blue-blazed road to the nearby top of Mohawk Mountain. The peak is cluttered with an array of several telecommunication and microwave towers and the state's ambient air quality monitoring site. There are also memorial benches, foundations of old fire towers, picnic facilities, and a paved parking area for motorists who arrive on the gravel road. A March trip will reward you with a clump of pussy willows adjacent to the paved area. The summit is worth the clutter as you also have an expansive view. Mounts Everett, Race, and Bear punctuate the Riga Plateau to

A RED EFT, THE TERRESTRIAL STAGE OF THE RED-SPOTTED NEWT

your right and follow them north, coming again to the Mohawk/Mattatuck Trail junction. Here turn right on the Mohawk trail. The remainder of today's hike involves retracing your steps back to the car from here following the blue blazes.

## OTHER HIKING OPTIONS

**Additional Resources:** A state park trail map can be found at www.ct.gov /deep/mohawk. Use the Summer Park Map, Northern Section.

**Nearby:** Cathedral Pines, once the premier stand of white pines in New England, is still an impressive array of pines and hemlocks, even though a tornado knocked down much of the stand in July 1989. This is a worthwhile 1-mile side trip. Take CT 4 west 0.5 mile from its junction with CT 125 in Cornwall. Turn sharply left onto Bolton Hill Road and bear right immediately onto Jewell Street. After 0.5 mile go left at the fork up Essex Hill Road 0.2 mile to a pullout on your left. The blue-blazed Mohawk Trail enters the woods at the south end of the pullout by a NATURE CONSERVANCY sign. Start the hike by climbing steeply up the hillside, aided by wooden stairs that keep the soil from washing away. The giant pines and hemlocks that survived the storm surround you immediately. Be careful of the trail when it is wet; don't step on exposed roots as they can be very slippery. You'll walk a short distance along a hilltop and then descend coming face to face with a large four-foot diameter white pine. The trail climbs again and you reach a crest where you'll angle around to the right and head downward. Turn right onto paved Essex Hill Road and walk back to your car.

the north. The Catskills rise on the western horizon. Farther to your left, in the distance, is the mountainous Hudson Highland in New York. The large, flat-topped mass in the middle distance to the right of the Riga Plateau is Canaan Mountain.

When your eyes have drunk their fill, descend on the paved road to the east, which loops back west down the north slope of the mountain (or alternatively you may reenter the woods the way you came and retrace your steps on the blue trail). Chestnut sprouts are common along the edge of the road. A little way down the road you pass a clearing to your right opposite two imposing stone gateposts flanking a grass-covered tote road to your left. This road leads to Cunningham Tower, which was visible earlier. Rejoin the blue blazes of the Mattatuck Trail at the small picnic area on

# Ragged Mountain

**LOCATION**: Southington

**DISTANCE**: 6 miles

**VERTICAL RISE**: 1,000 feet

**TIME**: 3.5 hours

**RATING**: B

**MAPS**: USGS 7.5-minute New Britain, Meriden

Ragged Mountain Preserve is a popular recreation spot found on the beautiful traprock ridges unique to Connecticut that run through the center of the state from Branford to the Massachusetts border. The craggy, reddish peak is made up of tough, volcanic basalt rock with many cliffs and viewpoints. The preserve is open to hiking, rock climbing, snow-shoeing, and other outdoor pursuits. Please note that swimming and diving in the reservoir is strictly prohibited. The blue-blazed New England Trail (once the Metacomet Trail) goes through the park and traverses the scenic ridge of Ragged Mountain.

## GETTING THERE

To get to this area of volcanic cliffs, start from the junction of CT 372 and CT 71A in New Britain. From CT 372 (Corbin Avenue), take CT 71A (Chamberlain Highway) south for 1.1 miles. Turn right onto West Lane. Proceed on West Lane for 0.6 mile to Ragged Mountain Memorial Preserve (563 acres) to your right. There is room for parking alongside the road.

## THE HIKE

Today's loop follows the blue- and red-blazed trail south until it reaches the blue-blazed New England Trail. There it heads north until the New England Trail goes west, whereupon our loop continues on the blue- and red-blazed trail which takes us south back to our car.

After parking, follow the blue-and-red blazes of the Ragged Mountain Preserve Trail about 100 yards to the beginning of the trail loop. You will start out on the left arm of the loop and return on the right.

Immediately bear left off the woods

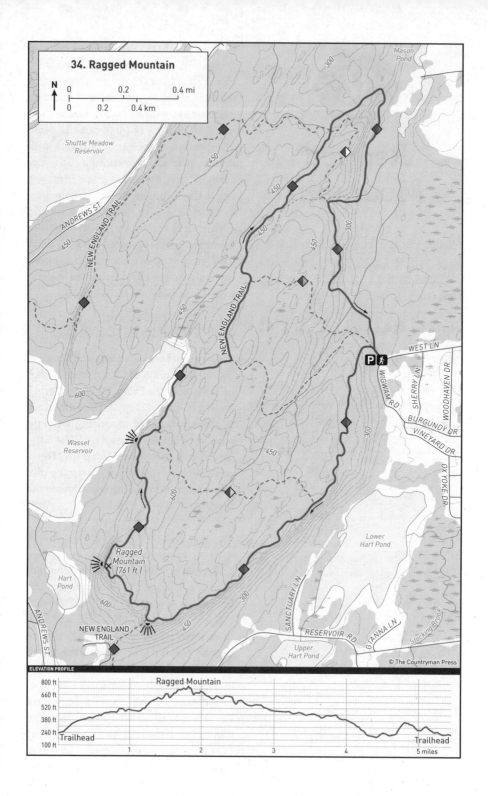

## 34. Ragged Mountain

N

| 0 | 0.2 | 0.4 mi |
|---|-----|--------|
| 0 | 0.2 | 0.4 km |

Mason Pond

300

Shuttle Meadow Reservoir

450

ANDREWS ST

NEW ENGLAND TRAIL

450

450

300

450

NEW ENGLAND TRAIL

450

450

WEST LN

P ☗

450

SHERRY LN

WIGWAM RD

BURGUNDY DR

WOODHAVEN DR

VINEYARD DR

600

Wassel Reservoir

450

300

OX YOKE DR

600

450

Lower Hart Pond

Hart Pond

600

Ragged Mountain (761 ft.)

450

300

SANCTUARY LN

RESERVOIR RD

GIANNA LN

Stocking Brook

ANDREWS ST

NEW ENGLAND TRAIL

600

450

Upper Hart Pond

© The Countryman Press

**ELEVATION PROFILE**

| | Ragged Mountain | |
|---|---|---|
| 800 ft | | |
| 660 ft | | |
| 520 ft | | |
| 380 ft | | |
| 240 ft | Trailhead | Trailhead |
| 100 ft | | |

1    2    3    4    5 miles

WASSEL RESERVOIR

road. Be careful not to continue blithely along the well-defined woods road and miss the trail turn, which is easy to do. Be sure to follow the well-marked blue- and red-blazed trail. The hike now progresses with a moderate climb. You'll then level out and proceed due south, then continue climbing past an old woods road on your right, before leveling out yet again.

Pass over a rise, and then turn sharply right onto a footpath, which leads to more old woods roads. After another brief stint on a woods road, bear left and climb to a rocky ridge where the Hart Ponds are visible through the trees. Continue on the ridge, soon climbing to an excellent lookout above the ponds. Drop down briefly, and return to the ridge-top dotted with numerous cedar trees, reaching another fine viewpoint above Reservoir Road. Be cautious of side trails on the ridge—they are well worn

but not marked with blazes. Continue on open ledges with beautiful views to the south where West Peak (one of the highest traprock ridges in Connecticut; hike #36), with its towers, can be seen in the distance.

The trail drops into and then climbs out of another small ravine. Permanent water is rare in traprock—snowmelt and rain soon run off this impervious stone, leaving most ravines stark and dry. Continue south along a small, rocky ridge, and then turn down and left off the end of the ridge before climbing again to more views and a freestanding wall—difficult to describe but unmistakable when you see it—1.2 miles from the start. The tops of central Connecticut's traprock ridges provide exhilarating hiking with excellent views.

You will reach the end of the blue- and red-blazed trail on top of Small Cliff, south of Ragged Mountain's summit, about 1.5 miles from the start. You'll see a tree with a double blaze (stacked next to each other, not staggered like a turn blaze) and a large rock cairn in front of you. Here you'll join the blue-blazed New England Trail, formerly the Metacomet Trail, where you'll turn right to head north on our loop. Follow the blue blazes down into a ravine, and then you have a hand-and-foot scramble up the traprock to the top of the cliffs, which are largely wooded here. In another quarter-mile or so of gentle ups and downs, you will come out into the open on the summit of Ragged Mountain. Here, of necessity, many of the blue blazes are painted on rocks instead of trees. Also on occasion you may see the old blazes of this trail, red dot on blue.

We've sat atop the cliffs and watched seagulls play follow-the-leader above the reservoir. Large birds often use the thermals associated with cliffs to soar for hours with nary a wing beat. Far below you can see strollers sauntering along the reservoir dike.

Bear right away from the cliffs, drop down, and climb again as the trail undulates along the ridge. A final lookout offers views of the northern end of Wassel Reservoir. Soon you'll reach a junction with the blue- and yellow-blazed trail on your right. Continue straight to follow the blue blazes (or to shorten your hike, you can turn right here as noted in *Other Hiking Options*).

Volcanic ridgetops are usually not good places to find large varieties of flowers, but we have found one especially favorite flower in Connecticut's traprock (though rarely elsewhere): pale corydalis, a member of the poppy family, closely related to bleeding heart and Dutchman's-breeches. Whenever you traverse these ridges, be on the lookout for this striking rose-and-yellow flower.

REACHING THE SUMMIT OF RAGGED MOUNTAIN

Wind along the ridge and the reservoir's shore. The rugged trail surface requires proper hiking footgear—not street shoes. Near the end of the reservoir on an open rocky ledge, you'll come to an unmarked trail junction with a blocked trail on your left. This now closed trail used to connect to another section of the Metacomet (now New England) Trail down very steep ledges. It is no longer maintained and can be dangerous for hikers. Continue following the blue blazes, again being alert to more unblazed woods roads and trails along the way.

Soon you'll reach another trail junction with two yellow blazes. Turn left, continuing to follow the blue-blazed New England Trail along the western edge of the Ragged Mountain Preserve.

After about a half-mile more, you'll reach another junction with a blue-and-orange trail on your right. Bear left to stay on the blue-blazed trail. (Turning right is another option to shorten your route.)

This stretch of the hike is a lovely woods walk with your path often wide and rocky. The trail has a few minor turns but is easy to follow with the blue blazes. You'll arrive at another trail junction on a little ridge. Your first right will be the blue- and white-blazed trail (taking this route would trim 0.3 mile off your loop), while the second right is another part of the blue- and red-blazed preserve trail. For this hike, take this second right. The trail ascends gently, and you'll pass a driving range on your right. Then the path veers right uphill over medium-sized loose traprock. The trail can be hard to follow here; watch for the blue-and-red blazes. Your path then veers left as it continues to climb back on a ridge, an easier climbing trail than earlier with fewer rocks to negotiate. Again continue to watch for blazes as the trail intertwines with woods roads and other unmarked paths, and then crosses over a large dry streambed. You'll reach a woods road where you bear right and then descend back to the original main junction at the start of the hike. At the junction, go left to your car.

## OTHER HIKING OPTIONS

**Additional Resources:** There is a protected bulletin board with a map at the West Lane entrance. There are also a few places online to find printer-friendly maps. One can be found on the Berlin town website (town.berlin.ct.us) and another somewhat clearer map, but with less detail, can be found on the Connecticut Forest and Parks website.

**Short & Sweet #1:** You can still hike Ragged Mountain with a shorter loop (a little less than 4 miles), follow as instructed and at the second intersection with the blue- and yellow-blazed trail, just after that last viewpoint over Wassel Reservoir, turn right. This will bring you back to the blue- and red-blazed preserve trail. Turn left here, and follow back about 0.7 mile to the main junction and then right down the hill to your car.

**Short & Sweet #2:** Another way to shorten the original loop is to take the blue-and-orange trail right about 3.5 miles into the hike. This 0.6-mile trail will bring you down to the main junction where you continue straight about a hundred yards to your car.

# Sleeping Giant State Park

| | |
|---|---|
| **LOCATION**: Hamden | |
| **DISTANCE**: 6 miles | |
| **VERTICAL RISE**: 1,600 feet | |
| **TIME**: 4 hours | |
| **RATING**: A/B | |
| **MAPS**: USGS 7.5-minute Wallingford, Mount Carmel | |

**Disclaimer:** Due to damage sustained during a tornado in May 2018, the hike description for Sleeping Giant will have some inaccuracies. After the tornado, Sleeping Giant State Park was closed to the general public. Once the park has reopened, the author will revise the hike description to reflect the significant changes the tornado wrought on the landscape of the park. Please contact the author at 50hikesCT@gmail.com if you would like a copy of the revised version.

Some hikers belittle the size of the Sleeping Giant, for he rises only 739 feet above sea level. They forget that he is lying down; were he to awaken and get to his feet, he would stand some 2 miles tall!

A series of folded, angular volcanic hills just north of New Haven defines the shape of the reclining titan. Legend has it that the giant was first recognized and named from sailing ships in New Haven Harbor many years ago. From the various parts of his anatomy you can see numerous peaks and ridges that other hikes in this book traverse. The giant is now contained in a 1,500-acre state park. Only a short distance from downtown New Haven, it is a popular spot with campers, picnickers, and hikers. In 1977 the Sleeping Giant Trail System was dedicated as a National Scenic Trail.

The park's trail system is well maintained by the active Sleeping Giant Park Association (SGPA). Formed in 1924, the SGPA is an all-volunteer organization whose mission is to protect and enlarge Sleeping Giant State Park. They maintain over 30 miles of trails in the park and offer many guided hikes each year. They sponsor a Giant Master Program where members can earn a patch and certificate if they hike all the marked trails and record them on an official log.

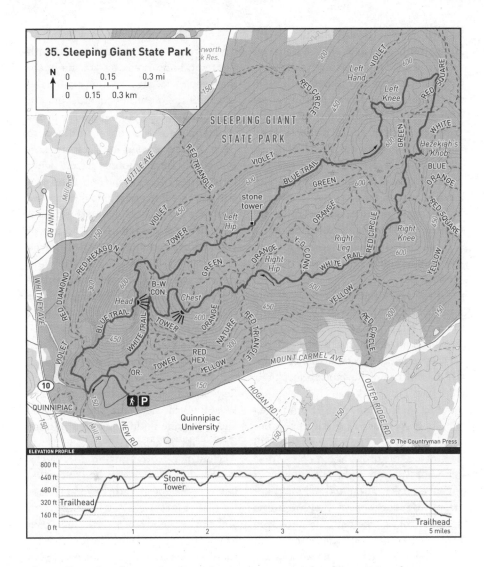

Three of our family members are Giant Masters.

## GETTING THERE

From I-91, take exit 10 (Hamden/ Mount Carmel) onto CT 40 north. After 2.6 miles on CT 40, follow CT 10 north (right) 1.3 miles to its junction with Mount Carmel Avenue. Turn right and follow it 0.3 mile to the park entrance on your left. There is a large parking lot on your right after passing the entrance kiosk.

## THE HIKE

The 32-mile park trail system, designed by Norman Greist and Richard Elliot of the Sleeping Giant Park Associa- tion, is ingeniously laid out in a series of loops. The traprock outcrops and ridges are named for parts of the slum- bering giant's anatomy and are labeled as such on maps (head, chin, chest, etc.). No matter how long or short a hike you wish, you need never retrace your steps. Six east–west trails, marked with blue, white, violet, green, orange, and yellow blazes, join the opposite ends of the park. Five north–south trails marked with red diamonds, squares, hexagons, circles, and triangles cut across the park. The loop combinations you can devise seem endless.

We favor the Blue-White Trail combination loop of about 6 miles in length. It is the most strenuous, covers most of the giant's anatomy, and affords the best views.

There are numerous other options and we highlight a few in *Other Hiking Options*. The Connecticut Chapter of the Appalachian Mountain Club has offered all the trails in this state park on a single day to those who want to test their hiking ability!

Start up the right side of the paved picnic loop road through the pine-shaded grove. (The tornado of 2018 decimated this grove and no pine trees remain.) To your right is a cluster of great red oaks. These tall oaks did not "from little acorns grow"; they are stump sprouts from a tree cut long ago. Tree clusters like this one are common in Connecticut's much-cutover woodlands.

You'll take a blue-blazed feeder trail on your right just before the park road veers uphill. The white trail also enters the woods here. Follow the blue blazes to soon join the main blue-blazed Quinnipiac Trail, the oldest of Connecticut's Blue Trails. Your route curves downhill and then bears right away from Mill River on a blue-blazed path.

Shortly the first ascent takes you onto the giant's elbow. The trail follows the cedar-spotted basalt ridge of his crooked arm to the right, dropping down

steeply. This 15-foot drop within the woods requires a careful descent with strategic hand holds as you navigate the steep rock. The trail then begins the ascent of the giant's head, crossing the red diamond trail. An old quarry drops off steeply to your left. The Sleeping Giant Park Association was formed in 1924 to protect the mountain from being torn down by a quarrying operation; you still see the damage of this industry as you climb the head. This stretch is a long, difficult scramble—a good test of your hiking condition. Avoid this area in winter; the slope is usually icy and treacherous. An alternate route around the steepest ledges is available to your right; this route is not recommended in bad weather, either.

Back to your right you will see two ridges. The Quinnipiac Trail runs along the closer mass of shapeless hills; the Regicides Trail follows the long ridge of West Rock farther right. The neat lawns and collegiate buildings of Quinnipiac University lie below.

Continue to the jutting cliff of the giant's chin. The wide path in the valley below is the Tower Path; beyond it rises the giant's massive chest. Looking north you can see the traprock ridges known as the Hanging Hills of Meriden, where the Metacomet and Mattabesett Trails join. West Peak, a large rock mass with a crown of towers, lies at the left just beyond the rock tower of Castle Crag (hike #36). The flat-topped peak to the right is South Mountain. The city of Meriden fills the break in the ridge; the two hills farthest to the right are Mount Lamentation and Chauncey Peak (hike #32). Lava flows formed all these traprock peaks and plateaus some 200 million years ago.

The trail zigzags steeply down the north end of the giant's head, crosses the Red Hexagon Trail and then the Tower Path. You'll pass the White/Blue Crossover Trail on your right. The crossover trails connect two different colored trails in the park. The blazes are different colors in different directions. This crossover trail is blazed in white as you head to the white trail, but if you came in the opposite direction you would see it is blazed in blue as it heads to the Blue Trail. Follow this to the white trail—our route then crosses the Red Triangle Trail, and then the Tower Path again before it climbs the giant's left hip, also known as Mount Carmel.

Perhaps the best view in the park is from the top of the stone tower found on the left hip. This large open-air field-stone building, at 739 feet above sea level, is the highest point of the park. Built in the 1930s by the Works Progress Administration (WPA), it is the second largest state park structure built by federal relief labor in the Depression era. Take some time to explore the details of this ramped 30 foot tall tower—can you find the iron spider web in the third floor window? Can you find the Doberman dog carved in the stone on the east side, between the second and third floors? In 1986, the tower was added to the National Register of Historic Places. There was also a large renovation project of the tower in 1996. You can learn more about the tower and the history of Sleeping Giant in the booklet "Born Among the Hills" by Nancy Davis Sachse.

After exploring the tower structure take time to enjoy the hilly panorama; starting with Mount Lamentation, you see the impressive cliff faces of Mount Higby (hike #20), the gap through which US 6 passes, and the long ridge of Beseck Mountain. Like the hills to the north, these ridges are traversed by trails.

A SCRAMBLE UP THE BLUE TRAIL

The barrenness of the land makes landowners more willing to give hiking clubs permission to cut trails on hills than on their more fertile property. Fortunately, hikers much prefer these barren hills to the low-lying fertile fields.

Follow the blue blazes past the tower and continue to the cliff edge, where you can look south to the giant's right hip, right leg, and right knee before dropping down to your right, where you cross the outlet of a swamp and the Red Circle Trail 0.4 mile from the tower. After a level spell through white pines, dip down and then ascend his left leg. Drop again and go up the left knee. Note the pitting that centuries of exposure have produced on the weathered rocks; they contrast sharply with the smooth faces of a few recently uncovered rock surfaces nearby.

Working down the far end of the giant's knee, you encounter the first section of smooth, rolling, rock-free trail. Footing makes a tremendous difference in hiking difficulty, and the angular volcanic-rock ridges of central Connecticut are particularly treacherous. The size of the dogwoods here attests to the depth of the rich soil beneath them. As the Blue Trail veers northward you'll pass the Violet/Blue Crossover Trail on your left. You'll see violet blazes from your direction. After the trail zig-zags for 0.4 mile it crosses the Red Square and Green Trails.

Begin your ascent of Hezekiah's Knob. As you near the top, look to the right for early-spring-blooming purple and white hepaticas with their characteristic three-lobed leaves left over from the previous summer's growth. The leaf's shape, supposedly like a liver, was the basis for its medicinal use for various liver problems.

The Blue and White Trails meet on the knob. This is where you begin the return portion of today's loop. Proceed to your right down the hill following the white-blazes. You cross the Red Square Trail again and then the Orange Trail. Soon after the Orange Trail you reach the top of his right knee; look north across the valley to the giant's rocky left side, where you hiked earlier. Descend the stone-strewn slope

WPA STONE TOWER

VIEW FROM THE CHIN OF THE GIANT

and then climb up and down his right leg and right hip crossing the Red Circle Trail and the Green-Yellow Crossover Trail. The Red Triangle Trail cuts across the park by the base of the sleeping titan's chest—after crossing this path (and the Orange Trail) you begin the last climb of this circuit. The trail winds up around great boulders passing a vista marked by a large rock cairn on your left, and then reaching the bald rocky-top of the chest with numerous views.

Here you leave the green blazes behind and twist down off the giant's chest on the white-blazed trail. You'll pass the Blue-White Crossover Trail and then descend on impressive stone steps built by the SPGA trail crew. Turning left, the White Trail then joins the Tower Trail for a short distance (30 yards) before heading down right back into the woods. This downhill stretch is steep over rough loose rock terrain. Soon you will reach the paved park road where you turn left back to your car.

## OTHER HIKING OPTIONS

**Additional Resources:** An excellent internet resource for Sleeping Giant State Park is the website of the Sleeping Giant Association (SGPA), www.sgpa.org. This website provides excellent information from the history of the park, trail maps, organized hikes, the nature trail pamphlet to information about their Giant Master Program. Another map resource is The Connecticut Department of Energy and Environmental Protection (DEEP) website for Sleeping Giant State Park, www.ct.gov/deep/sleepinggiant.

**Short & Sweet:** The most popular hike on the Giant is the Tower Path. This 3.2-mile round trip hike on the Giant is a gentle climb on a wide clear path that leads to the stone tower. The Tower Path starts just off the main parking lot beyond the bulletin board. It is unblazed but easy to follow, as it is a wide path that is well maintained by both the state and the SGPA.

# 36

# West Peak and Castle Craig

**LOCATION**: Meriden

**DISTANCE**: 6.4 miles

**VERTICAL RISE**: 1,200 feet

**TIME**: 4 hours

**RATING**: B

**MAP**: USGS 7.5-minute Meriden

Rising like cresting waves over the Quinnipiac River Valley, the Hanging Hills of Meriden are a well-loved natural landmark of central Connecticut. Today's hike takes you among these hills to their two highest summits: West Peak (1,024 feet) and East Peak (976 feet). The latter of these hosts a small stone tower at its summit—the source of the name Castle Craig.

Today the Hanging Hills are located within Hubbard Park—1,800 acres of parkland donated to the people of Meriden in 1900 by wealthy industrialist Walter Hubbard. It was Hubbard who funded the distinct castle at the crest of East Peak, a structure supposedly influenced architecturally by towers seen during his travels in Europe. The roads, lawns, and lake of the lower park grounds are also Hubbard's doing: here he collaborated with the Olmsted family, the most famous landscape architects of *fin de siècle* America (responsible for, among other things, New York City's Central Park). Perhaps most extraordinarily, the charitable Hubbard also stipulated that entrance to the park should always remain free of charge—a status that it still holds today.

With a peaceful lakeside walk, grand traprock cliffs, and a vigorous, woodland ascent rewarded with spectacular views, the Hubbard Park trail to West Peak and Castle Craig showcases some of the best elements that hiking in Connecticut has to offer. However, be warned that the path can get rather strenuous—an easy beginning to the hike gives little warning of the later scrambling, steep ascents along the Metacomet trail. Save this one for a day when you're feeling fit and the weather is clear, and you'll be rewarded with a grand day hike.

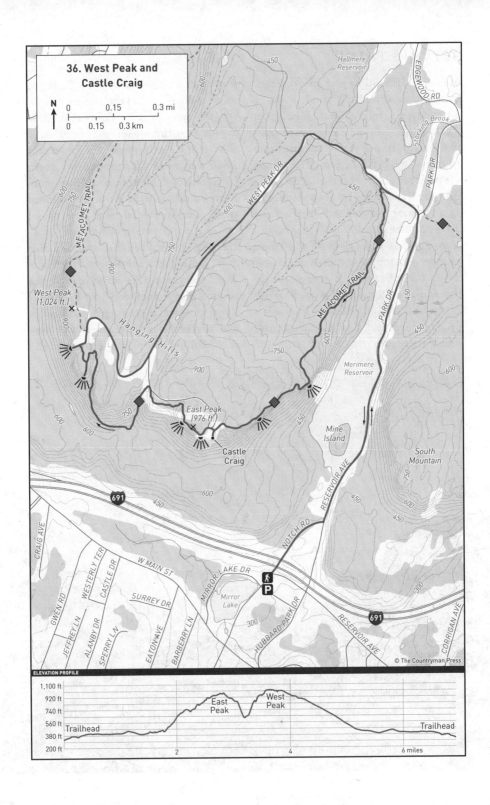

## 36. West Peak and Castle Craig

N

| 0 | 0.15 | 0.3 mi |
| 0 | 0.15 | 0.3 km |

Hallmere
Reservoir

EDGEWOOD RD

Stocking Brook

PARK DR

WEST PEAK DR

METACOMET TRAIL

West Peak
(1,024 ft.)

Hanging Hills

METACOMET TRAIL

Merimere
Reservoir

East Peak
(976 ft.)

Castle
Craig

Mine
Island

South
Mountain

RESERVOIR AVE

NOTCH RD

691

CRAIG AVE

WESTERLY TER

CASTLE DR

W MAIN ST

SURREY DR

GWEN RD

JEFFREY LN

ALANBY DR

SPERRY LN

EATON AVE

BARBERRY LN

MIRROR LAKE DR

Mirror
Lake

HUBBARD PARK DR

RESERVOIR AVE

691

CORRIGAN AVE

© The Countryman Press

**ELEVATION PROFILE**

| | | | |
|---|---|---|---|
| 1,100 ft | | | |
| 920 ft | East | West | |
| 740 ft | Peak | Peak | |
| 560 ft | | | |
| 380 ft | Trailhead | | Trailhead |
| 200 ft | | | |
| | 2 | 4 | 6 miles |

## GETTING THERE

Today's trailhead is just off of I-691. From either direction, you'll want to take exit 4 and follow West Main Street east toward downtown Meriden (a right off the exit ramp if you're coming from I-691 east, a left off the ramp from I-691 west). After about three-quarters of a mile you'll see the entrance to Hubbard Park on your left (named Mirror Lake Drive on some maps). Turn left here, and drive along a ways keeping the small lake to your right. As you reach the end of the lake, bear right—very shortly afterward you'll notice a large parking lot to your left, sandwiched between a playground and a public swimming pool. Park here.

## THE HIKE

As you lace up your boots, you'll notice an abandoned, gated road below a highway overpass in one corner of the parking lot. Take this paved road north under the interstate highway to Reservoir Road and bear left, continuing north between South Mountain and Merimere Reservoir. This road is open to summit traffic during the warmer months, so use caution. On summer weekends, this road can get quite a bit crowded, but don't let the automobiles get you down. You'll soon leave this paved road for the rugged Metacomet; consider Reservoir Road as a warm-up or prelude to the main event. Note that the reservoir here is a public water supply, so you aren't

VIEW OF SLEEPING GIANT ON THE HORIZON

allowed to enter the water, and the poison ivy along the roadside is more than sufficient to reduce the temptation. The views across the water to the west of Castle Craig and its cliffs are outstanding. Keep an eye out for birds—hawks and turkey vultures can often be sighted circling among the traprock cliffs, while herons and egrets can sometimes be spotted near the shore.

One mile from the start, turn left to cross the dam at the north end of Merimere Reservoir. Here you can enjoy the fine view of the lake, and the notch it sits in. At the dam's end, turn left off the paved road to follow the blue-blazed Metacomet Trail across a small stream, up a traprock embankment and into the woods. Note that this turnoff is rather poorly marked—in the summer of 2017, the only indicator was the word 'trail' spray-painted in blue on the side of the road! After crossing an attractive rock-bound rill, you edge up the long west side of the reservoir. Then follow near the twisting shore of the lake—the route is peppered with volcanic rocks. After leaving the shore, the way at first is very steep and rocky, but gradually the slope eases. Watch your footing—sections of the scree-covered Metacomet here can be quite treacherous, especially after a recent rain.

After 2 miles, you emerge on cliffs that rise 400 feet above Merimere Reservoir. Evergreen-covered Mine Island below you seems lifted from the Maine coast. Gerry first saw this island in the early 1960s on an autumn morning as the ground fog was lifting. Some sights plant themselves so firmly in your mind's eye that they are always there to delight you.

South Mountain rises from the far shore of the reservoir, and Mount Higby's northern cliffs poke up at left (hike

CASTLE CRAIG

#20). To the far left, you can just make out the jagged Hartford skyline.

As you continue uphill along the cliff, several unmarked paths on your left lead to similar viewpoints with slightly different perspectives; all are spectacular on a clear day. One last lookout provides a glimpse of Castle Craig's tower. Follow the blue-blazed trail across a final dip before arriving at the base of the tower, 2.2 miles from your car. Climb the tower on metal stairs for a panoramic view from East Peak.

The vista west is blocked by West Peak. Sleeping Giant (hike #35) and West Rock lie to the south, and the Metacomet Ridge is to the north. Talcott

MINE ISLAND ON MERIMERE RESERVOIR

Mountain (hike #47) is readily identifiable with its Heublein Tower. In the far distance, you can see the east-facing cliffs of Mount Tom in Massachusetts, the Connecticut River gap, and the humps of the Holyoke Range. It may be tempting to stop here for lunch, but a healthy push to the summit of West Peak still remains. Tuckered hikers can end the hike early here by following the peak road down (see *Other Hiking Options*).

Leaving the tower, continue on the Metacomet Trail across the parking lot. Be careful here; your route can be hard to locate. The trail goes across the near corner of the lot and continues up the slope near the cliffs. The entrance is marked with a white metal sign discouraging unprepared drivers from venturing too far on the trails. The route soon crosses more open cliffs and then drops down almost to the tower's access road.

Just before the road, a descending blue-blazed trail that avoids road walking by way of a series of ups and downs bears left away from the road. This path soon drops downhill rather dramatically—take this trail, and at the bottom turn right onto a wide tote road. You won't be down in these lower elevations for long; almost immediately, you'll turn right again, climbing diagonally left up an overgrown scree slope. A recent mid-March trip revealed a garter snake enjoying the early-season warmth of the hillside's southern exposure. Bear right and ascend a rather strenuous but rather attractive draw. The great traprock boulders scattered around you appear to flow down the intersection of the scree slopes. Look back—the sides of the draw frame the Sleeping Giant with his head to the right.

Near the top of this draw are a large elderberry bush and a stand of American yew. This is the largest, most southerly stand that we have encountered. New England is at the southernmost range of this northern shrub, so this may be one of its more southerly appearances.

The trail levels out before bearing left a short way up the steep side to the open plateau top of West Peak. Here, the Connecticut Chapter of the Appalachian Mountain Club was formed in June 1921. You'll emerge onto an old road, which you'll follow left to a formerly fenced, rocky point. You can see the Tunxis Ridge to the west. Several cliffs and headlands invite your careful exploration.

After a leisurely lunch—the surrounding thickets make nice spots for a nap—join up with the park road (next to a slew of radio towers) and follow it down the north side of West Peak. As with most of Connecticut's traprock ridges, the side opposite the cliffs tends to slope gently as a result of the tipping of the layer of traprock. The break in the traprock is then exposed as a cliff. Be sure to keep left at the road junction that leads right to Castle Craig. When you reach Merimere Reservoir, cross the dam and follow Reservoir Road south, retracing your steps to your car.

## OTHER HIKING OPTIONS

You can easily shorten this hike by heading down West Peak Drive from the summit parking lot at Castle Craig—missing the fantastic views from West Peak, but also skipping its deceptively rigorous ascent.

The opening walk along the Merimere Reservoir is in the notch between the Hanging Hills' East Peak and South Mountain. Taking a right on the blue-blazed Metacomet after reaching the Park Drive dam, and then another right onto a red-blazed trail a quarter-mile later, will lead you to the summit of South Mountain (767 feet). While not as grand in elevation as its neighbors, a lookout here provides superb views of the reservoir, Mine Island, and Castle Craig.

For those with young children or in the mood for something less strenuous, Hubbard Park has a wealth of shorter hiking paths. One good option would be the white-blazed trail. Follow the directions above to start, but just before the reservoir take a left off of Reservoir Avenue onto the white-blazed dirt carriage road. Following white takes you on a pleasant 2.5-mile, 1.5-hour hike featuring a pleasant brook crossing and a stone pavilion with views of Meriden.

# 37

# Bear Mountain

**LOCATION**: Salisbury

**DISTANCE**: 6.8 miles

**VERTICAL RISE**: 1,600 feet

**TIME**: 4.5 hours

**RATING**: A/B

**MAP**: USGS 7.5-minute Bash Bish Falls
(MA-CT-NY)

A rugged, windswept mountain with views into three states awaits you at the high point of this hike. Along the way, you'll hike a portion of the justly famous Appalachian Trail (AT). At the top of Bear Mountain sits a once-magnificent stone monument, partially crumbled but nevertheless an imposing landmark. In late 1983 the rubble was stabilized, creating a lower monument. The original tower was erected in the late 1880s by a man named Robins Battell, who was reportedly incensed that the Encyclopedia Britannica had published that no place in Connecticut rose above 1,000 feet. After hiring a surveyor and determining the peak was 2354 feet, he secured a long-term lease of the summit and recruited a mason to erect a tower. It took three years to haul 350 tons of native stone to the summit to build the 22.5-foot tower (39 feet if you include the lightning rod topped by a little metal ball). The original tower tapered upward, measuring 20 foot square at its base and 10 foot square at the top, and was built using no mortar. It was adorned with a plaque proclaiming it "the highest ground in Connecticut, 2354 feet above the sea."

Unfortunately, neither assertion was true. In the 1940s, it was discovered that the highest point in Connecticut is, in fact, on a shoulder of Mount Frissell at 2,380 feet. Mount Frissell is another peak on the Riga Plateau just west of Bear Mountain, the summit of which is in Massachusetts. This spot is unceremonially marked by a green-colored metal stake drilled into the ledge. Bear Mountain may not be the highest point in Connecticut, but it is the tallest peak in Connecticut at 2,316 feet. The monument has suffered from over

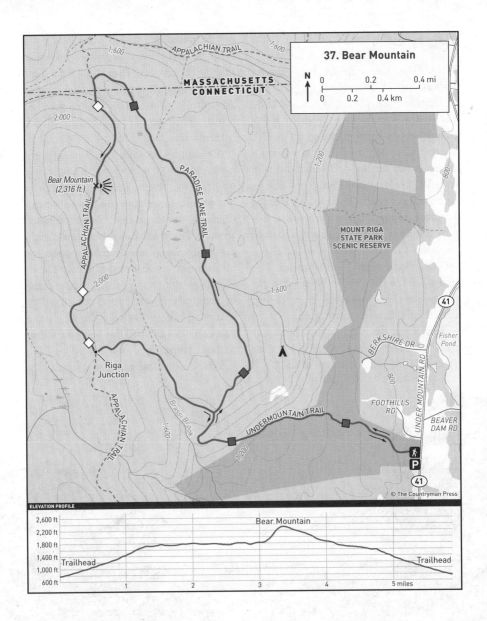

## 37. Bear Mountain

MASSACHUSETTS
CONNECTICUT

APPALACHIAN TRAIL

Bear Mountain
(2,316 ft.)

APPALACHIAN TRAIL

PARADISE LANE TRAIL

Riga
Junction

APPALACHIAN TRAIL

Brass Brook

UNDERMOUNTAIN TRAIL

MOUNT RIGA
STATE PARK
SCENIC RESERVE

BERKSHIRE DR

UNDER MOUNTAIN RD

FOOTHILLS
RD

BEAVER
DAM RD

Fisher
Pond

41

41

© The Countryman Press

**ELEVATION PROFILE**

Bear Mountain

2,600 ft
2,200 ft
1,800 ft
1,400 ft  Trailhead                                        Trailhead
1,000 ft
600 ft
          1          2          3          4      5 miles

a century of harsh winters and increasing vandalism, and has collapsed into a mound of rubble. Numerous efforts from the 1960s through the 1980s to rebuild the monument culminated in a decision in 1983 to stabilize rather than rebuild what was left of the tower. The once grand monument can be visited today, and serves as a good spot to have some lunch and enjoy the panoramic view of the area.

## GETTING THERE

To reach the start of this hike, drive on CT 41 3.2 miles north from its junction with US 44 in Salisbury. There is a small hikers' parking lot on your left.

## THE HIKE

Today's hike is a loop that takes you to the summit of Bear Mountain via the Undermountain Trail to Paradise Lane then up the Appalachian Trail (AT). The hike descends by continuing on the AT down the south side of the peak, meeting up again with the Undermountain Trail. We prefer this direction when hiking to the summit. The climb upward is the more rugged, as you'll have to use your hands to scale large expanses of rock. We find that sections like these are easier to ascend than descend. The hike down the summit is also rugged but steady, and the grade is easier, requiring no real need to use your hands.

Today's hike begins on the blue-blazed Undermountain Trail, a feeder trail to the AT, which starts at the back of the parking lot and soon passes a large bulletin board carrying the latest trail information. There is also a box with a frequently replenished supply of AT information folders. These provide handy parking, camping, and route information.

Proceed through these relatively new woods—50 years ago, this starting point was an open field. The trail then enters older woods and soon begins to climb, gently at first, and then more steeply. There are long stretches of this hike with steep steady climbs good for testing one's wind and muscle. These climbs present an excellent opportunity to practice the mile-eating trick used by seasoned hikers: Set a comfortable pace you can maintain all the way to the top without stopping.

After a quarter-mile, you'll pass an

A VIEW OF MOUNT EVERETT AND MOUNT BRACE WHILE DESCENDING BEAR MOUNTAIN

FINE TRAIL WORK ON THE UNDERMOUNTAIN TRAIL

eroded gully on your right that parallels the trail for most of the ascent along the Undermountain Trail. As you climb, you may notice that this trail is an old tote road whose surface has eroded several feet into the hill. This erosion was probably caused by countless horse and wagon trips scoring the surface, making it susceptible to rain and snowfall. Hikers then added to the erosion. The constant tramping of feet killed the stabilizing vegetation, and the deeply eroded road prevented the diversion of running water off the trail. Take notice of the excellent trail work, performed mostly by volunteers of the Appalachian Mountain Club (AMC), to manage this erosion with water-bars, stone steps, and even trail re-routing and reforestation areas.

At some point you'll notice yellow paint marking some trees across the trail. These are not trail blazes, but rather mark National Park Service land protecting the Appalachian Trail corridor in perpetuity.

After 1.3 miles from the start, you will reach a turnoff to the Paradise Group Camping area. Soon after this, you'll find yourself at a junction with the Paradise Lane trail. Turn right off the Undermountain Trail onto the blue-blazed Paradise Lane. Blazed trails may exhibit many different colors, but along this corridor white blazes are reserved for the AT, while AT side trails are blazed with blue.

Paradise Lane starts roughly parallel to the AT. In a short distance, the trail turns left off the old tote road and zigzags steeply up the hill. This trail has the densest population of chestnut sprouts we've seen in Connecticut. Prior to the twentieth century, chestnut trees comprised about 25 percent of New England forests. Unfortunately, by the 1930s the chestnut was all but decimated due to the spread of a fungus, the chestnut blight. You'll still see chestnut sprouts in the woods because the blight does not affect the roots of the tree and in fact only affects trees that have grown enough to develop bark with cracks.

You'll be walking the full distance of the 1.9-mile Paradise Lane, much of which travels gently up and down around the side of Bear Mountain. The path is well worn, but you'll find the blazes are often fairly far apart.

After about 0.3 mile the trail descends; pass another sign signaling the group camping area. Along this section of the trail Gerry once startled a ruffed grouse, which took off with the usual thunder of wings but without having run a bit (as they usually do). Why did it hold in one spot so long before flying? Having noted where it took off, Gerry went over and found a well-camouflaged, roughly circular nest with nine buff eggs in it.

You'll reach a relatively flat, somewhat swampy area where you will see the very steep south side of Bear Mountain at left. You'll cross a small seasonal stream and continue curving gently left. Soon you'll reach a small (dried-up) pond mostly filled with bushes and grasses. After crossing the pond's dried-up outlet stream on a log bridge, note the northeast corner of Bear Mountain as you walk through an open ledge decorated with laurel and huckleberry. You'll see many of the yellow, boundary blazes along this trail as well.

Descend though hemlocks to the junction with the AT, and then turn left (south) following the white blazes. (A right turn would take you to Mount Katahdin in Maine in about 800 miles.)

Go diagonally left up the white-blazed, rocky AT on Bear Mountain.

Some fine trail work has been done here to stabilize this steep route with large, erosion-proof rocks. After a long, steady uphill stretch, you'll turn directly up the steep, ledge-dominated slope. Scramble over several steep pitches where you'll have to use both hands and feet, and then enter some stunted pitch pines that perch precariously on rather bare open ledges. Soon you will come to the monument on top of Bear Mountain.

While you rest on the monument, watch for large, dark, soaring birds—turkey vultures. These birds, with a six-foot wingspan, are the largest of North America's vultures. They are common in the adjacent Hudson River Valley and are spreading throughout the Northeast. They use rising columns of air along the edge of the Riga Plateau to soar for hours without flapping their wings.

From the summit, the views are superb. To the east lie the Twin Lakes and Canaan Mountain. For the best view to the north, follow the AT north to a ledge on the edge of a stand of scrub pines. From there, the mountain with a tower is Mount Everett (2,602 feet), the apex of the second highest mountain mass in Massachusetts. The hulk in front of Everett is Race Mountain (2,365 feet).

As you sit on the monument, you'll see several clumps of gray birches below you. These trees stand out because of their nearly triangular leaves. These dowdy cousins of the sparkling white birch have a grayer bark that does not peel with age. A short-lived tree, the gray birch is an early colonizer of uncultivated, open fields.

When you are ready, follow the AT south off the top. Just as the trail starts seriously downward, there is a grand view to the south and west. Ahead is the relatively level Riga Plateau. To the right

the mountains you see are, from left to right, Gridley Mountain (Connecticut), North and South Brace Mountains (New York), and Round Mountain (Connecticut), with Mount Frissell (Massachusetts) behind it; north of Frissell (you will have to go down the path a bit to see past obstructing trees) is Mount Ashley

STABILIZED ROCK MONUMENT ON THE SUMMIT OF BEAR MOUNTAIN

(Massachusetts). The body of water left of Gridley is South Pond (1,715 feet), and the Catskills can be seen off in the distance on a clear day. It usually takes several visits before these mountains become old friends, but the journeys are definitely worth the effort!

Continue south, passing several pitch pines whose wind-distorted shapes would do credit to a bonsai artist. All lean east, away from the prevailing west winds. The cold, desiccating gusts have sheared off any upward shoots that braved the elements so that the tops are flattened and bent eastward—the path of least resistance.

As you progress downward, the various hardy oaks rise slowly to obscure your view. Then you rise into the open again to a partial view of the mountains. Each dip, however, carries you into higher and higher trees until the trees win this game of hide-and-seek. About 0.6 mile from the summit, a tote road comes in on your right; bear left onto the AT. In another 0.2 mile, you'll come to the well-signed Riga Junction. Here you'll leave the AT and follow to the left the blue-blazed Undermountain Trail steeply downhill. Over the first part of this trail, you'll cross some seasonal streams with plank bridges over muddy sections. The dampness of the area nourishes a rich display of ferns, laurel, and moss on either side of the trail. You'll start to see very large oaks and maples as you descend. After 0.8 mile, you'll pass the Paradise Lane junction (which you took toward the summit earlier); continue on the Undermountain Trail. From here, you'll retrace your steps back to your car.

## OTHER HIKING OPTIONS

We think the hike outlined above is the best loop around and over Bear Mountain. You could take a longer, more rugged loop of 9.8 miles that covers more of the AT, but that route involves a car spot. To try it, you would park a car on CT 41 (just north of the junction with CT 44) and then proceed in the other vehicle to the parking area described at the start of the original hike. Follow our description to the summit of Bear Mountain and descend on the AT as directed. When you reach the Undermountain Trail junction, do not turn. Instead continue south on the AT. You'll pass the Brassie Brook Lean-to, the Ball Brook group campsite, and the Riga Lean-to. The AT then climbs Lion's Head (1,734 feet) and ascends down to where you parked your first car.

The best map for this area (besides the one we provide) can be found in the 20th edition of the Connecticut Walk Book published by the Connecticut Forest and Parks Association.

# 38

# Westwoods

| | |
|---|---|
| **LOCATION**: Guilford | |
| **DISTANCE**: 6.5 miles | |
| **VERTICAL RISE**: 700 feet | |
| **TIME**: 4 hours | |
| **RATING**: B | |
| **MAP**: USGS 7.5-minute Guilford | |

You are going to want to explore every nook and cranny of this magical woodland in Guilford. Westwoods contains 39 miles of trails with a wide diversity of natural formations. You can find cave structures, waterfalls, salt and fresh water marshes, an inland tidal lake, carved rock sculptures, and evocative rock formations. As you hike the labyrinth of trails, gulls wheel overhead. Because it is so near to Connecticut's overdeveloped coast, Westwoods is especially prized. The 1,200-acre preserve consists of state forest and Guilford Land Conservation Trust (GLCT) land. All trails are beautifully maintained by the Westwoods Trails Committee of GLCT, a volunteer-run nonprofit that has been purchasing conservation land in Guilford since 1965. To learn more about their work, and to support the organization's efforts, please visit their website (guilfordlandtrust .org).

This hike is best in the summer, fall, or winter. Be warned that spring is mud season at Westwoods, and the paths can get quite messy. This hike can be especially beautiful in the winter—the woods are so peaceful that time of year. However, be aware that ice can accumulate on these rocky trails, and take care when hiking in the colder months.

## GETTING THERE

From the junction of CT 77 and CT 146 in Guilford, follow CT 146 west to Sam Hill Road on your right. Parking for the Westwoods Trail entrance is at this corner on your right. The white-circle trail starts here.

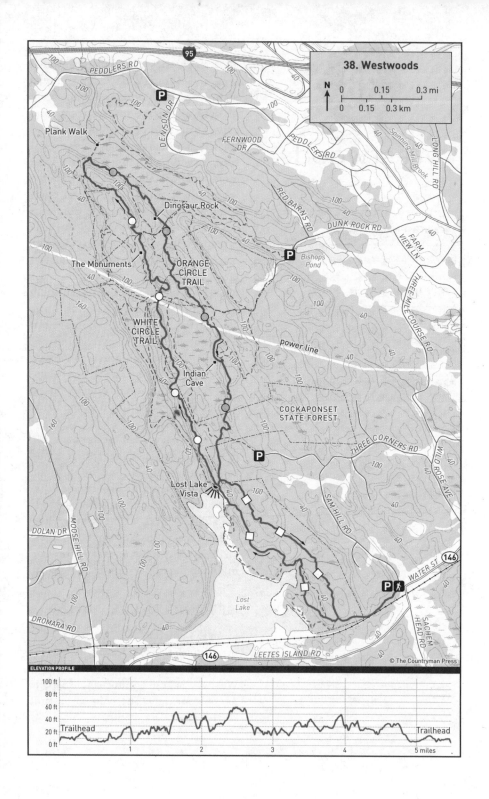

ELEVATION PROFILE

## THE HIKE

Westwoods, like Sleeping Giant (hike #35), has an extensive trail system. The hike described here is a lovely loop that covers many points of interest. In particular, you get to visit Lost Lake and explore the many rock outcroppings found at Westwoods. You'll follow the white-circle out and then return on the yellow-circle. The trails are blazed with paint and also in well-traveled areas with circular discs nailed to trees. If you see a colored X marking a tree, oftentimes with an arrow in the same color, that is a connector trail from where you are to the trail in that color. It is very helpful to have a color-coded map when you do this hike so you can see exactly where you are.

Follow the white-circle-blazed trail west from the parking lot along an old woods road paralleling the railroad tracks. Soon after the tracks, you'll see a vernal pond on your right, an important ecosystem for amphibians and insects in Connecticut's woodlands. You'll pass a number of trail junctions with the white square trail in this first part of the hike; in general, follow the white circle trail. You'll walk past an old quarry bearing the drill marks where feather wedges split the rocks. You'll soon head north away from the tracks and rise into a dry, thin-soiled area covered with old mountain laurel and hardwood. The woods you'll be passing through used to have multiple hemlock trees, which since the 1980s have been decimated by the woolly adelgid. You'll see many downed trees (both naturally fallen and some cut down) with succession growth filling in with the increased sunlight. The trail also flirts with a multitude of

DINOSAUR ROCK

SPLIT ROCK

Soon you'll climb over an abandoned quarry up a series of rock outcropping and come to an open ledge, dubbed Lost Lake Vista. You'll have a good view south over Lost Lake, a tidal marsh-turned-brackish lake created when the railroad builders passed through.

Continue on the white-circle-blazed trail as you leave the vista. Over the next mile, you'll pass a number of trail intersections with the white-square-blazed trail and some connector trails. Keep a watchful eye out for the white circles as you hike. The trail will pass a power line, and soon an intersection with the red-triangle and the blue-rectangle trails. Over the next stretch, there are numerous rock outcroppings and giant mounds that the white-circle trail takes you over. This section of the preserve is called The Monuments. If you find the various climbs daunting, bypass them by taking the white-square trail. The white-circle blazes over the outcroppings can be a little tricky to follow in this section. The white-circle and the white-square meet up after this rocky section. Staying on the white-circle-blazed trail, you'll then cross the green-rectangle-blazed trail. Eventually, you will reach the intersection with the yellow-circle, orange-circle, and white-circle trails. This is the northern-most (and roughly half-way) point of the hike. You'll return back to your car via the orange-circle-blazed trail.

Your return route on the orange-circle trail soon brings you to Dinosaur Rock. Nature carved this clever formation, and humans applied paint to visualize the dinosaur's face. The orange-circle blazes lead you along the top of more rock ledges. At times, you'll notice the trail forks and both options will display the orange-circles. These forks provide alternate paths

rocks, ledges, and glacially rounded outcroppings; these were laid out with much thought and care. The terrain that made Westwoods a farmer's wasteland has given birth to a hiker's wonderland.

About 0.6 mile into the hike, you'll see a split boulder with a cedar tree growing out of it. There are numerous, interesting rock formations such as this throughout this hike. The trail will also be bordered by mountain laurel and sweet pepperbush (summer-sweet, clethra alnifolia). Enjoy the pink blooms of the former in June and the highly fragrant white blooms of the latter from July through September.

LOST LAKE

through especially difficult areas; one of the fork's choices will clearly bypass a tricky route through rock outcroppings and rejoin the original trail soon after. Over the next 0.5 mile, you'll often climb in and out of nooks and crannies and pass between boulders that create eerie narrows. The many caves and rock formations of this section keep the hike interesting.

The next intersection you will pass is the green-rectangle-blazed trail. Remember that you will be following the orange-circle-blazes for the remainder of the hike. The route continues through a hiker's wonderland of rocky outcroppings and mounds. You will also see a forest in transition. Before their demise, the hemlock's combination of dense shade and tannin-rich needles nearly excluded understory shrubs. Now the underbrush is filled with felled hemlocks—some naturally fallen and

some taken down by chainsaw—and a healthy forest succession is taking place. Note the numerous white pine seedlings lining the trail and young hardwood trees competing for the newly available sunlight. Overall, the GLCT has done a good job managing the decline of the hemlocks in this preserve.

You'll then pass the blue-rectangle-blazed trail. Soon the orange-circle trail will parallel and then pass a power line. Keep an eye out for the nearby rock ridge: go up to it and peer into the cave at its base (Indian Cave). The next section of the orange-circle-blazed trail can be somewhat poorly marked with an uncomfortable distance between blazes (although the path is well worn). The trail next climbs over a large rock ridge before descending back down. You'll pass marshland on your right and see the red rectangle trail come in on your left. You'll cross the red-triangle-blazed trail and soon see something of a clearing of trees on your right. This is Lost Lake again. The orange-circle trail does not go right up to the water, but you will see a very short connector trail on your right that will bring you out to the Lost Lake Vista. Take this side trip to enjoy the view once again before returning to your car.

Head back to the orange trail connector, and turn right onto the orange-circle-blazed trail. At this point on the trail, you'll start to notice the ubiquitous stone walls found in Connecticut's woodlands. There is certainly no shortage of stones in this preserve! Interestingly, it appears that a farmer took advantage of the small rock ridges on their property to incorporate their stone walls into the natural structures of the land. This clever stone wall will parallel the trail for most of the route back to your car. You'll encounter a seasonal stream crossing (usually dry except in the spring) and turn left onto the white-circle-blazed trail. You'll once again parallel the train tracks—you may even see a train whoosh by. Soon you'll reach the parking lot where you left your car.

## OTHER HIKING OPTIONS

There are numerous other hiking options in Westwoods offered on the GLCT website; they describe 14 different loops from 1.25 to 3 miles in length.

**Short & Sweet:** Beginning at the same starting point, follow the white-circle trail to the Lost Lake overlook. After enjoying the overlook return back to your car via the white-square trail. This loop is about 2 miles in length.

**Alternative Starting Point:** You can begin your hike on the Peddler's Road entrance for a slightly shorter loop that follows the white-circle trail along a quarter-mile-long Plank Walk (over a boardwalk through a large marsh with a small stream flowing through it). After you walk the plank, you'll turn left on the orange-circle trail and follow it to Lost Lake. Take some time to enjoy the vista, then you will return along the white-circle trail. This is similar to the loop in our guide, but you'll be doing the second half first from the northern ends.

Maps of the many trails in Westwoods may be obtained at the following locations in Guilford:

- Bishops Orchards—1355 Boston Post Road, opposite Dunk Rock Road
- Community Center—32 Church Street, North of Town Green
- Breakwater Books—81 Whitfield Street, on Town Green
- Page Hardware—9 Boston Street, on Town Green
- Town Clerk, Town Hall—31 Park Street, on Town Green

Or you can print a map from the Guilford Land Conservation (GLCT) Trust website (guilfordlandtrust.org).

# 39

# Natchaug State Forest

**LOCATION**: Eastford

**DISTANCE**: 6.6 miles

**VERTICAL RISE**: 300 feet

**TIME**: 4 hours

**RATING**: C/D

**MAP**: USGS 7.5-minute Hampton

One of the state's most famous civil war soldiers is honored along the Natchaug trail in the wilds of eastern Connecticut. General Nathaniel Lyon was the first Union general to die in the Civil War. In the stifling heat of a Missouri summer morning, at the Battle of Wilson's Creek, the general's last words were: "Come on my brave boys, I will lead you! Forward!"—before falling from his horse, struck down by a bullet to the heart. Part of the Natchaug Trail runs from a large chimney marking the site of his home to a small cemetery with his grave guarded by partially buried cannons along the perimeter of his family lot. As you stand in the cemetery imagine that over 10,000 people attended his funeral, where the governors of both Connecticut and Rhode Island served as pallbearers. The general's death inspired a swell of intense patriotism in Connecticut, resulting in many volunteers rallying to support the Union.

Our hike today is along the Natchaug Trail through the Natchaug State Forest. The Natchaug Trail is part of the blue trail hiking system in Connecticut and is 19.5 miles in total length, traveling through two state forests and the Nathaniel Lyons Memorial Park. Natchaug comes from a Native American Nipmuc word meaning "land between the rivers," referring to the Still and Bigelow Rivers which join to form the Natchaug River. The park is popular for hiking, trout fishing, and picnicking. Backpackers may obtain camping permits.

## GETTING THERE

From the junction of CT 198 (Chaplin Road) and US 44 in Phoenixville (part of Eastford), drive south on CT 198 for a half-mile. Turn sharply left onto General

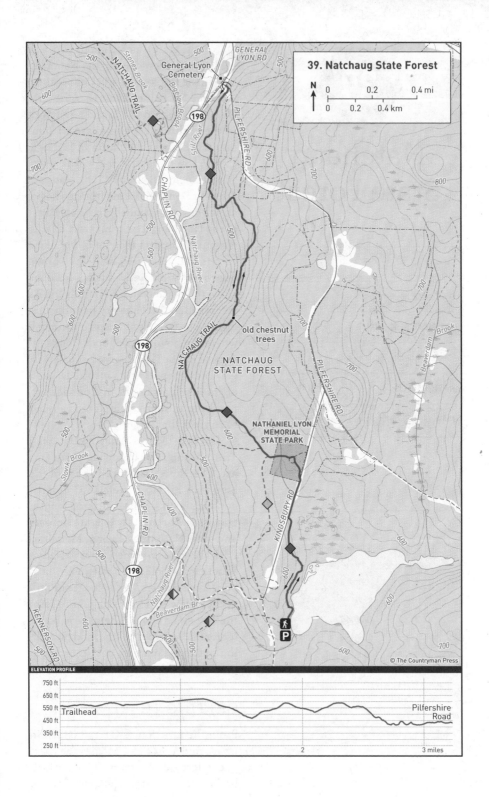

### 39. Natchaug State Forest

N
0        0.2        0.4 mi
0    0.2    0.4 km

General Lyon
Cemetery

GENERAL
LYON RD

PILFERSHIRE RD

NATCHAUG TRAIL

Stones Brook

Bigelow Brook

Still River

198

CHAPLIN RD

Natchaug River

old chestnut
trees

NATCHAUG
STATE FOREST

Slow's Brook

Beaverdam Brook

PILFERSHIRE RD

NATHANIEL LYON
MEMORIAL
STATE PARK

KINGSBURY RD

198

Natchaug River

Beaverdam Br

KENNERSON RD

P

© The Countryman Press

**ELEVATION PROFILE**

750 ft
650 ft
550 ft
450 ft
350 ft
250 ft

Trailhead

Pilfershire
Road

1                    2                    3 miles

BEAVERDAM MARSH

Lyon Road; in a tenth of a mile, turn right onto Pilfershire Road (shown on some maps as Pilshire Road), and then turn right again in 1.7 miles onto Kingsbury Road where there is a sign for the state forest unit headquarters. In about three-quarters of a mile, this road becomes dirt. In another 0.2 mile, you'll turn left on a gravel road to the Beaverdam Wildlife Management Area (there is a sign that says BEAVERDAM MARSH). You'll see blue-blazed trees on the side of this road. There is a sizable parking lot at the end of this road, which you'll reach shortly.

## THE HIKE

Today's hike follows the blue-blazed Natchaug Trail along a pond, through a historic park, and then alongside a river to the northern terminus of route, where there is an old cemetery for you to rest and explore. Then the hike has you retrace your steps back to the car with a slight detour at the end to a brook (noted in *Other Hiking Options*). The entire route follows the blue-blazed Natchaug Trail.

Facing the pond, the hike starts with you bearing left out of the parking lot to follow the Natchaug Trail. But first explore the earthen dam backing up the pond to your right. A stone-and-concrete apron accommodates the pond's spring overflow, but a vertical corrugated pipe, which also acts as a debris screen, usually handles the summertime water flow. The croak-jump-splash of a multitude of frogs here heralds your approach to the water's edge. In the pond, near the far shore, is a brush, stick, and mud beaver lodge. You may see beaver cuttings along the start of the trail. The pond's surface is almost completely covered in summer with floating and emergent

STILL RIVER

vegetation, especially the rather dull, yellow-blossomed bullhead lily and the exotic white-flowered water lily. Tall, emergent purple spires of pickerelweed line the shallow shoreline.

Return to the blue-blazed trail that parallels the pond. Several highbush blueberry shrubs tempt you to dally, and the summer perfume of the pepperbush lightens your way. In late summer, the woodland birds are quiet; they anticipate the coming of fall sooner than we do.

After walking along a lovely trail dotted with small glacial boulders and through woods populated by maple and oak (mostly seedlings), the trail veers away from the pond, and in about 0.6 mile from the start you reach Kingsbury Road.

The trail crosses the road and enters the woods. After about 0.2 mile more, you will enter Nathaniel Lyon Memorial Park. Nathaniel Lyon was born in nearby Eastford, Connecticut, and was mourned by his community as the first Union general to die in the Civil War (at the battle of Wilson's Creek in Missouri). The park features picnic tables, outhouses, a water pump, and a great stone fireplace. Just past the fireplace, bear left down an old tote road. Soon the trail veers right, and on your left you'll see a lean-to with a picnic table for backpackers hiking this trail. As you continue along the blue-blazed trail, you'll wander through mixed hardwood forest, pass occasional stone walls, and finally invade the stillness of a hemlock grove. After about 1.5 miles from the start, you'll see the blue- and yellow-blazed trail on your left. Continue on the blue-blazed trail.

Earlier editions of this book highlighted the last standing trunks of old chestnut trees, killed almost a century earlier by the blight that destroyed all of the chestnuts in the forests of our country. In 1.9 miles you'll see all that remains of one of these giants—the large rotting stump of a tree once more than 15 feet in circumference, with its seemingly indestructible wood now broken down and returned to the forest. Soon this last vestige of one of the natural wonders of eastern Connecticut will no longer be recognizable for the giant it once was.

GREAT STONE FIREPLACE AT NATHANIEL LYON MEMORIAL PARK

About a quarter-mile further along the trail and about 50 feet into the woods, you'll see a smaller chestnut tree trunk still standing. Identification of dead chestnuts depends upon an unusual dissolution sequence: Most dead trees rot from the outside in—the chestnut rots from the inside out. The hard, intact surface hides a rotting interior. Even in death, you can witness the chestnut's extreme durability that made it highly sought after for beams and lumber.

At 2.3 miles, you'll come to a group of circular piles of stones, many perched on large rocks embedded in the ground. In the days of small hand-tool harvesters like scythes, piling stones in small piles was an efficient method of clearing fields, quicker than building a wall; with today's straight-line mowing machines a field with small piles of stones throughout would be unacceptable. Of course, running a mowing machine on these rocky hillsides would be a feat in itself.

In about 2.6 miles, turn left down a rutted road. Follow along the edge of a hemlock grove, which offers a welcome break from cold, northern winds on the hillside. Soon turn right into the woods, and bear right again at a wooded, grassy remnant of a field dotted with eastern red cedars (many of them now dead). Carefully follow the blue blazes through these reforested fields.

Dropping steeply down a bank through a mature hemlock grove where the ravages of the woolly adelgid can be seen, you'll soon reach the Still River and follow it upstream. (This trout stream is a tributary of the Natchaug River.) In the next half-mile, you alternately pass through typical woodland and grassy woods.

After 3.3 miles, you'll reach Pilfershire Road at a bridge. If you cross the road, you will come to the General Lyon Cemetery. This small, hillside cemetery contains the grave of General Lyon as well as many other soldiers killed in the civil war. The general's grave is clearly recognizable by the cannons positioned around the perimeter of his family lot.

Retrace your steps following the blue Natchaug Trail down along the Still River and then up the steady incline. Be careful to turn right off the rutted tote road as you climb upward about three-quarters of a mile along. It is an easy turn to miss as you walk this steady rise with your head down. Enjoy a short rest at the memorial park you saw earlier, arriving full circle having now seen both General Lyon's gravesite and his birthplace. In a short distance, the trail crosses the road and veers down to the pond. You will parallel the pond until you reach the parking lot and your car.

## OTHER HIKING OPTIONS

**Additional Resources:** A state park trail map can be found at www.ct.gov /deep/natchaug.

**Extending Your Hike:** For a short side trip (0.4 mile in total) take a hike down to a lovely woodland brook. Head out of the parking area along the gravel road to Kingsbury Road. Across the street, you'll see the blue blazes enter the woods. About a tenth of a mile downhill, you'll reach a bridge over Beaverdam Brook. If you cross the bridge, you can follow the trail for about another tenth of a mile, paralleling the brook and enjoying the water gently cascading over diagonal slabs of rock. When the trail veers left from the brook, turn around and retrace your steps back to the road and down the gravel drive to the parking area at Beaverdam Marsh and your car.

# Macedonia Brook State Park

| | |
|---|---|
| **LOCATION**: Kent | |
| **DISTANCE**: 6.7 miles | |
| **VERTICAL RISE**: 1,550 feet | |
| **TIME**: 4 hours | |
| **RATING**: A | |
| **MAPS**: USGS 7.5-minute Ellsworth, Amenia (NY-CT) | |

Separated by Macedonia Brook, a cluster of hills 1,000 to 1,400 feet high make up Macedonia Brook State Park. This 2,300-acre park boasts 13 miles of trails. The famed Appalachian Trail (AT) used to run through Macedonia Brook, but was relocated in the late 1980s. Now what was the AT is part of the Connecticut Blue Trail System.

The park began as a 1,500-acre gift from the White Memorial Foundation in 1918 (hike # 42). This area was once the domain of the Schaghticokes, descended from Sassacus's Pequots and dispersed after the 1637 Pequot War, the first of America's Indian Wars. During the Revolutionary War, more than 100 Schaghticoke warriors joined the American cause; serving as a signal corps, they used drums and signal fires to relay messages from Stockbridge, Massachusetts to Long Island Sound. Macedonia became a thriving community that supported the iron industry in nearby Kent. Due to excessive charcoal production to feed the blast furnaces, all the local timber had been consumed by the 1840s. Competition with the larger Pennsylvania mines closed down the local iron operation in 1865. In the 1930s, Macedonia Brook State Park, like many of Connecticut's state forests and parks, was home to a Civilian Conservation Corps company. The legacy of the CCCs work in the park continues through the beautiful forest road they constructed and which you'll use as part of your hike today.

## GETTING THERE

Macedonia Brook lies just inside Connecticut's western boundary. From the junction of CT 341 and US 7 in Kent, take CT 341 west for 1.7 miles to Macedonia Brook Road, where you'll turn right,

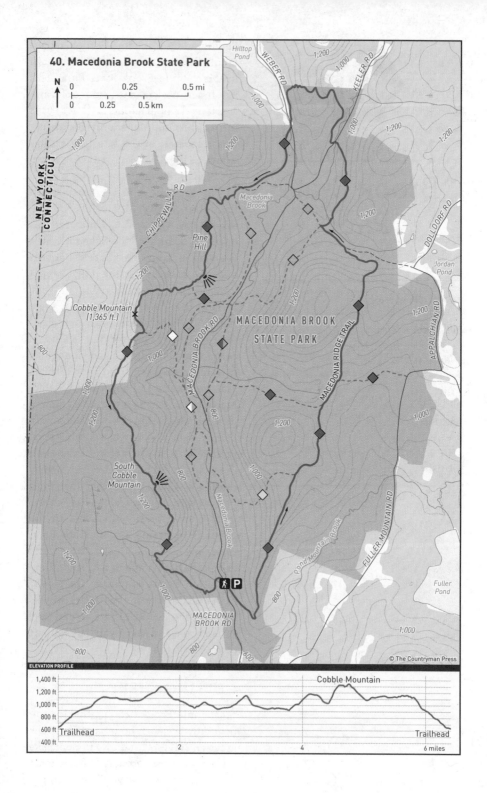

**40. Macedonia Brook State Park**

N

| 0 | 0.25 | 0.5 mi |
| 0 | 0.25 | 0.5 km |

NEW YORK
CONNECTICUT

Hilltop
Pond

WEBER RD

KEELER RD

CHIPPEWALLA RD

Macedonia
Brook

Pine
Hill

DOLLDORF RD

Jordan
Pond

Cobble Mountain
(1,365 ft.)

MACEDONIA BROOK RD

MACEDONIA BROOK
STATE PARK

MACEDONIA RIDGE TRAIL

APPALCHIAN RD

South
Cobble
Mountain

Macedonia Brook

Pond Mountain Brook

FULLER MOUNTAIN RD

Fuller
Pond

P

MACEDONIA
BROOK RD

© The Countryman Press

**ELEVATION PROFILE**

| | | Cobble Mountain | |
| 1,400 ft | | | |
| 1,200 ft | | | |
| 1,000 ft | | | |
| 800 ft | | | |
| 600 ft Trailhead | | | Trailhead |
| 400 ft | 2 | 4 | 6 miles |

following a park sign. You'll see Fuller Mountain Road forking right 0.8 mile from CT 341; stay on Macedonia Brook Road. After another 0.6 mile, you'll have passed through the park entrance and will reach the blue-blazed Macedonia Ridge Trail at a bridge over the brook. Park here to begin your hike; there are spaces for cars on both sides of the bridge.

## THE HIKE

Today's route is a rugged 6.7-mile loop that circles around the Macedonia Brook Valley, going over and between many of the hills in the park. You'll be following the main trail, which is blazed in blue throughout. The first two-thirds of this lovely woodland trail have steady but moderate ups and down; the last third of the hike, however, has you traversing the Cobble Mountain range with very strenuous terrain and some intense scrambling over rock faces and ledges. We've included an alternative ending to the hike (see *Other Hiking Options*) so that you can still enjoy this beautiful woodland park without the intensity of the last stretch of the trail.

Enter the woods, following the blue blazes, on the east side of the valley (to your right as you drive in from CT 341). Ascend the woody hillside through a field of scattered glacial erratics. The trail turns sharply left and climbs the ridge through open oak forest. On an early-morning hike in July, a large hawk flew out of a tree ahead on the ridge.

After 0.9 mile, you follow the blue-blazed trail as it bends to the right. You'll walk on the level through this

HIKING ALONG THE OLD CCC FOREST ROAD

peaks. On your left, you'll see a large ruin of stones arranged in a circular layout, possibly an old foundation or pit for making charcoal. In spring along this trail, the greenish-yellow flowers of the many striped maples here lend a faint but delightful fragrance to the woods. The flower clusters dangle from the branches like exotic earrings.

From the col, the ridge trail drops steeply down to a deeply worn, old town road (the former AT); turn left to follow it downhill. At a simple gate, the trail turns right. Just ahead of the gate is a junction with the orange trail on your left and a large clearing straight ahead. The clearing is one of the many camping spots in the park.

Turn right off the woods road following the blue-blazes. Cross a stream before climbing over a rise. Then descend and turn left to cross over a bridge on dirt Keeler Road. Turn right after crossing the bridge, and follow Macedonia Brook before curving left to ascend a hill near the northern boundary of the park. We found a box turtle here on one of our recent hikes. The little six-inch-long specimen was probably more than 60 years old! Adult turtles have relatively few enemies except cars and can live to ripe old ages of more than 100 years.

A 30-FOOT SLOPING ROCK FACE ON COBBLE MOUNTAIN.

open forest and then drop down the east side of a hill, ultimately joining a green-blazed trail that comes in at your left from the park road. The blue- and green-blazed trails run together briefly, passing through openings in a couple of old stone walls. At the beginning of the next rise, bear left onto the blue-blazed ridge trail where the green-blazed trail continues down the road and out to Fuller Mountain Road.

Your trail climbs easily and steadily up and over a col between two unnamed

Pass over the crest of the ridge and drop steeply through an old hemlock stand using switchbacks. Turn left onto the gravel surface of Weber Road. Then, at a park sign, turn right to follow blue blazes onto the gated old CCC forest road. Follow the shaded, grass-covered road through a gated crossing of the partially paved Chippewalla Road. Continue on CCC forest road by following the blue blazes, and then turn right off the road to follow a footpath steeply up Pine Hill. Beneath an ash tree on

ONE OF MANY STONE WALLS FOUND AT MACEDONIA BROOK

the right we once found two morels. Acclaimed as Connecticut's best-tasting local wild mushroom, this hollow, light-brown fungus with its exterior raised latticework is the elusive treasure of the dedicated mycologist. Always make a positive identification with a mushroom expert before nibbling!

At the top of the grade, the trail turns left into the woods, climbing steadily and fairly steeply. Threading through the laurel undergrowth, the grade eases as you near the top of Pine Hill. As on most Connecticut hills, the steepest slope on Pine Hill is in the middle of the grade. The fact that there are no pines on Pine Hill, which is now covered with oak, birch, and hop hornbeam, is evidence of the changing nature of forests. On a recent trek up this hill in mid-August, we sighted numerous frogs and toads and wondered if perhaps it should be called Amphibian Hill!

From the ledges on Pine Hill's far side, you have an excellent view down the Macedonia Brook Valley. Close by, from right to left, are Cobble Mountain, South Cobble Mountain (both of which you climb on this hike), and Chase Mountain. In the center distance are Mounts Algo and Schaghticoke.

Follow the trail down over steep ledges, passing the green-blazed Pine Hill Trail to your left just before reaching the col. Continue uphill, passing through boulders before reaching the ledges above. It is very important to have footwear with good traction on this stretch. Scramble over a boulder and climb a challenging eight-foot-high ledge with minimal handholds. This route is not recommended when wet or icy. Just above that ledge, follow the blue-blazed trail up a 30-foot sloping rock face. You'll have to either find a way around or use a crack for traction. This is definitely not recommended in adverse conditions. If you're uneasy with these ledges, see *Other Hiking Options* for a way to bypass them while still having an enjoyable loop through this park. Your ascent moderates but still climbs steadily as you pass by several large beds of wild oats with their drooping, bell-shaped flowers.

You then reach the top of Cobble Mountain, a rock-covered summit whose views have been obscured somewhat by the trees. Continue along the rocky summit ledges, and you'll see white blazes start to be paired with your blue blazes. At this point, you do have an excellent view to the west. The ridge across the valley is in New York, and beyond it are the Catskills.

Continue on the blue- and white-blazed trail a little further along the ridge until the white-blazed Cobble Mountain Trail descends on your left. Stay on the blue-blazed ridge trail, and drop steeply down the ledges into the col before rising up the side of South Cobble Mountain. The trail passes to the left of the summit on a wooded trail lined with mountain laurel and huckleberry.

As you circle around the summit, the trail goes along a ridge and views open up to your left across the valley over to the hills we hiked earlier in the day. You'll then descend steeply along a route with rock ledges (a section not as challenging as our earlier ascent but still rugged). In midsummer, our trek was punctuated by the bright-yellow blooms of woodland sunflower and goldenrod. As the climb down moderates, the blue trail veers left, paralleling and then crossing a multi-branched stream.

Leaving the stream you'll continue to climb steadily downhill along the side of the mountain. You'll follow a slight switchback section to lessen the steepness until the trail heads straight down and veers left at the bottom to cross a footbridge. Just ahead you'll see the privy, and the park road where you left your car.

## OTHER HIKING OPTIONS

**Additional Resources:** A state park trail map can be found at www.ct.gov /deep/macedoniabrook.

**Shortening the Hike:** If you wish to avoid the strenuous final third of this hike but still enjoy a woodland loop around this park, you'll want to take the orange trail left off the CCC forest road just after Chippewalla Road. You'll follow the orange trail through the valley, paralleling the park road. After a half-mile, you'll pass the green trail on your right. Another 0.4 mile later, you'll see the white-blazed Cobble Mountain Trail on your right. Here the orange trail is double-blazed with the white. After 0.2 mile, the trail switches to only orange, before reaching the park road in another 0.3 mile. Turn right to head back to your car, which you'll find about a half-mile down the park road.

# Peoples State Forest

| |
|---|
| **LOCATION**: Barkhamsted |
| **DISTANCE**: 7 miles |
| **VERTICAL RISE**: 1,000 feet |
| **TIME**: 4 hours |
| **RATING**: B/C |
| **MAPS**: USGS 7.5-minute Winsted, New Hartford |

Established in 1924 through the efforts of the Connecticut Forest and Park Association, Peoples State Forest is located in the Pleasant Valley section of Barkhamsted and offers four-season fun for the outdoor enthusiast. The west branch of the Farmington River, designated as a Wild and Scenic River by the National Park Service, runs through the western portion of the forest and offers the possibility for many recreational activities including trout fishing, canoeing, kayaking, and tubing. There are over 11 miles of hiking trails, snowmobile trails, and area for cross-country skiing. The forest boasts some beautiful stands of 200-year-old managed pines throughout the park. There is also camping at nearby American Legion State Forest.

Peoples State Forest provides an example of an excellent trail system benefiting from a combination of volunteers and state funding. The trails are well blazed with large, wooden signs at each trailhead. Trails are named after individuals who had key roles in establishing the park. Not only are the trails in good shape, but the Stone Nature Museum described in *Other Hiking Options* has been restored as well, and provides displays and programs for summer visitors.

## GETTING THERE

From the junction of CT 318 and US 44 east of Winsted, proceed east on CT 318 across the Farmington River, and go across the steel bridge. Take the first (immediate) left onto East River Road. In 0.8 mile by the PEOPLES FOREST sign, fork right onto the paved, state-forest Greenwoods Road. You have missed your turn if you come to a picnic area on your left. Then, in 0.2 mile, turn left up a short gravel road to a parking lot next to the

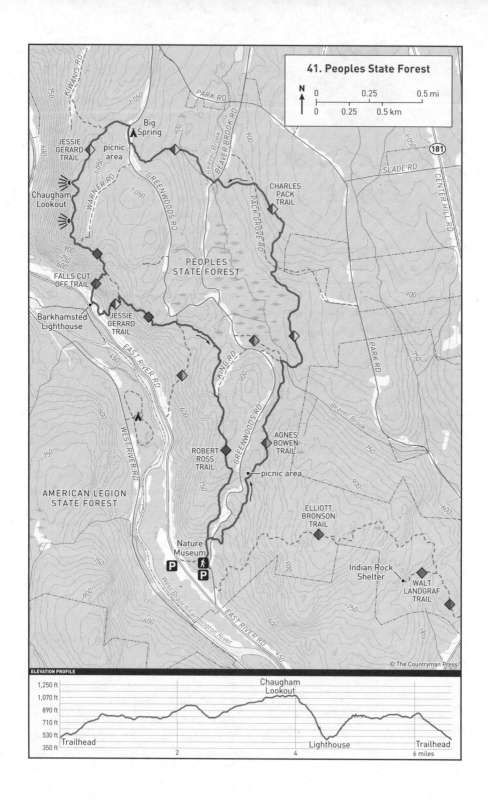

41. Peoples State Forest

N

| 0 | | 0.25 | | 0.5 mi |
| 0 | 0.25 | | 0.5 km | |

KIWANIS RD

PARK RD

Big Spring

JESSIE GERARD TRAIL

picnic area

WARNER RD

GREENWOODS RD

Chaugham Lookout

FALLS CUT OFF TRAIL

Barkhamsted Lighthouse

JESSIE GERARD TRAIL

EAST RIVER RD

WEST RIVER RD

AMERICAN LEGION STATE FOREST

Beaver Brook

BEAVER BROOK RD

CHARLES PACK TRAIL

PACK GROVE RD

PEOPLES STATE FOREST

181

SLADE RD

CENTER HILL RD

KING RD

GREENWOODS RD

ROBERT ROSS TRAIL

AGNES BOWEN TRAIL

picnic area

PARK RD

Beaver Brook

ELLIOTT BRONSON TRAIL

Nature Museum

P

P

West Branch Farmington River

EAST RIVER RD

Indian Rock Shelter

WALT LANDGRAF TRAIL

© The Countryman Press

ELEVATION PROFILE

Chaugham Lookout

1,250 ft
1,070 ft
890 ft
710 ft
530 ft
350 ft

Trailhead

Lighthouse

Trailhead

2

4

6 miles

VIEW FROM CHAUGHAM LOOKOUT

stone-sided nature museum. This is a legacy of the Civilian Conservation Corps' labors in the 1930s. Try to park efficiently so others visiting the museum can park here too. When the forest is busy, or in winter (when Greenwoods Road is not maintained), it is recommended that hikers park on East River Road at Matthies Grove and take the blue-blazed Ross Trail directly across the road from the parking lot uphill to the museum.

## THE HIKE

Today's route is a 7-mile loop that follows the blue/orange-blazed Agnes Bowen Trail, the blue- and yellow-blazed Charles Pack Trail, the blue- and yellow-blazed Jesse Girard Trail and the blue-blazed Robert Ross Trail. All the trail heads are marked with large brown wooden signs and have weather-protected trail maps on display.

The Agnes Bowen Trail, named for the person who suggested the original site of Peoples State Forest and marked by blue blazes with orange dots, starts into the woods across the parking lot from the museum. Follow this path through a stand of huge white pines. We found porcupine tracks in the snow near the museum on a recent December visit. Porkies are notable for their waddling gait and are active during warmer stretches of the winter.

Shortly the blue-blazed Robert Ross Trail breaks off to your left; stay on the orange-on-blue-blazed Agnes Bowen Trail as it curves downhill to the tar forest road. Turn right and follow the road for a few yards, then go left into the woods. Almost immediately, you'll cross a small stream, which the now rocky trail follows uphill to your left. In a half-mile the trail passes through a roadside picnic area. The trail crosses a muddy brook. After another two-thirds of a mile, you will intersect the Charles L. Pack Trail (yellow dots on blue blazes). Charles L. Pack was the president of the American Tree Association and an early supporter of public forests. Among other things, he helped save a beech-tree grove along the now-appropriately named Pack Grove Road.

Turn right to follow this yellow-dot-on-blue-blazed Charles Pack Trail. In a few yards you'll reach Beaver Brook, which you cross on a footbridge (use caution—it can be slick when wet) built by the Youth Conservation Corps in 1976. On your right you can see the old high-water double-cable crossing; the cable crossing was used by walking on the lower cable and holding on to the upper one for balance. Along the brook, you'll find the red cardinal flower, a really striking midsummer bloom.

After crossing the footbridge, bear

MAGNIFICANT WHITE PINES

left across the hillside, keeping Beaver Swamp on your left, and then curve to your right uphill, still following the yellow-on-blue blazes. At the top of the rise, the trail bears left. Beaver Swamp (on your left along this trail) was once a meadow, and some of the Charles Pack Trail follows the wagon path used to haul hay from these fields at the turn of the twentieth century.

You'll continue on this trail passing through a magnificent pine forest with double- and triple-trunk giants. You'll pass a large foundation to your right, all that remains of a dwelling built before 1806 and torn down in 1880.

Next you'll cross gravel Pack Grove Road. Climb among the beech trees, the original grove that Charles L. Pack helped save, and zigzag through a wet area with exposed roots along the trail. Be careful not to step on wet roots—they can be very slippery even when wearing heavy-duty hiking boots. You'll then descend to join Pack Grove Road again. Turn right onto the gravel road, and then quickly bear left to leave the road and continue downhill to Beaver Brook Road. Turn left and cross Beaver Brook again on a bridge. Turn right off the road, and reenter the woods on the stream's far side on a woods road. You'll also see orange-diamond blazes nailed onto trees, a snowmobile trail. After a short while, the orange-blazed snowmobile trail heads straight (to Kiwanis Road), and our blue- and yellow-blazed route continues to the left. Another half-mile of woods walking brings you to Greenwoods Road, where this trail ends.

Turn right to follow the pavement through Big Spring Youth Camping Area, and then turn left into the woods. Here you pick up the blue- and yellow-blazed Jesse Gerard Trail, which leads you to the escarpment along the Farmington River.

A LARGE FOUNDATION OF A DWELLING FROM THE 1800s

Jesse Gerard was a longtime director of the Connecticut Forest and Park Association who helped raise funds to purchase land for Peoples State Forest.

This trail traces an old tote road for a short distance before taking a path uphill. After passing between two huge glacial boulders a half-mile from Greenwoods Road (the Veeder boulders, named for Curtis Veeder, an inventor from Hartford who helped raise money for Peoples Forest land purchases), the trail turns right toward Chaugham Lookout. These open ledges provide an excellent view northwest across a wide, wild, wooded valley. The canoe-dotted Farmington River winds sinuously below. Chaugham was a Native American whose cabin in the valley below, lit up at night, was a familiar landmark for stage drivers heading for New Hartford. From the fact that it was a well-lit nighttime beacon, it received the name of the Barkhamsted Lighthouse; you'll be hiking along to it a bit later.

The well-worn trail continues through hemlocks along the ledge escarpment, reaching another overlook in a half-mile. Proceeding steeply downward, you'll find sweet low-bush blueberries flanking the trail over erosion-bared basalt. The blue- and yellow-blazed Jesse Gerard and blue-blazed Robert Ross Trails run together here. They split about three-quarters mile from Chaugham Lookout. A yellow-blazed trail descends down on your right. Follow this Falls Cut-Off Trail down to the Barkhamsted Lighthouse Loop Trail, a short trail through an abandoned village where James Chaugham lived with his wife Molly Barber.

You'll follow the Lighthouse Loop back up to the blue-blazed Ross Trail. Turn right and continue your steep and rocky descent. Pass over a rise, and notice a large rock ledge on your left that the trail passes by. Your path soon meets up with the Agnes Bowen Trail on your left. Here you will bear right downhill, and then take a quick left into the woods, following blue blazes to stay on the Robert Ross Trail. Robert Ross was a forester who sponsored the first Forestry Work Camp in the 1930s, which was later used as a model for the CCC.

The trail will come to Kings Road on your left; turn right, following the blue blazes. Continue downhill on the

PASSING THROUGH THE VEEDER BOULDERS

blue-blazed trail to the orange-on-blue-blazed trail near the stone Nature Museum. Follow the blazes to your right back to your car.

## OTHER HIKING OPTIONS

**Additional Resources:** There are trail maps posted throughout the park at many trail junctions. A state park trail map can be found at www.ct.gov /deep/peoples.

**Nearby:** If you have time and you find it is open, visit the Peoples State Forest Nature Museum, located in a stone-faced building built by the CCC in 1935. The museum has limited weekend hours: it is recommended you double-check by calling the Peoples State Forest office 860-379-2469. The museum has displays on native plants and animals as well as on area pioneers, Native Americans, logging, quarrying, and the CCC.

**A Shorter Hiking Option:** You can hike the Elliot Bronson Trail, a red- and blue-blazed trail that starts just below the nature museum. This trail is a total of 2.2 miles, going over a forested summit and then down to the intersection with the Walt Landgraf Trail. This half-mile spur trail is worth the extra distance as it brings you to an old soapstone quarry used by Native Americans as long as 4,000 years ago. You'll pass many boulders on the way, and will then reach the cliffs of the former quarry. This long, shallow cave was where the Indians once quarried the green soapstone to be carved into cooking vessels, smoke pipes, ornaments, and bowls. You can then retrace your steps back to the car. Alternatively, a shorter option of this Elliott Bronson/Walt Landgraf route would have you start on the park road off of CT 181 (east of East River Road).

# 42

# White Memorial Foundation

| | |
|---|---|
| **LOCATION**: Litchfield | |
| **DISTANCE**: 7 miles | |
| **VERTICAL RISE**: 100 feet | |
| **TIME**: 3.5 hours | |
| **RATING**: D | |
| **MAP**: USGS 7.5-minute Litchfield | |

The White Memorial Foundation and Conservation Center in Litchfield was established in 1913 by Alain and May White in order to preserve for generations to come the countryside they so loved. Located in the northwestern Connecticut foothills of the Berkshire Mountains, this wildlife sanctuary welcomes individuals, families, and groups to its wide range of facilities for outdoor study and recreation. Within its 4,000 acres of fields, waters, and woodlands, you'll find more than 35 miles of crisscrossing trails, a Nature Museum, campgrounds, boating facilities, and special areas for large outdoor educational and recreational gatherings.

The foundation's property contains a maze of hiking trails, including the blue-blazed Mattatuck Trail, part of Connecticut's blue trail system (6.2 miles of this nearly 35-mile-long trail are within the property). Since the numerous trails through the foundation's land twist, turn, and cross each other with bewildering abandon, a map is a good investment. This can be purchased at the bookstore within the Nature Museum Building. The Nature Museum exhibits provide a rewarding half-hour look over the area's interesting wildlife, geology, history, and Native American artifact (there is a fee to enter).

Over 200 acres of the White Memorial Foundation have been set aside in four untouched natural preserves. These areas provide bases against which environmental changes on adjacent tracts can be judged. The hike described here explores only a small part of this special sanctuary.

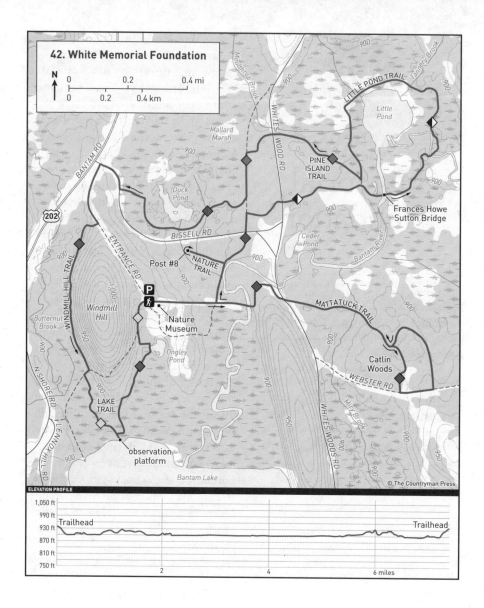

## 42. White Memorial Foundation

N

0        0.2              0.4 mi
0    0.2      0.4 km

Mallard Marsh

Duck Pond

BANTAM RD.

202

ENTRANCE RD.

WINDMILL HILL TRAIL

Post #8

NATURE TRAIL

P

Windmill Hill

Nature Museum

Ongley Pond

Butternut Brook

N SHORE RD.

LENNOXHILL RD.

LAKE TRAIL

observation platform

Bantam Lake

BISSELL RD.

Ceder Pond

Moulthrop Brook

WHITES WOOD RD.

LITTLE POND TRAIL

Tansey Brook

Little Pond

PINE ISLAND TRAIL

Frances Howe Sutton Bridge

Bantam River

MATTATUCK TRAIL

Catlin Woods

WEBSTER RD.

WHITES WOODS RD.

Miry Brook

© The Countryman Press

**ELEVATION PROFILE**

1,050 ft
990 ft
930 ft — Trailhead                                    Trailhead
870 ft
810 ft
750 ft
        2            4            6 miles

## GETTING THERE

Follow US 202 west 2.2 miles past its junction with CT 118 in Litchfield, and turn left by the signs for White Memorial Foundation. The park road then is a quick right after your turn. The entrance road proceeds for a half-mile to a parking area just beyond the carriage house to your right.

## THE HIKE

Today's walk involves a number of trails near the main area of the sanctuary. You'll loop through Catlin Woods (a forest untouched for three centuries) via the Mattatuck Trail, then walk up to Little Pond with a boardwalk trail more than 1 mile long. Then you'll trek through a woodland to Duck Pond and

BANTAM RIVER LEADING TO LITTLE POND

over to Bantam Lake with its historic ice house trail and lake observation tower before returning to the main parking area via Ongley Pond.

The hike begins by following the gravel road east from the parking area toward the information kiosk and past the bookstore and Nature Museum. As recommended, consider stopping in and purchasing a map. Also useful are the self-guided interpretive trail and "Ice-cutting at Bantam Lake" brochures.

Continue past the museum on the road. Large sugar maple, white oak, and white ash grace the road to your left. As you walk along, you'll see a post with the number 12 on it from the interpretive trail. This stop highlights a magnificent, old-growth white pine tree. About 20 feet above you, the left trunk hosts a wild honeybee colony. On a warm August day, we watched worker bees fly in and out of the small holes safely above us in the trunk.

Continue on the gravel road when you reach a gated entrance flanked by two large cement-and-stone posts. Follow this road through the entrance, now the blue-blazed Mattatuck Trail, east to the edge of the Bantam River, and then cross the slow-moving river over an old truss bridge. You may see kayaks in the water here and perhaps a fisherman or two on the bridge. Darting dragonflies skim over the water catching small insects like mosquitoes for lunch—never hurt a dragonfly!

On the other side of the bridge the Mattatuck turns left. Continue following this blue-blazed trail. You'll cross a private driveway and then the busy Whites Woods Road. The trail continues through the woods on a lovely, wide forest road. You'll then cross a marshy area (part of Cranberry Swamp) and enter Catlin Woods.

Catlin Woods harbors 200-year-old hemlocks and white pines on land that was never cultivated, as indicated by the ancient pillows and cradles, or mounds and depressions, formed by the uprooting and decomposition of trees. At various points in these woods, especially at the outer edges, you'll pass large bull pines with multiple lower branches. These great white pines gained their early growth in an open field, with little or no competition for sunlight; the numerous large branches create the wood known as knotty pine.

You'll then come to Webster Road, a hard-packed, public dirt road. Turn right, and then about a tenth of a mile down the road, you'll turn right on an unblazed gated woods road. You are back in Catlin Woods; enjoy this peaceful walk on pine-cushioned forest roads.

After another tenth of a mile, you'll come to a fork; bear left. You'll soon reach another fork; go left again to return to the blue-blazed Mattatuck Trail. You'll follow this path back to the truss bridge you crossed earlier. Continue on the trail until you reach and pass through the gated entrance flanked by two large cement-and-stone posts.

Turn right and continue to follow the blue-blazed Mattatuck Trail north on a gravel road. Soon you will reach an interpretive nature trail to your left. Take a short detour down this trail, and follow it into the woods. You'll soon enter a stand of old-growth pines—trees more than 200 years old. These majestic giants tower 100 feet above the forest floor and are well worth the visit. Continue along the interpretive trail to post #9. This stop directs you to look at a few trees on the trail that bear the marks of hungry beavers. Not only do they use trees to

THE BOARDWALK TRAIL AROUND LITTLE POND

build dams and lodges, beavers also eat a nutritious inner layer of the tree trunk known as the cambium. Humans are not the only species to modify their environments—much of the landscape around you has been modified by beavers.

Continue a bit further on the interpretive trail until you reach post #8, directing you to examine a "lovely" white pine. You'll see a heart-shaped swelling on this tree, formed when the tree's cells started dividing rapidly in response to a virus, fungus, bacterium, or insect infestation.

Return to the gravel road by retracing your steps, and then turn left to continue along the Mattatuck north. Cross Bissell Road and continue north to the Little Pond Trail. Turn right to follow the black-on-white-square-blazed Little Pond Trail along another tote road. Cross the paved Whites Woods Road. You'll then hike along the edge of a clearing to the swampy edge of Little Pond, and bear right onto the mostly boardwalk-covered loop trail, which soon passes through phragmites and crosses the arched Frances Howe Sutton Bridge. Follow the boardwalk around the pond. A late August visit featured the bright-red berries of honeysuckles along the way, as well as the occasional, tasty blackberry.

The boardwalk is an elevated, wooden walkway that gives you a fascinating look at one of nature's most interesting but least accessible areas—too wet to walk, too dry to canoe! Open year-round, the boardwalk is particularly interesting in the spring and fall during bird migrations, and in the spring and summer when the numerous wildflowers bloom. In season, you'll encounter innumerable buttonbushes, purple loosestrife, cardinal flower, meadowsweet, lily pads, pickerelweed;

in terms of annual vegetation per acre, a swamp is one of the most productive ecosystems of all. After passing around the pond, the trail veers away from the open water but continues in a marshy area with frequent boardwalk-covered portions.

You'll reach a junction with the red-triangle-blazed Pine Island Trail. Turn sharply right to follow it through hemlock woods to Whites Woods Road. This Pine Island Trail along with the Mattatuck Trail will lead you to Duck Pond, but be warned that the route does have a few turns and overlapping bits with relatively short distances between the turns (the map will help you see where you are going).

This Pine Island route begins by crossing Whites Woods Road and continuing on a woods road following the red-triangle blazes. You'll see the red-triangle-blazed trail goes right; continue to follow it. Then you'll reach another junction; turn left to stay on the red-triangle-blazed trail. Next, where the red triangles bear off the road to your right, continue straight to walk along the blue-blazed Mattatuck Trail (which is also the diamond-shaped-sign, green-square-blazed Greenway trail). Soon you'll come to an intersection where the blue-blazed trail goes right or straight. Turn right at this junction (the green blazes also go right) to head toward the pond. Follow the Mattatuck Trail west, and following the blue blazes to Duck Pond. The Mattatuck trail circles Duck Pond on its south side—not as grand as Little Pond but you'll still have a lovely view of the water. You'll next reach paved Bissell Road, where you'll turn right and walk along until you reach the entrance road for White Memorial Foundation. Turn left on this hard-packed gravel road, and walk 0.2 mile until you see a gated wood

BANTAM LAKE WITH THE REMAINS OF CONCRETE SUPPORTS FOR OLD ICE CONVEYOR SYSTEMS

road on your right. Turn onto this the woods road past the Pine-Grove I youth camping area, following green rectangle blazes on the Windmill Hill Trail.

Descend past the lean-to, and walk around the thickly wooded base of Windmill Hill along a lovely, grass-covered forest road. On a hot August day, we saw a large deer in the woods while enjoying this section of the route. The trail reaches a tote road T-junction with the yellow-blazed Lake Trail where you will turn right. You'll start to see numbered posts on this trail—this is where the Ice House Trail overlaps the Lake Trail. During the winters of 1908 through 1929, the Berkshire Ice Company cut large cakes of ice from Bantam Lake. An enormous icehouse stood along this trail (you'll see the foundation marked by white and orange posts), 36 feet high and able to hold a total of 60,000 tons of ice. You can take a short detour to follow the numbered posts using the interpretative brochure

from the bookstore to learn more about ice-making on Bantam Lake.

Soon you'll turn left, following the yellow-rectangle blazes of the Lake Trail (you'll also continue to see numbered posts). You'll take this path down to Bantam Lake, passing a narrow, old, concrete canal that was part of the ice-cutting operation of the early twentieth century. When you reach the lake, you'll come to an observation platform on the shore (notice it is built upon concrete supports from the old ice-conveyor system). White Memorial Foundation owns almost 60 percent of the property bordering the lake, including nearly all of the visible shoreline.

Leaving the platform, turn right on the yellow-rectangle-blazed Lake Trail, and bear right onto the green-rectangle-blazed Windmill Hill Trail past several large oaks. You'll come to a tree with a double-green blaze marking the end of the Windmill Hill Trail. Turn left here to take the orange-blazed Ongley

Pond Trail, which skirts the western shore of the small pond on a boardwalk-punctuated trail. When you reach the northwest corner of the pond, turn left on a grassy trail heading away from the pond. You'll notice a stone wall paralleling this trail on your right (parts are heavily covered with vegetation). At the top of a slight rise, you'll reach a crushed-stone, covered woods road; turn right. This is the yellow-rectangle-blazed Lake Trail again. As you continue along, another woods road will merge with yours as you head back toward the carriage house. Soon you'll reach the end of this hike and your car.

## OTHER HIKING OPTIONS

**Short & Sweet:** You can hike to Little Pond and boardwalk, with a total round-trip hiking distance of approximately 3.5 miles. Follow the gravel road away from the museum. Turn left just before the gated entrance flanked by the two large cement-and-stone posts and walk along the Mattatuck Trail (blue blazes) to Bissell Road. Cross Bissell Road, past the wooden gate, and follow the Mattatuck Trail for about 300 feet. Take the first trail to your right. This is the beginning of the Little Pond Trail (blazed with black inside a white square). Follow the Little Pond Trail for a sixth of a mile to the paved Whites Woods Road. Cross the road, and follow the blazes for a quarter-mile to the beginning of the boardwalk, bearing right to circle around the pond. You'll come back to an intersection with the Pine Island Trail (red triangle) and a fork with the incoming branch of the Little Pond Trail (black inside white square). Go left on the Little Pond Trail, and retrace your steps back to the museum.

**Extending Your Hike:** A small add-on is to circle around Ongley Pond after the Bantam Lake observation platform. Where you turned left, you would instead turn right around the pond. This detour doesn't add much mileage and gives you a fuller view of the pond. This path forms a loop and meets back up on the western side of the pond with the yellow-rectangle-blazed Lake Trail, where you'll turn right to finish your hike as described earlier.

**Something Completely Different:** There is a pleasant 2-mile trail (4 miles round trip) in the southwest corner of the sanctuary that climbs up Apple Hill. Park at the base of Apple Hill on East Shore Road in a lot three-quarters of a mile north of CT 109. You can reach CT 109 by going south on CT 209 from Bantam, off CT 202; then turn left on CT 109 where East Shore Road is on your left. Travel the steady incline of Apple Hill, which culminates at one of the most beautiful destinations in the sanctuary—a view overlooking Bantam Lake. With cross-country skiing opportunities in winter, unique birding opportunities in spring and summer, and a majestic panorama of leaf colors in fall, Apple Hill enthralls in every season. Climb the viewing platform during dawn, and witness the moon setting in the west and the sun rising in the east.

There are over 35 miles of trails traversing this park. You can personalize your route by shortening or adding on to this hike. Indeed, you may want to take a completely different route—look over the park map and get creative!

# 43

# Devil's Hopyard State Park

**LOCATION**: East Haddam

**DISTANCE**: 7.5 miles

**VERTICAL RISE**: 800 feet

**TIME**: 4 hours

**RATING**: C

**MAP**: USGS 7.5-minute Hamburg

Water dominates the 860 acres of Devil's Hopyard State Park, located in the Millington section of Haddam—water in the form of the rushing, turbulent Eightmile River and its tributaries, and water as the agent that shaped this rugged scenic area.

Devil's Hopyard became a state park in 1919 and is fully developed; with picnic tables, pedestal cooking grills, picnic shelters, a campground (not always operating, it depends on the state budget), and several miles of hiking trails. The origin of its colorful name is lost in a welter of fanciful stories, ranging from the simple corruption of Mr. Dibble's hopyard to tales of mist-shrouded forms seen dancing on the ledges amid spray from the falls. Early settlers also attributed the pothole formations to the supernatural. They thought the Devil passed by the falls and accidentally got his tail wet. Supposedly that made him so mad he burned holes in the stones with his hooves as he bounded away.

Today, most people come to this park for the beautiful main waterfall, Chapman Falls, which drops more than 60 feet over a series of steps in a Scotland–schist stone formation. For more than a century prior to its inclusion in the state park, this main waterfall powered a mill on the river; remains of mills and milldams such as this abound in New England. To get the full impact of these falls, you should view them from both above and below. The rocks beside the trail reveal many circular holes (called pothole formations) formed when hard, loose rock got caught in a small indentation in the ledge. The force of the flowing water caused this rock to gyrate in the cavity, eventually wearing a circular hole. After the first rock has worn away, often another one falls in to continue the erosion.

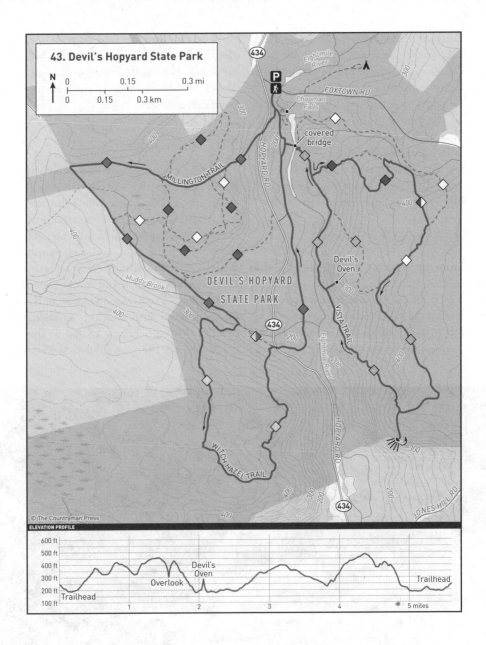

43. Devil's Hopyard State Park

ELEVATION PROFILE

Indeed, a trip to Devil's Hopyard State Park is one of the most geologically interesting hikes in Connecticut. Alongside its potholes and waterfalls, one also encounters features unique to the underlying rocks of this area. In keeping with the rather infernal theme, Devil's Hopyard is set in the Brimfield Formation, a geological layering of iron-sulfide bearing schist and gneiss. Devil's Oven, found on the Orange Vista Trail, is an impressive cave formed from the sulfide weathering typical to this kind of formation.

The park also offers some of the finest birding in the state, and fishermen find the clear, cool stream water an excellent source of brook trout. Throughout Devil's Hopyard, there are several lovely trails to hike as well as some beautiful spots to settle down and enjoy the quiet serenity of the woods and water. This park is especially beautiful in the fall with its vibrant foliage. But it is also worth a visit in winter, when you can enjoy the quiet peace and wonder of hiking in the snowy woods.

## GETTING THERE

From the junction of CT 82 and CT 156 in East Haddam, drive east a tenth of a mile on CT 82 to Hopyard Road, following the signs to the state park. Turn left (north); follow this road 3.4 miles past the picnic entrance, and then turn right to the campground (signed) on Foxtown Road. Park in the small, paved lot on your left, just off Hopyard Road. The campground will be just beyond the pond on your left.

## THE HIKE

This hike encompasses two separate loops. Our narrative will describe them in one way, but see *Other Hiking Options* for alternate approaches to hiking in this beautiful park. The first loop visits the main attractions of Devil's Hopyard, traveling on the orange (Vista Trail), blue, blue/white, white, and orange trails, respectively. The first loop has recently been reblazed with weather-resistant, plastic, rectangle blazes nailed to the trees. The second loop follows the red

CHAPMAN FALLS

Millington Trail, to the yellow Witch Hazel Trail, before returning to the red trail and back to your car. The second loop is less spectacular and less traveled than the first, but it lets you stretch your legs a bit more. You'll find the blazing has not been updated (as of summer 2017), and that there are a number of fallen trees across the trail with a few side trails having been forged around these blow-downs.

Start your hike by leaving the parking lot, crossing the road, and heading down the trail past the covered bulletin board. Follow the gravel trail past an unmarked path to your right that passes under a bridge. Shortly you'll pass the red-blazed Millington Trail going uphill to your right (you'll follow this later when starting out your second loop). Bear left on the gravel path, and descend gently past Chapman Falls. Be sure to save some time to explore the falls area after your hike.

You'll soon join the park road, and continue below the picnic shelter bearing left to the covered footbridge. Cross the river through through the bridge, and ascend the woods road away from the brook by turning right onto the orange-blazed Vista Trail (left is the white trail).

Soon you'll turn left on a blue-blazed trail. When the trail forks, bear right (still blue) and continue climbing. Next you will pass a large white oak with outstretched side limbs, indicating that the tree matured in a clearing or pasture (note the stone walls around this area as well, more evidence of pasture land).

After descending briefly you will come to a T-junction; turn right onto the blue/white trail. You'll see signs pointing to a vista on this route, but note that you won't reach the vista until further along on the yellow trail. Resume a steady climb on this blue- and white-blazed trail. After topping the rise, come to another T-junction; here you'll turn right onto the white-blazed trail (formerly blazed orange, you'll see some old orange blazes at times).

Cross a muddy stream, and pass over a rise with a cleared area, leveling out along a ridge until you come to a T-junction with the orange Vista Trail. Proceed left on this trail (where you will once again see signs for a vista). You'll continue on this trail for about a half-mile until you see an orange-blazed footpath that breaks off the main trail toward the vista. The vantage point is a rocky outcropping on the edge of a steep drop. From here, you'll see the rolling hills of the Eightmile River Valley, a classic example of the north-south valleys that formed all over Connecticut when Europe and Africa jutted North America, folding the rocks into ridges perpendicular to the collision direction. The valley was then steepened and widened by the southward movement of glacial ice, giving it a characteristic U-shape. The valley is especially beautiful in the fall with the multi-colored foliage to delight you.

After enjoying the view, retrace your steps to the main trail. Pass where you came in, and continue straight on the main orange trail. You'll walk downhill along a wooded trail, passing a small ledge-outcropping on your right. Bear left downhill to follow the orange trail through a dying hemlock forest—macabre evidence of the woolly adelgid. Keep an eye out for orange blazes throughout this stretch as you bear right toward the river. Once you reach the river you'll turn right to continue on the orange trail.

After crossing the stream, you'll see a signpost that encourages you to take a right for a side trip to the Devil's Oven.

We encourage you to view this impressive set of ledges and caves. You'll climb up a very steep hill of loose rock. Bear left at the first fork, and then right at the second fork. Soon you'll be right under the ledges. Walk carefully around and explore the weathered and fractured ledges that make up the Oven and other cave formations. Return to the main trail by walking carefully down the side trail; we found the trail to the left had better foot and hand-holds for the steep trek.

When you are back on the orange trail, turn right to head to the bridge. The trail follows the river—follow the blazes carefully as the path weaves around, parallel to but a bit above the river. You'll see another orange-blazed trail come in on your right; continue straight. You'll also pass the blue trail on your right; again continue straight until you come once more to the covered bridge. Cross the bridge, and go right up the road toward the parking lot where you left your car.

Just before reaching the rock ledge on your left, the second loop begins by turning left onto the red-blazed Millington Trail. Follow this trail just below the impressive stone embankment, and then across the road. This well-used foot trail appears to be a dry, sunken streambed; it continues diagonally left by slabbing gently up the hill. Follow the path, passing the white trail coming in on your right and then two four-way intersections with the green trail. After 0.6 mile, you'll reach the far western point of the red trail. Here turn sharply left, still following the red-blazed trail. The trail can be quite muddy over the next half-mile with slight detours available to avoid the worst of the muck. You'll see the white trail come in on your left. After another tenth of a mile, cross over a curved footbridge. Soon the woods road you've been following goes

left, but the red trail goes right—continue on the red-blazed trail. Descend into another dying hemlock stand, and cross a plank bridge over Muddy Brook just below Baby Falls. Immediately on the other side, a yellow-blazed trail cuts in; turn right to climb uphill away from the well-worn woods road. You'll soon pass the falls, which are on your right. Enjoy a short respite at this less impressive yet tranquil spot.

When ready, continue following the yellow-blazes uphill. You are now on the Witch Hazel Trail. The faded blazes have not been updated and can be difficult to follow at times. Proceed up the steep grade moving away from the stream. Your climb will level out and cross the top of a rise, passing through an area lush with ferns—Christmas, cinnamon, beech, and New York. The woods here are a mixture of oak, black birch, and hickory.

Turn downward; at one point, you'll pass under a canopy of ancient mountain laurel bushes. The tops reach 10 to 15 feet above you, supported by boles almost as thick as your leg.

When you reach the southern end of the Witch Hazel trail, you'll see a blue trail branch off to the left. This is a blue loop trail that is not on the DEEP map. At this point in the hike, you are far from the busy crowds around the main falls; enjoy the peace and quiet of these unsullied woods. On a recent hike here, we sighted a pair of ravens in this area—they have a more throaty *kraaa* sound as compared to a crow's *caw*.

After passing the blue loop trail, you'll begin to descend down through a tableau of forest succession: large dead hemlocks interspersed with hardwoods. The shade once cast by the tall evergreens no longer blocks out the sunlight. The tall, straight deciduous trees in this stand will spread out their branches more, and new trees will emerge now that sunlight is again plentiful. The dead trees do create a bit of an obstacle course through the woods—be watchful of the yellow blazes, and look for detours around blow-downs.

As you level out, you'll see a paved road ahead of you through the woods. As you emerge from the trees, the yellow blazes steer you left to a red-blazed woods road. You'll follow this to the right, crossing the paved Hopyard Road. You'll now follow the red-blazed woods road, as the yellow blazes ended at the tar road. The woods road will then become a trail (still blazed in red), and you'll soon cross a stream on a footbridge. Curve to the left as the path becomes a woods road again before ultimately meeting up with a paved park road. Follow the road through several picnic areas, and pass the covered bridge on your right through the parking lot. Ascend up the dirt road past the falls and back to your car.

## OTHER HIKING OPTIONS:

**Additional Resources:** A state park trail map can be found at www.ct.gov /deep/devilshopyard.

**Short & Sweet:** For a nice 2-mile walk that includes the falls, the vista, and the Devil's Oven take the orange-blazed Vista Trail after you cross the covered bridge; do not turn on the blue trail. Continue following the orange blazes for your whole hike, bearing left at a fork and heading down to the vista turnoff. The trail loops around and heads back to the falls via the turnoff to the Devil's Oven.

PASSING THROUGH AN AREA LUSH WITH FERNS

# Mansfield Hollow State Park

**LOCATION**: Mansfield

**DISTANCE**: 8 miles

**VERTICAL RISE**: 600 feet

**TIME**: 4.5 hours

**RATING**: C/D

**MAP**: USGS 7.5-minute Spring Hill

Because of its proximity to the University of Connecticut at Storrs, Mansfield Hollow State Park and Wildlife Area is sprinkled with jogging professors, strolling students, and young families with toddlers. The park borders the 500-acre Mansfield Hollow Lake reservoir. The Army Corps of Engineers created the lake in the late 1940s by damming the Natchaug River, substantially reducing the flooding in the area. It is popular for boating and fishing, but no swimming is allowed since part of the lake is used for public water supply.

In addition to picnic tables, fireplaces, ball fields, bridle paths, rest rooms, and boat-launching facilities, Mansfield Hollow also encompasses one of the two southern terminals of the Nipmuck Trail, which stretches 34 miles north to Bigelow Hollow State Park (hike #46) near the Massachusetts border. This park is delightful all year, each season providing different natural wonders for the hiker.

Please note that regulated hunting is allowed in the Mansfield Hollow Recreation Area, with the majority of hunting occurring in the early morning (before 10 a.m.) from mid-October through late December. Refer to the book introduction section on *Hunting in Connecticut* for more information.

## GETTING THERE

From the junction of CT 89 and CT 195 in Mansfield Center, drive south on CT 195 for a half-mile to Bassetts Bridge Road, and turn left. Or from the junction of CT 6 and CT 195, head north for 2.1 miles, and turn right onto Bassetts Bridge Road. After 0.8 mile on Bassetts Bridge Road, you'll turn left into Mansfield Hollow State Park. There will be a parking lot immediately on your right.

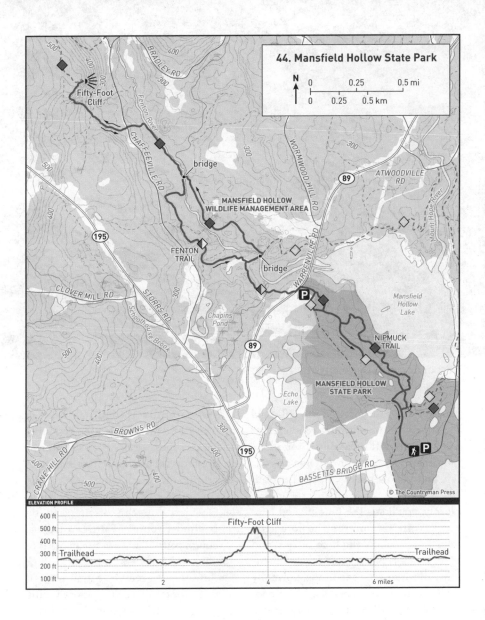

**ELEVATION PROFILE**

## THE HIKE

Today's hike follows the blue-blazed Nipmuck Trail through a flood-control area and rolling countryside extending to Fifty-Foot Cliff, a nice little lookout. The return route takes the blue- and white-blazed Fenton Trail, and the yellow trail for some variety. Much of the terrain is relatively easy and flat, but there are a few sections of moderate ups and downs as well as one steady, steep climb up to the Fifty-Foot Cliff. The trail can be muddy at certain times of the year, due to its proximity to the Fenton River.

To reach the start of the Nipmuck Trail, follow the paved entrance road through an open field fringed with white pine woods, keeping the flood-control

THE FENTON RIVER ON A COLD WINTER DAY

causeway to your left and the ball field to your right. The entrance road ends at a yellow gate. After passing through the gate, there is a large stone levee on your left and yellow-blazes marked prominently on trees on your right. Looking closely, you'll see the blue-blazed Nipmuck Trail also enters the forest on your right. Follow the blue blazes, and enter a forest remarkable for its understory of white-pine seedlings, normally a shade-intolerant species. The flood-control reservoir is visible to the east.

The trail starts on sandy soil, where white pines grow very well. You'll reach a woods road in a tenth-mile; the blue blazes lead to the right before turning left into the woods. For a view of the reservoir, Mansfield Hollow Lake, take a short detour down the woods road before turning left.

Return up the woods road, and turn right into the woods. Follow the blue

blazes carefully through this maze of trails and woods roads. You may encounter recent relocations designed to prevent abrupt meetings between hikers and mountain bikers.

On your right are patches of shinleaf, which you can distinguish by their almost round evergreen leaves. Although you will not see their spikes of nodding white flowers until June or July, the flower buds may be found nestled beneath forest litter, here mostly pine needles, in early May. This plant derives its name from the early custom of applying its leaves to sores and bruises—any plaster, no matter where applied, was called a shin plaster.

As you wind your way up onto a flat, the trail touches and then heads left off a bridle path. You will come across numerous bridle paths strewn with strawberry plants and cinquefoils through the first part of the hike. The mixture gives you a chance to distinguish between these two plants with similar leaves: The strawberry has three-leafed bunches, and the local cinquefoils, five.

Beneath a blue-blazed white pine, you will find the first of many hawthorns along the trail. This shrub is characterized principally by formidable two-inch thorns, as well as attractive white flowers with a rather disagreeable odor and fall pomes suitable for making jelly. You'll encounter and cross a second bridle path, pass through another wooded section, and emerge once again on a bridle path.

At this junction, turn right and note that the path is now blazed with both blue and yellow blazes as the two trails coincide for the next half-mile. After curving left through a small patch of woods, you'll come to another junction with a woods road where you'll turn right, heading toward an open area. The trail continues along the right side of a ball field, Southeast Park (adjacent to Southeast Elementary School), on CT 89, 1.5 miles from the start. This is the starting point if you choose a shorter loop along the Fenton River for your hike (see *Other Hiking Options*).

Follow paved CT 89 to your left briefly, and then cross to a grassy area along the road. Bear right into the woods, still following the double blue-and-yellow blazes. Continue downhill by an old well and cellar hole located on your right, and then cross an abandoned tar road. Soon the trail goes left on a dirt road to the bottom of a large, dry dike. In times of high water, the central gates of the flood-control dam can be closed to limit downstream flow. Several such dikes are found in this area. Bear right to cross the stream beside the flood-control gate, and head uphill still following the double blue- and yellow-blazed trail.

Reenter the woods. White oaks (their bark is actually light-gray) stand sentinel on the trail. Follow a gravel road, and then turn right onto another road. An unmarked park road veers to your left. Still following the blue-and-yellow blazes, your path continues through a wooded area and curves uphill to the right. You'll reach another woods road where you'll bear right downhill following the double blue-and-yellow blazes. To the left is the blue- and white-blazed Fenton Trail, which you'll follow on the return route.

THE BLUE-BLAZED NIPMUCK TRAIL ALONG THE FENTON RIVER

A new steel-truss footbridge carries the trail across the Fenton River. After crossing the bridge, the blue-blazed Nipmuck leaves the yellow-blazed trail by turning left. Your path will now go over some wet ground before reaching a woods road that follows along the east side of the Fenton River Valley. Blue blazes and painted wooden arrows

CROSSING A STEEL-TRUSS FOOTBRIDGE OVER THE FENTON RIVER

guide you through this stretch. Robins fly ahead of you in the grass, and the soulful cry of the mourning dove echoes around you.

The path now angles up onto a small gravel ridge deposited by the glaciers, with the river below you at left, and ponds and wetlands below you at right. To your left, a small stream widens into swamp pools populated with frogs and painted turtles. Dropping off the ridge, you'll continue through a meadow brilliant with the yellows of the goldfinch and the swallowtail butterfly. Turn left into the woods just before you reach a second gravel ridge.

Shortly thereafter, you'll come to the Fenton River again, which is spanned by another new (1997) steel-truss footbridge. The trusses of these sturdy bridges are recycled from older bridges in the area, this one from the Cider Mill Road Bridge (circa 1914). The blue-and white-blazed Fenton Trail rejoins the Nipmuck Trail on the west side of the bridge. After crossing, follow this 30-foot-wide trout river upstream (turning right), keeping a cornfield on your left. Follow the blue-blazed trail as it winds among numerous anglers' paths along the riverbank—watch the blazes carefully to avoid straying. A variety of ferns grace the low spots, while the interrupted fern stands tall throughout. The interrupted fern gets its name from the distinct interruptions found in the center of many fronds of the plant. Two miles from CT 89, the trail crosses a woods road, cuts to your left away from the river, and then proceeds uphill to Chaffeeville Road. The trail crosses the road and ascends through hardwoods and hemlocks. Soon you will cross a stream and begin a steady uphill ascent toward Fifty-Foot Cliff. You'll come to a second stream crossing, after which the path is level for a short stretch before continuing its steady uphill climb. A half-mile or so from Chaffeeville Road, you'll emerge on the uppermost ledges of Fifty-Foot Cliff. This lookout offers fine views of eastern Connecticut woodlands. Enjoy your lunch with a view while sitting on the marble bench. Then retrace your steps south back to Chaffeeville Road.

To add variety to your return trip, when you reach the steel-truss bridge over the Fenton River, do not cross. Instead, follow the blue- and white-blazed Fenton Trail straight. This 0.9-mile route follows the river on the opposite bank whence you came, then veers away from the river to the right, taking you through marshland and then to higher ground. Eventually, you will rejoin the Nipmuck Trail, now double-blazed with yellow once again. You'll follow this path down to the base of the dike, crossing the stream and heading back up to the abandoned tar road. After going through the woods for a short stretch, you will once again reach CT 89 across from Southeast Park. Walk around the left side of the ball field, continuing to follow blue and yellow blazes. Enter the woods as the trail continues along a woods road. Soon the blue- and yellow-blazed trails split, with the blue going left and the yellow going right.

Follow the yellow-blazed trail for variety and a pleasant walk back along a level woods road to the levee we saw at the beginning of the hike. When you reach the base of the levee, go left through the yellow gate, and follow the park road back to your car.

## OTHER HIKING OPTIONS

**Additional Resources:** A state park trail map can be found at www.ct .gov/deep/mansfieldhollow. If you have interest in exploring the geology of this park, you can find a detailed write-up describing interesting geologic features of the last glacial period linked on the above website.

**Short & Sweet:** You can trim the hike to about 3 miles and still enjoy the beautiful river-walk along the Fenton River. This route starts at Southeast Park and Elementary School located on CT 89 about three-quarters of a mile north of its junction with CT 195. In front of the school, you'll see the oval Nipmuck Trail road signs (posted where blue trails cross highways). You'll take the trail across CT 89, following the double blue-and-yellow blazes (see the route above for details). Continue until you reach the first steel-truss bridge, veering left to stay on the blue-blazed Nipmuck Trail. After crossing the second steel-truss bridge, you'll take a hard left to loop back on the blue- and white-blazed Fenton Trail. This 0.9-mile trail takes you along the opposite side of the river, through marshland and up to higher ground. Soon you'll meet up again with the double-blazed, blue-and-yellow Nipmuck trail. Follow this path back to CT 89 and Southeast Park where you parked your car.

# Seven Falls
# State Park

**LOCATION**: Middletown

**DISTANCE**: 8 miles

**VERTICAL RISE**: 900 feet

**TIME**: 4.5 hours

**RATING**: A/B/C

Laying out a hiking trail is more an art than a science; the shortest distance between two points does not necessarily provide the most interesting hiking. A trail that is properly laid out directs you to the best of an area's natural features, thus offering you the finest hike possible. This stretch of the Mattabesett Trail, which starts at Seven Falls south of Middletown, does just that. Its corkscrew route approaches, circles, and often climbs the boulders and rock ridges that are so characteristic of the local terrain.

The Mattabesett Trail is a 50-mile-long, hook-shaped, blue-blazed hiking route and is part of the New England Scenic Trail. This portion of the Mattabesett Trail offers pleasant vistas, numerous streams, glacial erratics, and many stands of mountain laurel (Connecticut's state flower, which blossoms mid-June).

Another attraction of this hike is the number of loop trails. The main trail is blazed with blue rectangles; the loop trails, generally shorter, are marked with blue-and-yellow blazes (blue square above connected to a yellow square for a stacked, two-color rectangle). Our route departs on the main trail and returns on the loop trails to maximize hike variety.

## GETTING THERE

The hike begins by the Seven Falls State Park on CT 154 south of Middletown. Leave CT 9 on exit 10 (Aircraft Road), and follow CT 154 south (right) for 0.8 mile. The park is on your left with roadside parallel parking available. Seven Falls State Park may not be what you expect. It has a modest picnic area and parking lot. According to the Haddam Historical Society, the park

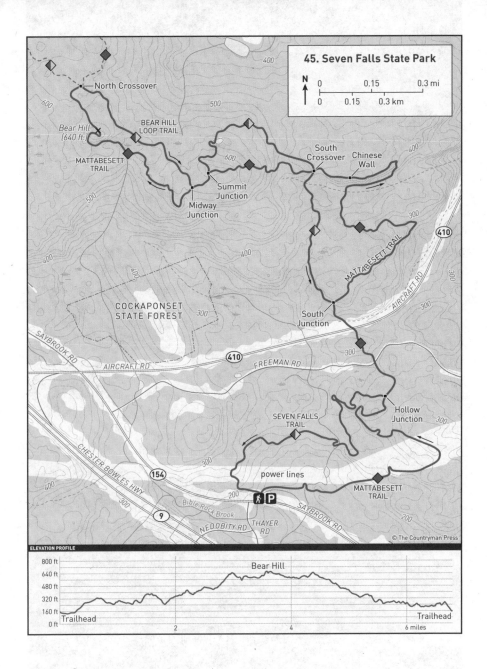

Map caption / labels:

45. Seven Falls State Park

North Crossover
Bear Hill (640 ft.)
BEAR HILL LOOP TRAIL
MATTABESETT TRAIL
South Crossover
Chinese Wall
Summit Junction
Midway Junction
MATTABESETT TRAIL
410
COCKAPONSET STATE FOREST
South Junction
SAYBROOK RD
AIRCRAFT RD
410
FREEMAN RD
AIRCRAFT RD
Hollow Junction
SEVEN FALLS TRAIL
CHESTER BOWLES HWY
154
power lines
MATTABESETT TRAIL
Bible Rock Brook
9
NEDOBITY RD
THAYER RD
SAYBROOK RD
© The Countryman Press

ELEVATION PROFILE
800 ft / 640 ft / 480 ft / 320 ft / 160 ft / 0 ft
Bear Hill
Trailhead
Trailhead
2    4    6 miles

"derives its name from a series of small cascading falls in Bible Rock Brook. The stopover was the state's first rest area and was extremely popular when Route 154 was the main road from Hartford/ Middletown to the Connecticut shoreline." If you are hiking in the summer, Bible Rock Brook is an excellent spot to soak your feet after finishing this hike!

## THE HIKE

This Seven Falls hike starts on the Mattabesett trail in the woods just north of

HIKING ALONG THE CHINESE WALL ON THE MATTABESETT TRAIL

the park on the same side of CT 154. The rectangular blue blazes head right into the woods. Soon you'll pass the blue- and yellow-blazed trail on your right; continue on the main trail (blue blazes). Picnickers have worn an aimless labyrinth of trails through this section; most go nowhere, so be careful to stick with the well-marked, blue-blazed main trail.

You'll cross a small stream, and take the main trail left onto a gravel access road along a power line. The trail parallels the power line for a distance, and at times wanders inward to take advantage of the numerous ledges and boulders it skirts, surmounts, and circles. Note that there may be some hand-assisted scrambling here—an uncharacteristically difficult stretch in what is otherwise a less strenuous hike. Many of the blazes are painted on rocks or on wooden posts. You will also see an occasional stone cairn marking the way. The forest edges along the power line are frequently the best places to view wildlife—this was underscored during a recent fall visit when we flushed two bucks!

When you reach Hollow Junction, about 1.5 miles from your car, the blue- and-yellow trail bears slightly uphill to your left, while the blue rectangular blazes continue straight, gently downhill. Go straight here on the main trail to descend to paved Freeman Road in about a tenth of a mile, then the busier, paved Aircraft Road. Climb the hill to South Junction (1.9 miles from the start), where a second loop trail bears left. Keep to the main trail, which forks uphill to your right.

The path crests a rise and then heads downhill, bearing sharp left at a stream to the edge of a logging operation (which we could not see but could hear at this point in the hike). You'll then ascend along that stream for a way before crossing it several times and leveling out on a worn woods road. You'll then climb another ridge about a mile from South Junction. Cross another brook, and scramble over ledges and across the top of the Chinese Wall, a long uniform escarpment that ends at a stream crossing just before reaching South Crossover, about 1.4 miles from South Junction. The blue-and-yellow trail crosses the main route here.

Continuing on the main trail, you'll

TUFTS OF NEEDLES GROWING OUT OF THE TRUNK OF A PITCH PINE

A TRAIL CAIRN MARKS THE ROUTE

reach Summit Junction—on an open, rocky hilltop with blueberry bushes lining the trail. In the fall and winter after the leaves have fallen off the trees, you'll have a good view west across to Bear Hill. Stay to your left to descend the ledge; in another a tenth of a mile, bear left onto the main trail at Midway Junction. After another half-mile, you'll climb to the top of Bear Hill (elevation 640 feet) on the main trail (blue rectangles) about 4.4 miles from the start. Look for the two US Geological Survey bench markers (metal discs set into the rock)—one to your right and one to your left. The profusion of huckleberries here would have been a major attraction for bears, hence the probable origin of its name. Continue on the blue-blazed trail, turning left to descend on an old woods road and then bearing left off the road to stay on the ridge. Drop abruptly to another junction a quarter-mile from

the summit, the North Crossover. This is the furthest most point of the hike. You'll bear right onto the blue- and yellow-blazed trail, the Bear Hill Loop Trail.

The Bear Hill Loop Trail winds its way through a large stand of mountain laurel. After a half-mile, you'll rejoin the main trail at Midway Junction, and ascend to the rocky hilltop and Summit Junction. Bear left to follow the blue- and yellow, fern-lined trail as it crosses the main trail at South Crossover and then heads down to South Junction. From there, follow the main trail to retrace your steps across Aircraft and Freeman Roads. At Hollow Junction, you'll bear right onto the blue-and-yellow blazed Seven Falls Loop, which passes over and around ledges, then skirts a small pond just above a small cascade. Here, the trail once again clambers around boulders and rock outcroppings. You'll veer close to the power line but will then head back into the woods until you go under the power line about 1.2 miles from Freeman Road. Take care while crossing to watch for your blue-and-yellow blazes. The undergrowth is thick and can obscure the trail. Once you go past the power line, you'll descend to the main blue-blazed trail, which you follow briefly to CT 154 and your car.

## OTHER HIKING OPTIONS

**Short & Sweet:** You can shorten the hike by taking only the first loop (heading back at the yellow junction) for a total distance of 2.5 miles.

You can also shorten the hike by taking the first two loops (heading back at South Crossover after going on the Chinese Wall) for a total distance of 5.5 miles.

# 46

# Bigelow Hollow State Park

**LOCATION**: Union

**DISTANCE**: 8.5 miles

**VERTICAL RISE**: 800 feet

**TIME**: 5 hours

**RATING**: B

**MAPS**: USGS 7.5-minute Westford, Eastford, Wales (MA-CT), Southbridge (MA-CT)

In the quiet border town of Union in northeastern Connecticut, there lies some beautiful park and forest land which are well worth the drive. Bigelow Hollow State Park is nestled within the larger Nipmuck State Forest, from which it was carved out and designated a state park in 1949. The park and forest are located in a large hollow, approximately 700 feet below the surrounding ridge line. Breakneck Pond provides a sense of undeveloped nature, with its long narrow waters nestled within the hollow. This secluded 92-acre lake is accessible only by foot. There are backcountry campsites along the water that make this area an appealing overnight destination for serious hikers.

The park also has two other sizable bodies of water: Bigelow Pond (25 acres) and Mashapaug Lake (287 acres)—both accessible by park roads for boating and fishing (year round). There are over 35 miles of hiking trails and numerous picnicking spots in the park and surrounding forest. This hike ventures out to the remote Breakneck Pond, starting from the northeastern corner of Bigelow Pond.

Please note that hunting is allowed in Nipmuck State Forest. Refer to the book introduction section on *Hunting in Connecticut* for more information.

## GETTING THERE

From I-84's exit 73, follow CT 190 east to CT 171 in Union. Turn right, and follow CT 171 south to the park entrance about 1.5 miles on the left just past the pond. Turn left onto the park road and follow it 0.7 mile to the picnic area and trail parking at the north end of Bigelow Pond. You'll pass a boat launch on your right just before the parking area.

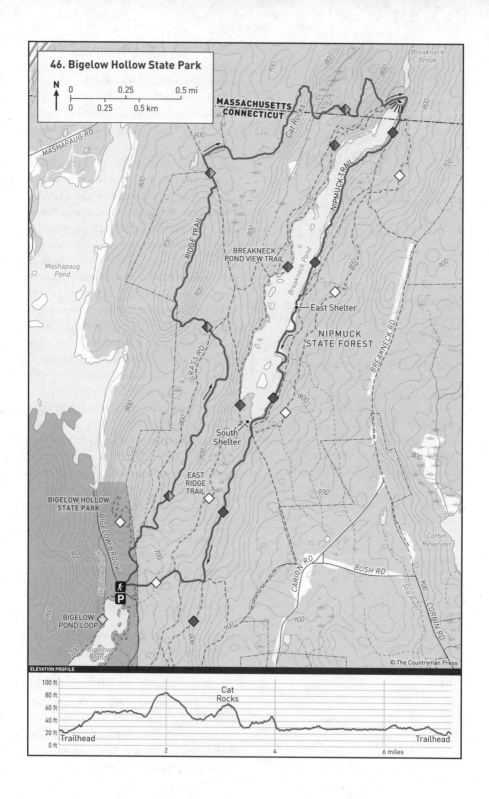

## 46. Bigelow Hollow State Park

N

| 0 | | 0.25 | | 0.5 mi |
| 0 | 0.25 | | 0.5 km | |

**MASSACHUSETTS**
**CONNECTICUT**

Breakneck
Brook

beaver
pond

MASHAPAUG RD

RIDGE TRAIL

Cat Rocks

NIPMUCK TRAIL

BREAKNECK
POND VIEW TRAIL

Mashapaug
Pond

Breakneck Pond

East Shelter

NIPMUCK
STATE FOREST

GRASS RD

BREAKNECK RD

South
Shelter

EAST
RIDGE
TRAIL

BIGELOW HOLLOW
STATE PARK

Corbin
Reservoir

CARION RD

BUSH RD

Bigelow Brook

BIGELOW
POND LOOP

Still River

CORBIN RD

Bigelow
Pond

© The Countryman Press

**ELEVATION PROFILE**

| | | Cat | | |
| 100 ft | | Rocks | | |
| 80 ft | | | | |
| 60 ft | | | | |
| 40 ft | | | | |
| 20 ft | Trailhead | | | Trailhead |
| 0 ft | | 2 | 4 | 6 miles |

## THE HIKE

Today's route is a loop that heads north over a ridge following the blue- and orange-blazed Ridge Trail, down to a swampy beaver pond area and then onward to Breakneck Pond. The hike will then follow the blue-and-red trail (once blue-and-white) for a short distance until you come to the blue-blazed Nipmuck Trail. You'll continue south along the east side of Breakneck Pond and then further south until you travel back to your car by means of a woods road and the white trail. There are especially beautiful views of the long, narrow Breakneck Pond as you head south on the Nipmuck Trail.

Enter the woods opposite the parking lot beside a bulletin board with trail maps, taking the white-blazed East Ridge Trail uphill into the woods. In about 50 feet, you will turn left at a fork onto the blue- and orange-blazed Ridge Trail, hiking over a small hill featuring hemlocks and mountain laurel. Cross a small stream, and ascend the ridge on a cushioned surface of tree needles. The acid content of the needles helps the overstory hemlocks out-compete other tree species, and helps create a grove of trees. White pine needles contribute to the acidic nature of the soil, but white pines retain their dominance in the forest by growing faster and taller than New England's other tree species.

Follow the ridge north toward Breakneck Pond. The ridge features rocky soil, oak trees, and an open, park-like understory. After about 1.3 miles from the start of your hike, you may see the blue waters of the pond peeking through the trees. Leave the ridge, and ascend the 1,020-foot hill west of the pond. After a short, steep climb, you'll follow an interesting, rocky ridge before you crest the wooded hill. Next, descend through the familiar oak-hickory-hemlock forest, and observe a less common northern tree in the mix: striped maple, whose presence is probably due to the hillside's northern exposure. This maple, also called duck's foot maple for the shape of its leaf, does not grow to great size, and is easily recognized by its smooth green-and-white-striped bark. You'll see more seedlings than large, full-grown trees—look for the distinctive duck-foot shape of the leaves.

After about 2 miles from the start, you'll pass through a four-way junction with an unblazed woods road (called Grass Road on the DEEP maps). After about a tenth of a mile, the trail curves left through a small swampy area and then, punctuated by large rocks and boulders on either side of the trail, up a steady rise. Take caution following the blue-and-orange blazes as the trail veers left about a third of the way up your ascent; the turn is easy to miss. Along the top, you'll have a lovely woodland view.

After about 3.3 miles from the start, the trail turns left to follow an eroded woods road. Continue to follow the blue-and-orange blazes as the trail proceeds along the rocky woods road with other roads crossing and merging with your path. After a quarter-mile more, the trail bears right off the road to descend to a bridge crossing over a brook. From there, you'll ascend to Cat Rocks. Cat Rocks are a number of large rocks under the ridge that used to be home to wildcats, last confirmed seen in the area in the 1980s. Just before the top of the ridge, there is a little side trail on the right—this path is very steep as it goes below the rocks. The ridge you'll soon be walking along has numerous fissures and caves below, a perfect home for wildcats! From atop Cat Rocks, you'll notice there is a narrow valley on your right but the foliage obscures the actual view of Breakneck Pond. The

92-ACRE BREAKNECK POND—ONLY ACCESSIBLE BY FOOT

walk along the rocky ridge with its pitch pine and sunny exposure is well worth the 3.4-mile hike from Bigelow Pond. Follow the ridge north, and you'll zigzag back and forth between Connecticut and Massachusetts with little fanfare. Be cautious while following the blazes; they are spread out and can be hard to follow. After reaching the northern-most tip of the ridge, the trail descends, steeply circling beneath the ridge you were just walking upon on before veering left toward a beaver pond. The beavers have made a flooded area as they dam up woodland streams. Their diligent work can have dramatic effects on the surrounding ecosystem as seen by all the dead trees within this wetland area.

You'll follow the edge of the beaver pond south to your right; keep an eye out for beaver activity—gnawed trees along your route. Bear right (away from the wetlands), and you'll soon reach a junction with a woods road. Turn left and descend on the red- and blue-blazed

Breakneck Pond View Trail (once blue-and white-blazed). Cross the pond's outlet stream, a somewhat tricky endeavor, especially in spring. You'll then reach a clearing with a beautiful view south down the length of the pond. Take some time to have a rest and enjoy the view.

You'll pass the northern end of the pond, and then turn right to cross one last time from Massachusetts into Connecticut, this time marked clearly with a stone monument. Here your route becomes the blue-blazed Nipmuck Trail.

Follow the Nipmuck Trail south on the wide, unpaved East Shore Road. The white-blazed East Ridge Trail leads uphill to your left. Continue to follow the blue blazes south along the road, but watch carefully: your route soon leaves the road to follow the water's edge more closely. The trail then becomes a series of gentle ups and downs interspersed with feeder-stream crossings from the uplands to the east. The path is padded with evergreen needles, but take care as

STONE MONUMENT MARKING ONE OF MANY TRAIL CROSSINGS BETWEEN MASSACHUSETTS AND CONNECTICUT ON THIS HIKE

BEAVER ACTIVITY ALONG THE ROUTE: GNAWED TREES

you step over rocks and roots along this route. You'll continue to pass beaver-gnawed oak and black birches along the shore. Beavers tend to drop trees in the direction of the water, although they probably don't do this deliberately. Rather, the beavers are aided by a tree's natural tendency to grow toward sunlight, a resource more abundant over open water. You'll also see trees stripped of their bark along the lower circumference. Beavers don't actually eat wood, but they do enjoy bark, and the soft and smooth cambium layer just below it.

After about 1.75 miles along the blue-blazed Nipmuck trail, you'll reach East Shelter—an overnight camping spot with a beautiful view of the pond (camping permits are required). In 0.3 mile, you'll come to another clearing, the site of an old shelter that has since been dismantled. As you reach the southern end of the pond, the trail turns away to the left. You'll see the South Shelter up ahead to the right as you veer away. Continuing along, you'll soon reach a woods road and a large clearing (a helispot); here the white trail goes off to the left. The Nipmuck Trail continues straight across the helispot. The trail parallels a stone wall, and then turns right once you're back in the woods.

You'll continue to follow the Nipmuck Trail south of Breakneck Pond. After about 0.8 mile, you will turn right downhill onto an unblazed woods road. In another 500 feet, you'll come to a T-junction with another woods road where you will turn right. After another 500 feet or so, you'll come to a second junction where you'll turn left to follow the white blazes onto a woods road headed back to the parking area. Along the way, you'll cross an earthen dam with swamp on either side. After a quarter-mile, you'll reach the paved park road, where you'll turn right to get to your parked car just a short distance up the road.

## OTHER HIKING OPTIONS

**Additional Resources:** A state park trail map can be found at www.ct.gov/deep/nipmuck.

**Short & Sweet:** If you want a pleasant walk around a pond, but are not interested in a 9-mile hike then consider the Bigelow Pond Loop. This 2-mile loop follows the yellow trail around the pond. You can start this trail at the same parking location at which our described hike starts. On the same side of the road as the parking area, you will see the entrance to the yellow-blazed Bigelow Pond Loop trail. You can follow the loop either clockwise or counterclockwise around the pond.

# Talcott Mountain and Heublein Tower

| | |
|---|---|
| **LOCATION**: West Hartford | |
| **DISTANCE**: 8.5 miles | |
| **VERTICAL RISE**: 700 feet | |
| **TIME**: 4.75 hours | |
| **RATING**: C | |
| **MAP**: USGS 7.5-minute Avon | |

This hike will bring you through one of the more popular recreational reservoir lands in West Hartford before taking you along the Metacomet Trail over to Talcott Mountain to one of the state's most prominent landmarks, Heublein Tower.

Reservoir #6 is a large, attractive area of open reservoir land. Preserved to maintain water purity, areas such as this one in West Hartford are often open to nonpolluting activities. A nice day brings out an endless procession of walkers, joggers, bicyclists, hikers, and—in winter—cross-country skiers. The main trail loop (about 3.6 miles around) is a mixed surface trail (gravel, dirt, and some pavement).

Heublein Tower sits atop Talcott Mountain, a long traprock ridge named after the Talcott family. Standing 165-feet high, the tower was built as a summer home in 1914 by Gilbert Heublein. By the 1940s, ownership had shifted to the *Hartford Times*, and it became a place for parties and meetings for the newspaper. The paper's guests included many celebrities, including General Dwight D. Eisenhower who attended a barbeque here where he was convinced to run for president. Many of the structures built for that party (picnic pavilion, barbeque pit) are still standing. In the early 1960s, the tower was sold to a corporation that planned residential and commercial development of the property. Fortunately, there was a huge groundswell of support to "Save Talcott Mountain," and ownership ultimately shifted to the state. A non-profit group, Friends of Heublein Tower, was created to help restore the tower and grounds for public use. The park grounds are open year round from 8 a.m. until sunset, while the tower can be entered between Thursday and Sunday from 10 a.m. to

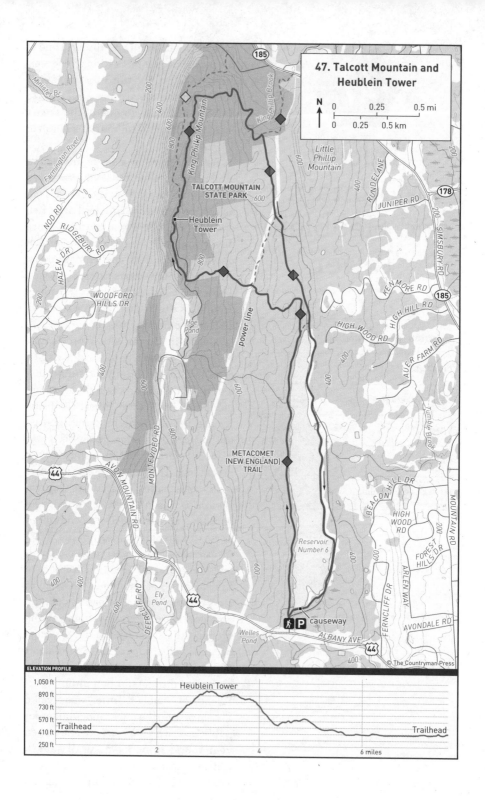

### 47. Talcott Mountain and Heublein Tower

N

| 0 | 0.25 | 0.5 mi |
| 0 | 0.25 | 0.5 km |

5 p.m. during the warmer months (June through the end of October). Admission to both is free and the tower has restored rooms and informative displays for the public to enjoy.

## GETTING THERE

From the junction of US 44 and CT 10 south in Avon, proceed east for 2.3 miles on US 44. On your left (north), a sign indicates RESERVOIR 6, METROPOLITAN DISTRICT. Turn here to park.

## THE HIKE

Walk to the far end of the parking lot, pass a mounted reservoir map, and bear left onto a dirt road barred to motor vehicles (there is an unmarked side trail on your left before the road—do not take it). Pass through the metal gate, and proceed north. This path soon becomes the blue-blazed Metacomet Trail (part of the New England Trail).

Along your route are the great rhubarb-like leaves of the burdock; its nondescript flowers yield the round, multi-hook burrs that dogs and hikers pick up in the fall. These plants usually grow alongside trails and at hikers' campsites; when hikers stop and remove the burrs from their socks or pants, they discard the burrs or seeds wherever they are. The fresh, green growth of grapevines edges out onto the dirt road, where it is soon beaten back by the pounding feet of joggers. Shaded by pine and spruce, this west shore of the reservoir is lovely any time of the year.

The wind-stirred wavelets on the reservoir reflect the sun in a sparkling glitter that adds life to this shifting scene. Along the shallow edges of the water swim numerous species of the sunfish family, including the black bass; this

RESERVOIR #6 DURING A SOFT RAIN

border area provides protection from its predators and is handy for snaring land-based insect life. The shiny-leaf vine on the reservoir side of the cement bridge is the harmless, five-leafed Virginia creeper; however, there is much poison ivy along the path.

Further along, the great torrent of water pouring into Reservoir #6 is ducted from another reservoir in an extensive system. Hartford gets most of its water from the Shepaug and Barkhamsted Reservoirs in northern Connecticut; the West Hartford reservoirs serve largely for holding and storage, rather than as primary sources of water.

Continue along the western shore of the reservoir. Before reaching the north end of the reservoir and its bridge, turn left at the double blue blazes (also marked with a blue sign as the Mattabesett Trail) to follow a woods road uphill away from the water. You'll continue uphill, crossing over a gravel road and under a power line. In summer, you'll see wild bergamot or bee balm growing there, notable for its beautiful lavender color. Not long after, you'll cross a gas pipeline clearing. Then you'll reach the paved ridge road; bear right briefly before reentering the woods. At this point, you'll pass a covered bulletin board and sign directing you to Heublein Tower. The trail ascends to the traprock ridge. Next you'll pass under a radio tower, and continue to the summit of Talcott Mountain. You'll see the summit development first: stone garages and picnic pavilions. Turn left to travel below the picnic platform and over rock outcroppings. You'll soon pass a town line sign for Avon/Simsbury and then a barbeque pit installed to entertain then General Eisenhower.

Before long, you'll pass to the left of Heublein Tower. If open, take some

HEUBLEIN TOWER, ONE OF THE STATE'S MOST PROMINENT LANDMARKS

time to climb up the tower and enjoy the view. The view encompasses nearly 1,200 square miles; on the northern horizon, you can pick out New Hampshire's Mount Monadnock (reportedly the most climbed mountain in North America) some 80 miles to the north, the Berkshires in western Massachusetts, the hills of eastern Rhode Island, and Long Island Sound to the south.

After your tower visit, follow the woods road north, and bear right to remain on the ridgeline. The blazes are blue with a faded-yellow blaze underneath. After following the crest with intermittent views to the west, turn right onto the blue-blazed Metacomet Trail, a winding, narrow path through thick mountain laurel. Leave the laurel, and follow a woods road down the east side of King Philip Mountain. After a stream crossing, turn right to stay on the trail and climb briefly over a small rise.

You'll next come to a woods road

where you'll turn right following combined blue and red blazes (blue on top, red underneath)—a connector trail that takes you back to Reservoir #6. This lovely trail ascends gently past a solitary stone chimney. It will then parallel and cross a power line. While crossing, you'll turn right onto the road and go down the hill about 250 feet to head back into the woods on the blue- and red-blazed trail.

At this point, the trail crosses another gas pipeline clearing. Go straight through a woods road crossing; this is the old tower trail on your right. Soon

A LONE STONE CHIMNEY ON THE WAY BACK TO RESERVOIR #6

your road reaches the reservoir and passes the bridge on the northern end to your right.

Leave the blue- and red-blazed trail that crosses the bridge, instead bearing left to follow the road along the reservoir's eastern shored. As you top a hill, the Metropolitan District Commission's filtration plant for Bloomfield comes into view below to your left. Beyond is the ever-growing Hartford skyline. From this point on, your route is in the open, fully exposed to cold winds in season. The dirt road joins and briefly follows the filtration plant's tar road along the wooded shore.

Keep along the reservoir, following the lesser-used tar road. This road turns to dirt in a few yards and follows the length of the reservoir bank. As you look back, the Heublein Tower rises up above the ridge.

When you come once more to a tar road, stay on the path between it and the water. Eventually you'll reenter the woods at a chained barrier. Soon at a fork, you'll bear left uphill on the narrow path away from the reservoir. After crossing a causeway, you'll quickly emerge on the road within sight of the parking lot.

## OTHER HIKING OPTIONS

**Additional Resources:** A state park trail map can be found at www.ct.gov /deep/talcottmountain.

**Short & Sweet:** Just have time to climb up to Heublein Tower? The Tower Trail is 1.25 miles long; a round-trip walk to the Tower takes approximately 60 to 80 minutes. Parking is on CT 185 in Simsbury (opposite Penwood hike #21).

**Loop Around the Reservoir:** This is a popular local walking spot. The loop is about 3.6 miles on a mixed surface trail (gravel, dirt, and some pavement).

# 48

# Windsor Locks Canal

| | |
|---|---|
| **LOCATION**: Suffield | |
| **DISTANCE**: 9 miles | |
| **VERTICAL RISE**: negligible | |
| **TIME**: 4.5 hours | |
| **RATING**: D | |
| **MAPS**: USGS 7.5-minute Windsor Locks, Broad Brook | |

By the middle of the nineteenth century, stiff competition from railroads brought about the collapse of New England's expanding canal system. The Windsor Locks Canal, built in 1829 to bypass the Enfield Rapids on the Connecticut River, was an exception. Here, the canal survived because water diverted from New England's biggest river not only served barge traffic but also provided power to mills, the last of which continued to operate until the 1930s. Today the Windsor Locks Canal still routes an occasional pleasure craft around the rapids, and its old towpath, now paved, offers a pleasant, level trail for walking or bicycling.

Please note that the towpath is open from April 1st to November 15th, from dawn to dusk. The towpath is closed late fall to early spring so as to not disturb wintering birds of prey. We recommend you double-check with DEEP (Connecticut Department of Energy and Environmental Protection) for any additional closures. For example, the southern end of the trail was closed in 2017 until late June specifically to protect a pair of nesting bald eagles in the area. The pair had nested along the canal trail since 2011 and through 2017, successfully raising five chicks in that time. During the 2017 closure, the first 3.5 miles of trail were still open to visitors.

## GETTING THERE

To reach the towpath, follow CT 159 south from its southern junction with CT 190 for a tenth of a mile, turning left onto Canal Road. The road ends in about 0.4 mile, with a large parking lot on your left. The size of the lot is not indicative of trail use, it is heavily used by anglers who congregate here from April to June. The famous Enfield Rapids provide the

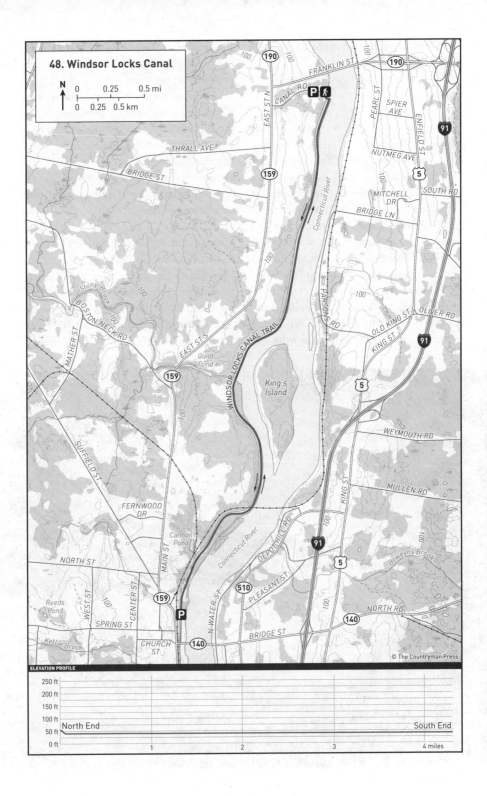

## 48. Windsor Locks Canal

N
0    0.25    0.5 mi
0    0.25  0.5 km

FRANKLIN ST

190

EAST ST N

CANAL RD

190

PEARL ST

SPIER AVE

ENFIELD ST

91

THRALL AVE

BRIDGE ST

159

100

NUTMEG AVE

5

SOUTH RD

Connecticut River

MITCHELL DR

BRIDGE LN

100

Stony Brook

BOSTON NECK RD

MATHER ST

EAST ST S

Guild Pond

WINDSOR LOCKS CANAL TRAIL

King's Island

PARSONS RD

100

OLD KING ST

OLIVER RD

KING ST

91

5

SUFFIELD ST

WEYMOUTH RD

FERNWOOD DR

Cannon Pond

Connecticut River

MULLEN RD

MAIN ST

N WATER ST

DEPOT HILL RD

KING ST

91

Boweyns Brook

NORTH ST

WEST ST

CENTER ST

Reeds Pond

SPRING ST

159

510

PLEASANT ST

5

NORTH RD

140

Kettle Brook

CHURCH ST

140

BRIDGE ST

100

© The Countryman Press

**ELEVATION PROFILE**

250 ft
200 ft
150 ft
100 ft
50 ft
0 ft

North End

South End

1    2    3    4 miles

best ocean-run shad fishing in New England.

## OUR HIKE

Your route simply follows the paved way 4.5 miles to its end; there are no side trails to mislead you. The towpath is a designated bicycle trail, so please give cyclists the right-of-way. The impressive Enfield Rapids dominate the scene to your left. The rapids provide a shallow area perfect for bald eagles to hunt their preferred prey of fish, and they can be seen along the river year-round.

Head south down to the river; pass through the gates and over the canal to the start of the towpath. While the plants and wildlife along the way are the chief attractions of this hike, human-made constructions along the canal are not without interest.

About 2 miles from the start, the blunt prow of heavily-wooded, mile-long King's Island comes into view. Notice here that the banks of the canal are made of soft Connecticut Valley red sandstone, best known as the rock used to build New York City's brownstone apartments. About a third of a mile along King's Island, you'll cross the Stony Brook Aqueduct, which was built in 1827 and rebuilt in 1998; this structure allows the water level of the canal to remain higher than that of the Connecticut River below—without it, the canal's water would drain into the river via the brook! A quarter mile below

THE CONNECTICUT RIVER

King's Island you'll pass venerable stone abutments supporting a trestle over the Connecticut River; several trains whistled by as we hiked the towpath.

As you walk, maintain an alert eye. This entire trip is a veritable oasis in an urban desert. While humans create monotonous conformity, nature, in all her diversity, moves in wherever possible.

We came upon a young woodchuck caught between the devil (us) and the deep blue sea (the canal). Butterflies were constant companions. Besides the cabbage white (the only butterfly that is a common agricultural pest), we saw various swallowtails, skippers, wood satyrs, and a beloved ally, the red admiral, whose caterpillar ravages nettles.

From a botanical point of view, this walk is one of the best in the state. We identified oxeye daisy, fleabane, yarrow, vetch, two varieties of milkweed, campion, Saint-John's wort, black-eyed Susan, several goldenrods, mullein, deadly nightshade, thimbleweed, Deptford pink, plantain (American and English), both bull and Canada thistle, roses, gill-over-the-ground, jewelweed, daylily, and lovely sundrop-like, giant buttercups with cross-shaped stigmas. The clovers, legumes with built-in nitrogen factories on their roots, are well represented. In addition to white and alsike clover, we found at least two varieties of yellow-blossomed hop clovers.

Vines, bushes, and trees abound: poison ivy, several varieties of grapes, Virginia creeper, Oriental bittersweet, sweet-smelling Japanese honeysuckle, scrub willow, various types of smaller dogwoods, elderberry, alder (both smooth and speckled), sassafras, juniper, slippery elm, and smooth and staghorn sumacs with their great masses of red-ripening acidic fruit. On a recent

May visit, the white bracts of flowering dogwood punctuated the various shades of green along the canal's edge.

Here also, treetops—growing along the riverbed or on the canal's steep sides to your left—present their seldom-seen tops for your curiosity. The round

WALKING ALONG THE CANAL PATH

buttons that give the sycamore one of its common names (buttonwood) are present at eye level, and the stickiness of the butternut tree's immature nuts can be tested in place. In mid to late May, the fluffs of cotton from the aptly named eastern cottonwood fill the air—in places, we have seen a gossamer layer of this cotton two inches deep on the ground. In early summer, you can pick with ease the tasty fruit of the red mulberry—if you can get there before the birds!

We talk of waste areas, but probably the only true wastelands are those areas sealed with concrete and asphalt—and even these are transitory. A constant rain of seeds awaits the smallest moistened crack, ready to sprout and grow. Near the end of the towpath, we found that a clump of field bindweed had wrestled a foothold in the junction between an old brick building and the asphalt drive. In the wild, the small, white morning glory–like flowers of this weed have little appeal for most of us, but here they lighten a dingy corner.

A second set of gates, 4.5 miles from the first, marks the end of the towpath near CT 140. Turn around, and retrace your steps to your car unless you have left a car at this southern end to shorten your hike (see below in *Other Hiking Options*).

## OTHER HIKING OPTIONS

**Additional Resources:** A state park trail map can be found at www.ct.gov /deep/windsorlockscanaltrail. Their map is not very detailed. Our map is clearer and more thorough. Since this is an easy route along a tow path, a map is not especially necessary except for getting there.

**Short & Sweet:** Nine miles can be daunting, even when the path is flat. You can cut this route in half, but still walk the entire canal trail by arriving at this hike in two cars. Leave one car at the southern end, and then drive to the northern end (CT 159 north to Canal Road on your right) to begin the hike as noted. When you reach the southern end and your other car, you're done. Directions to southern end parking: Take I-91 to exit 42 in Windsor Locks to CT 159. Take CT 159 north and turn right onto CT 140 east (Bridge Street). You'll soon cross over the canal bridge, and then take an immediate left into the roadway between the canal and a factory. A gravel parking lot is found at the north end of the factory complex.

# Cockaponset
# State Forest

**LOCATION**: Chester

**DISTANCE**: 10.1 miles

**VERTICAL RISE**: 900 feet

**TIME**: 5.5 hours

**RATING**: C/D

**MAP**: USGS 7.5-minute Haddam

At 15,000 acres, Cockaponset State Forest is the second-largest state forest in Connecticut. It is reportedly named after a Native American chief buried in the Ponset section of Haddam. The 7.4-mile, blue-blazed Cockaponset Trail runs the length of the park as it travels along beautiful rolling terrain, crossing brooks and wandering through mature forest. The Civilian Conservation Corps (CCC) built the first parts of this trail in 1934. In its heyday (1933–1942), Cockaponset Forest was home to three camps, with a workforce three times as large as is presently employed in the entire state forest system. The passage of decades has not obliterated the excellent stone trail work completed by the CCC, particularly on the northern section.

Cockaponset State Forest is also home to the Pattaconk Recreation Area, which offers swimming, picnicking, and additional hiking trails around the Pattaconk Reservoir. The forest is used for multiple other outdoor pursuits such as cross-country skiing, horseback riding, mountain biking, and letterboxing. Please note that hunting is allowed in Cockaponset State Forest. Refer to the book introduction section on *Hunting in Connecticut* for more information.

## GETTING THERE

This hike starts by Pattaconk Reservoir in Chester. From CT 9, take exit 6 to CT 148. Follow this road west 1.5 miles to Cedar Lake Road ,and turn right (just after the lake). Or, if you're traveling on CT 80 east, take CT 81 north to CT 148 east, and then go 3.3 miles to Cedar Lake Road and turn left (just before the lake). Travel 1.5 miles on Cedar Lake Road to the entrance of the Lake Pattaconk State Recreation Area (look for the brown state sign for Cockaponset

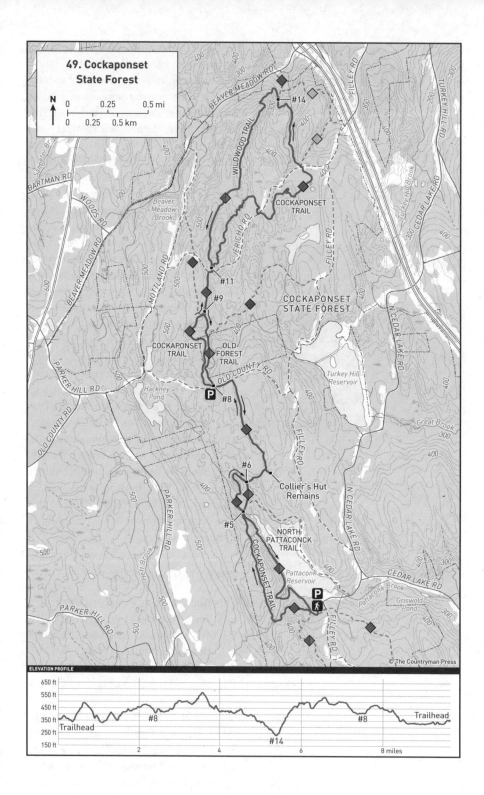

**49. Cockaponset State Forest**

N

0    0.25    0.5 mi
0    0.25    0.5 km

BEAVER MEADOW RD

#14

WILDWOOD TRAIL

COCKAPONSET TRAIL

Beaver Meadow Brook

JERICHO RD

MOTTLAND RD

#11

#9

COCKAPONSET STATE FOREST

BARTMAN RD

WOODS RD

BEAVER MEADOW RD

PARKER HILL RD

OLD COUNTY RD

Hackney Pond

COCKAPONSET TRAIL

OLD FOREST TRAIL

P  #8

FILLEY RD

Turkey Hill Reservoir

N CEDAR LAKE RD

TURKEY HILL RD

CEDAR LAKE RD

Great Brook

OLD COUNTY RD

PARKER HILL RD

Heft Brook

#6

Collier's Hut Remains

#5

NORTH PATTACONCK TRAIL

COCKAPONSET TRAIL

Pattaconk Reservoir

P

N CEDAR LAKE RD

CEDAR LAKE RD

Pattaconk Brook

Griswold Pond

PARKER HILL RD

FILLEY RD

© The Countryman Press

**ELEVATION PROFILE**

650 ft
550 ft
450 ft
350 ft
250 ft
150 ft

Trailhead

#8

#14

#8

Trailhead

2        4        6        8 miles

State Forest) and turn left. In 0.4 mile (past the beach), there are parking lots on both sides of the road; park in the lot on your right.

## TODAY'S HIKE

Today's hike follows the blue-blazed Cockaponset Trail from the reservoir up to the northern Beaver Brook junction with the Wildwood Trail. On your return, you will follow loop trails that parallel the Cockaponset Trail. These are blazed as blue-red trails—a blue blaze with a thick red under-bar. All the trail junctions were once posted with signs; very few of these remain. This write-up will still refer to junction numbers to help you use the provided map. This 10.1-mile leg-stretcher of a hike can easily be shortened into a shorter hike of either 2.3, 5.1, or 5.8 miles (see *Other Hiking Options*).

Proceed through the parking lot on the west side of the road (to your right as you're coming from Cedar Lake Road) to the far left end. You'll see a yellow-blazed trail that leads into the woods. Soon the yellow veers off to the left; you will continue to the right, following blue blazes to the Pattaconk Crossing (junction 4). Bear left to stay on the blue-blazed Cockaponset Trail, heading north. The trail crosses a series of three woodland brooks, each one more lovely than the one before; all three flow into Pattaconk Reservoir.

When we first scouted this trail, thousands of chipmunks enlivened these woods. Six years later, we didn't see any. Chipmunks, like many of the small mammals whose numbers are not effectively limited by predators, go through population cycles. From a very low point, their numbers increase steadily year by year until they seem to be everywhere; then disease and/or starvation decimates their population, and the cycle starts over again.

After crossing several more streams, the trail climbs and then descends gently to Pattaconk Brook at junction 5 (see map), 1.2 miles from your car. Cross the brook over an arched bridge, which may be slippery when wet. This is where you'll return on the Pattaconk Trail to your right if you wish to hike only the 2.3-mile option (see *Other Hiking Options*).

Remain on the blue-blazed trail to your left, reaching another brook crossing in 0.3 mile at North Pattaconk, junction 6 (see map). At this junction, you'll bear left to stay on the blue-blazed trail. You'll cross another stream and pass a large jumble of rocks on your left. Then in a tenth of a mile, you will see a side trail labeled with the sign COLLIER'S HUT REMAINS. In the eighteenth and nineteenth centuries, Connecticut was a prime producer of charcoal. Until the 1920s, Connecticut's forests were heavily harvested to make charcoal to dry tobacco, fuel brick kilns, and power iron and brass foundries. Charcoal was also a key ingredient in gunpowder and gas mask manufacturing. Up to 30 cords of wood would be covered with dirt and leaves and then burned from within for about two weeks. A collier maintained these slow-burning mounds.

Return back from this side trip, and follow the blue-blazed Cockaponset Trail north for about 0.7 mile to Old County Road. In spring, the ledges in this section are decorated with dwarf ginseng, white violet, wood anemone, Solomon's seal, and a profusion of mountain laurel.

Throughout this hike, you may see some areas of forest that appear to have been clear-cut. These are controlled

PATTACONK RESERVOIR AS SEEN FROM THE TRAIL

forestry operations by the State of Connecticut Department of Energy and Environment (DEEP) Forestry Division. The department clear-cuts some areas to promote the germination and development of young forest habitats, whose flora (including shade sensitive oak) are increasingly uncommon in Connecticut. The brushy habitat of young forests is also necessary for numerous at-risk bird species, such as the blue-winged warbler and the chestnut-sided warbler.

Turn left onto Old County Road, and proceed for a tenth of a mile before turning right at the bottom of a hill on a tote road. Pass Old County Road junction 8 (see map), where the Old Forest Trail blazed with red-spotted blue blazes bears to your right up a woods road. In *Other Hiking Options*, this is where you would begin a 5.1-mile northern loop hike.

As you follow the blue blazes, on your left is a laurel-covered hillside, and on your right a brushy swamp. You'll climb uphill off the tote road, soon passing a small rock outcropping to overlook a dammed-up swamp. Once populated by native cattails, this swamp has been overrun by invasive, non-native phragmites grass. The trail proceeds with the swamp pond on your left, soon crossing the old dam. Originally built by the Works Progress Administration in 1936, the dam's height was increased three feet in 1979.

Your blue-blazed trail bears left along the pond through azaleas and laurels. Passing a rock jumble to your right, proceed through a lovely laurel tunnel to another large rock jumble on your right. Notice the small circular piles of stones along the trail at this point. These are not naturally placed; rather, eighteenth century farmers piled stones in circular piles while they cleared fields. It was

quicker than building a wall and worked just fine with small, hand-tool harvesters like scythes.

Soon the trail joins a woods road and reaches Jericho junction 9 (see map), 3.1 miles from the start. Here is where you can shorten your hike to 5.8 miles (see *Other Hiking Options*). If you prefer to hike only 5.8 miles, head back to your right following the red-dot-on-blue-blazed trail (Old Forest Trail).

Just before you reach dirt Jericho Road, you'll pass a small stand of red spruce on your left; this is the only native spruce found in any number in Connecticut. Its needle-covered twigs, when boiled with molasses or a similar sweetener and fermented, yield spruce beer, a good scurvy remedy. The colonists also used spruce to flavor homemade ales before hops were common in America.

Bear right a short distance on Jericho Road past an old CCC water hole on your left, and then turn left back into the woods. Almost immediately, you'll reach Wildwood junction 11 (see map) just before some stone steps, where that trail goes to your left. Stay straight along the blue-blazed Cockaponset Trail, and ascend the stone stairs.

The next mile of trail to the second crossing of Jericho Road is a work of art—trail design and construction at its best. The path is stepped, curbed, graded, and routed by all points of interest. It was constructed only incidentally for the ease and comfort of the hiker; after more than 60 years of use, erosion here is practically nonexistent. Around Memorial Day weekend, lady's slippers are in bloom everywhere along this woodland path.

The trail in the midst of this scenic mile climbs and follows a rocky ridge covered with mountain laurel. At one point along this ridge are four spaced concrete blocks to your right, the underpinnings of an old fire tower. These remnants tell two stories: the prominence of this ridge as a lookout and the substitution of modern, efficient fire-spotting planes for these older structures. To reach a fire tower, with its warden standing his lonely vigil, was once a favorite goal for hikers, for both good views and good stories.

You'll then come to Jericho Road again where you'll turn left and continue for about 25 yards along the road before reentering the woods on your right. Shortly thereafter, the trail skirts a swamp on your left, which is sprinkled with tiny, yellow spicebush blossoms in early spring.

About a half-mile from the road crossing, watch the blue blazes carefully; several unmarked trails lead left to a campground. Soon you'll cross Jericho Road again, 5.1 miles from your car. Take the left fork across the road (on your right are orange blazes), and continue gently downhill, then uphill through the laurel. You will first hear, and then see, the brook rushing along to your left. The trail crosses the brook, and soon crosses another brook before coming to Beaver Brook junction 14 (see map), 5.6 miles from the start.

Here you'll begin your return. You will take the loop trail whenever possible, marked with blue-and-red blazes (really a blue blaze with a red underbar). At this junction, you'll bear left for a steady ascent on the Wildwood Trail. You'll meet and then cross a dirt road, turning south and climbing to a wooded hilltop. Descending, you'll soon level out and continue through a laurel tunnel, then through pines.

Cross Jericho Road for the fourth and last time just south of Wildwood

COLLIER'S HUT REMAINS

junction 11, about 1.5 miles from junction 14. Follow the Cockaponset Trail to Jericho junction 9, and bear left onto the Old Forest Trail, a deeply-rutted tote road. Your path will soon join up with purple blazes, but they then veer to the left as you continue to follow the blue-and-red blazes. Cross a wooden bridge just before rejoining the blue-blazed Cockaponset Trail at junction 8. If you were following the Northern Loop on *Other Hiking Options*, this is where you would end, meeting up with your car on Old County Road. Otherwise, proceed south past Old County Road, and bear left on the blue-and-red-blazed Pattaconk Trail at North Pattaconk junction 6. Follow this well-worn path, part of the old Cockaponset Trail, past junction 5 to the edge of Pattaconk Reservoir.

The rattling cry of the kingfisher frequently shatters the woodland silence here. From a well-chosen perch these brilliant blue-and-white birds spot a small fish and then plunge headfirst into the water to snare it.

Continue along the western edge of the reservoir, following the blue-and-red blazes. After nearly a mile, pass a beach to your left, and bear right uphill away from the reservoir. Soon you'll reach Pattaconk Crossover junction 4. Here take the blue-blazed trail, and on your left you'll soon see the yellow-blazed side trail that takes you back to the parking lot and your car.

## OTHER HIKING OPTIONS

**Additional Resources:** A state park trail map can be found at www.ct.gov /deep/cockaponset. Two maps encompass the route of this hike: Central Section, Haddam and Chester; and Southern Section, Haddam and Chester.

**Short & Sweet:** For a 2.3-mile option, follow the write-up to junction 5, and then return back to your car by turning right onto the blue- and red-blazed Pattaconk trail. This scenic route hugs the western shore of the Pattaconk Reservoir until you reach the short, yellow-blazed trail back that leads to the parking lot.

**Northern Loop Hike:** This hike begins on Old County Road and is 5.1 miles in length. To get to the start of the hike, you'll head north on CT 81 from its junction with CT 80 in Killingworth. You'll pass CT 148 (route to original hike). After 7 miles from the junction with CT 80, you'll turn right onto Beaver Meadow Road. This turns into Old Country Road, and after 0.2 mile becomes gravel. After another 0.8 mile, you'll see blue blazes and parking on your left. You'll follow the hike route as noted in the description up to Beaver Brook Junction, and then return back to your car following the loop trails.

**Southern Loop Hike:** following the hike from the original starting point. When you reach Jericho junction 9 (see map), 3.1 miles from the start, you will head back by following the blue- and red-blazed trail (Old Forest Trail) on your right. From there, you'll continue to junction 8 where you'll rejoin the blue-blazed Cockaponset Trail; proceed south crossing County Road. Follow the hike write-up from this junction back to your car. This southern loop option is 5.8 miles in length.

# 50

# Tunxis Ramble

| | |
|---|---|
| **LOCATION**: Burlington | |
| **DISTANCE**: 11 miles | |
| **VERTICAL RISE**: 970 feet | |
| **TIME**: 6 hours | |
| **RATING**: B/C | |
| **MAPS**: USGS 7.5-minute Thomaston, Bristol, Torrington, Collinsville | |

After hikers get their sea legs, short, flat, often comparatively monotonous trails no longer hold the appeal they once did. Aesthetic sense demands a more varied terrain; toughened muscles ask for more of a challenge and some distance to test one's stamina. This lengthy Tunxis Ramble should satisfy those needs nicely.

The first 2 miles offer some very strenuous hiking, as the trail leads you through the Mile of Ledges—a natural playground of rocky chasms between hulking granite slabs, stratified ledges, and scenic outlooks from atop expansive ridges of rock. The route also passes through the 43-acre Martha Brower Wildlife Sanctuary, skirting around Country Pond, which is layered with lilies and showcases a beaver's lodge at its center. The rest of the hike is much more subdued—a lengthy, leg-stretching woods ramble that also takes you through some meadowland and includes a little road walking to close up the loop.

This hike is difficult to categorize with a rating. The first 2 miles have some solid A-level terrain, requiring hand-assisted scrambling up and down steep pitches. Good, proper hiking footgear is essential for scaling the numerous rock outcroppings. The remainder of the hike is very much a C/D rating, with average terrain and easy-to-moderate footing.

Overall this loop route is a wonderful, full-day hike through the forest north of Bristol. June is a beautiful time of year to go when the laurel is in flower. Be cautious of taking on the Mile of Ledges in the winter months when conditions can be icy.

## GETTING THERE

From the junction of CT 4 and CT 72 west in Harwinton, proceed south on

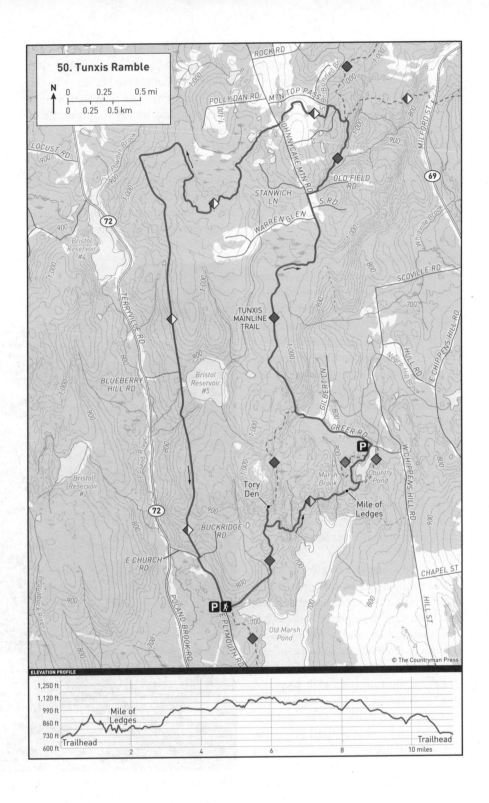

## 50. Tunxis Ramble

N

0        0.25        0.5 mi

0    0.25    0.5 km

POLLY DAN RD

ROCK RD

MTN TOP PASS

Br Burden Br

1,000

MILFORD ST

LOCUST RD

900

Powder Brook

JOHNNYCAKE MTN RD

OLD FIELD RD

69

STANWICH LN

S RD

WARREN GLEN

72

Bristol Reservoir #4

TERRYVILLE RD

TUNXIS MAINLINE TRAIL

SCOVILLE RD

E CHIPPENS HILL RD

700

HULL RD

Negro Hill Brook

Wildville Brook

Bristol Reservoir #5

GILBERT LN

GREER RD

BLUEBERRY HILL RD

Poland River

Bristol Reservoir #2

Tory Den

Marsh Brook

Country Pond

P

Mile of Ledges

Pequabuck River

BUCKRIDGE RD

72

E CHURCH RD

CHAPEL ST

HILL ST

W CHIPPENS HILL RD

POLAND BROOK RD

P

E PLYMOUTH RD

Old Marsh Pond

© The Countryman Press

### ELEVATION PROFILE

1,250 ft
1,120 ft
990 ft
860 ft
730 ft
600 ft

Mile of Ledges

Trailhead

Trailhead

2          4          6          8          10 miles

CT 72 for 4.4 miles. Turn left onto East Church Road; after 0.7 mile, the trail junction is on your left just before a gate. There is parking on either side of the road and in a small lot just before the gate. Or, from the junction of CT 6 and CT 72, proceed north on CT 72 for 2.8 miles. Turn right onto East Church Road, and follow the directions above.

## THE HIKE

Today's route is a loop that follows the Mainline Tunxis Trail to the blue-and-yellow-dotted trail through the Mile of Ledges and then the Brower Wildlife Sanctuary to Greer Road. After walking west on the road, you'll meet up again with the blue-blazed Mainline Trail; take that trail north to the blue-and-white-dotted trail, which you'll follow west and then south to your car. The blue blazes with either yellow or white dots are all side trails of the Tunxis Mainline Trail.

To start the hike, walk around the gate to follow the well-worn tote road blazed with blue with white dots. Soon the Mainline Tunxis Trail, here marked with solid blue blazes, enters from your right. Continue on the tote road, now the blue-blazed main line of the northbound Tunxis Trail.

Proceed along the tote road, which in late summer can be overgrown with vegetation on the sides but still has a well-worn path through the center. Gill-over-the-ground—a little flower whose fanciful name rivals its delicate, purple beauty—is plentiful here.

Follow the tote road as it passes a swamp dotted with ferns and skunk cabbage. As it gently ascends, continue following the tote road until you come to a Y junction; bear left here, following the blue blazes (the trail to your right is unmarked). About 0.6 mile from the

start, you'll reach a signed trail junction with the blue-and-yellow-dot trail. Follow the blue-blazed Mainline Tunxis trail briefly north to Tory Den, a small set of ledges with nooks and crannies to crawl through. This was a hiding place for Tories fearing retribution from local Patriots during the Revolutionary War. The famous Leatherman also reportedly stayed here. The Leatherman was a vagabond, famous for his handmade leather suit of clothes, who repeatedly traveled a

AN EIGHT-FOOT ROCK FACE IN THE MILE OF LEDGES

COUNTRY POND, PART OF THE MARTHA BROWER WILDLIFE SANCTUARY

364-mile circuit through Western Connecticut and Eastern New York from the mid-1850s until his death in 1889. In his travels, he was known to stay in rock shelters and caves such as this one.

Retrace your steps back to the junction, and turn left (east) to follow the blue- and yellow-dot-blazed trail to the Mile of Ledges. This part of the trail is a long series of boulders, ledges, and cleft rocks. You'll know you've begun this stretch when you climb through a small slot canyon. You'll then cross a stream over the remains of an old stone dam, climb up a rise, and continue through another smaller canyon between vertical slabs of rock. As the trail twists and turns through the jumbled rocky outcroppings, be on constant lookout for the blue-and-yellow-dot blazes on trees and rocks. Take your time and enjoy peering into crevasses and small caves. You'll then come to a long, slotted canyon called the Bear Den that comes to a dead-end (except for a small hole in the rocks above you—at first glance you'll wonder how you'll get through

that!). The trail actually turns right just before the end of the canyon—over an eight-foot wall. There are multiple foot and hand-holds to help you scramble up. The trail then descends and is much less rocky, a signal that you are leaving the Ledges. You'll pass a red-blazed trail on your right, and then start to spy a pond through the woods. This is Country Pond, part of the Martha Brower Wildlife Sanctuary owned by the Burlington Land Trust. The red-blazed trail soon joins up with our blue-and-yellow-dot trail as you parallel the pond. The red trail then veers left as you continue straight, looking down on the pond from atop a hill. You'll descend and follow along the shores of the pond. As you listen to the twangs and jug-a-rums of the green frogs and bull frogs echoing through the humid air, you'll spy a beaver lodge and numerous birds, including herons, enjoying the bounty of the 10-acre spring-fed pond. The red trail then rejoins from the left, and you'll soon reach Greer Road. Just before the road, there is a picnic table, a good place to have a rest or lunch break after the last challenging stretch of trail.

When you reach the paved Greer Road near the shore of the pond, 2.2 miles from the start, turn left. After about a half-mile, just before the road ends, turn left to follow the blue-blazed Tunxis Mainline Trail into the woods and up the wooded slope to reach a junction at the top of the rise along Bryda Ledge. Here you'll take the trail marked with blue blazes to your right up the hill. (To your left, this trail leads back to Tory Den—see *Other Hiking Options* for taking this shorter route.)

The trail then descends the mossy Bryda ledge and walks along a level path bordered with ferns and mountain laurel. You'll cross an old, dry steambed, and then join an eroded woods road, bearing slightly left. A well-formed old stone wall will parallel your route on the left, and you'll soon come to a four-way junction where you'll continue straight— still following the blue blazes. For a short stretch, the forest floor opens up so that the only undergrowth is a sea of ferns shaded by maple, black birch, and oak. In late 2017, we then came to a logging area marked with temporary signs cautioning to stay on the trail. There is selective logging in some areas abutting the Tunxis trail; these locations change but are clearly marked with signs.

About 2 miles from Greer Road, the blue-blazed Mainline Tunxis trail reaches a dirt road that then emerges onto the paved Johnnycake Mountain Road. You'll walk along this road past a few houses. Soon you'll take a right onto Old Field Road (also paved). After about 150 yards, the blue trail dips into the woods on your left (in late summer, this was a narrow path bordered by dense vegetation).

In previous editions, this hike stayed on Johnnycake Road and once went through a private game farm that has since been sold and developed into lots with stately homes. This new construction resulted in a rerouting of the trail which this hike now follows.

Continue following the blue blazes through the woods skirting the base of Johnnycake Mountain. After about a half-mile, you'll reach a junction with the blue-and-white-dot trail. Turn left at this junction. You'll come out onto a paved road; turn right. Blazes and arrows, marked on the road, lead your way through this new development. After 0.2 mile, the trail goes left into the woods, meandering over moss-covered rocks along a lush, fern-bordered trail. You'll cross a small stream and climb a small hill. The trail then changes to a wide, mowed path along the edge of a fenced-in field with more new construction around you. Please respect the rights of property owners; much hiking is done on private land, which is not a right but a too-easily-lost privilege.

You'll pass a pond on your right, and continue along a mowed grassland path through the backyards of this neighborhood. Another pond appears on your right, this one with a windmill likely used to aerate the pond, whether to keep it from freezing or to add oxygen to the water that retards algae growth and keeps fish from dying.

Once again, you'll reach Johnnycake Mountain Road; just before crossing it, you'll find a trail information box posted along the roadside. Inside, you'll find a map and information about the Burlington Land Trust.

Cross the road, continuing to follow the blue-and-white-dot trail; then cross a field to a low point where a white pine and maple stand together. Stay to the left, walking along a ledge in woods

SLOTTED CANYON IN THE MILE OF LEDGES

populated with dying hemlock trees. You'll see that black-birch seedlings are moving in to take advantage of the space cleared by these coniferous victims of the woolly adelgid. Your path is speckled with mica and white-quartz—beautiful, glimmering treasure in the sunlight. Soon you'll continue onto higher ground to the left of a swamp. Occasionally, you'll catch a glimpse of some trees killed when water from a beaver dam flooded them out.

This next stretch of trail is a bit of a rambling woods walk—level terrain but with some twists and turns in the route. Continue to follow the blue-and-white-dot blazes. Enjoy the peaceful meditation of walking along this quiet stretch.

After about a mile, the trail bears left on a woods road and gently descends. In a quarter-mile, turn left again onto another tote road. Continue over a rise past an old logging operation on your left, through the woods and over a small hill, then descend to a gate. Shortly thereafter, you'll pass a house on your right, and the road you've been walking briefly becomes paved. The pavement becomes a packed-dirt road you'll follow until you cross Blueberry Hill Road (about a mile) and pass through a gate. Reservoir #5 is on your left. Continue straight on the gravel road through the Bristol Water Department property. When the road bends left, proceed straight into the woods on an overgrown tote road still following blue-and-white-dot blazes. Proceed downhill on this trail, cross a brook with steep banks, climb once again, level out, and then descend gradually; you'll reach a driveway that leads downhill to a paved road.

Turn right on this new road, and th left onto East Church Road. Follow th paved road for 0.4 mile to where yo parked your car on the left.

## OTHER HIKING OPTIONS

**Short & Sweet:** Looking for a shorter hike (about 4 miles) that still includes the Mile of Ledges? Follow the start of the hike as described, but skip the detour to Tory Den (you'll pass it on last part of this shorter loop). Continue the hike until you reach Greer Road and climb to Bryda Ledge. At the junction on top of Bryda Ledge, turn left on the blue-blazed Mainline Tunxis trail to head back to your car. You'll reach the Tory Den in about three-quarters of a mile on this route. Continue until you reach that first main junction at the start of the hike; from there head straight back to your car.

**A Side Trip:** Explore the Martha Brower Wildlife Sanctuary. The mile-long, red trail circumnavigates Country Pond (and joins the blue-and-yellow-dot trail after the Mile of Ledges). This delightful trail zigzags through the Sanctuary over multiple rocky ledges, leading you to many natural points of interest, including a spur with lookouts over the pond. In the spring, you can find pink lady slippers in bloom along this trail. You can access this trail directly from the Greer Road entrance.

The Tunxis Trail is maintained by the Connecticut Forest and Parks Association. The organization recently (2014) completed a relocation and extension of the Tunxis Trail, and have updated trail maps on their website (ctwoodlands.org).